Human Rights
for
South Africans

Edited by
Mike Robertson
Professor and Director, Centre for Socio-legal Studies
Faculty of Law, University of Natal, Durban

Assisted by
Megan Seneque
Applied linguist and communications consultant

CONTEMPORARY SOUTH AFRICAN DEBATES

1991
Oxford University Press
Cape Town

Oxford University Press
Walton Street, Oxford OX2 6DP, United Kingdom

Oxford New York Toronto
Delhi Bombay Calcutta Madras Karachi
Petaling Jaya Singapore Hong Kong Tokyo
Nairobi Dar es Salaam Cape Town
Melbourne Auckland

and associated companies in
Berlin Ibadan

ISBN 0 19 570632 3

Published by Oxford University Press Southern Africa
Harrington House, Barrack Street, Cape Town, 8001, South Africa

DTP conversion by Theiner Typesetting (Pty) Ltd, Bellville, Cape.
Printed and bound by Galvin & Sales, Cape Town.

Preface

This book has been written for South Africans who are interested in human rights. Its aim is to provide basic information about international human rights standards and their relevance to a changing South Africa. Each chapter explains an aspect of the Universal Declaration of Human Rights, the famous document adopted by the United Nations in 1948. South Africa, the Soviet Union, and a few other states then abstained from voting on the document, and South Africa has failed to endorse it subsequently.

For at least the last 43 years South Africa's rulers have shown little respect for human rights. Hopefully this is about to change. Yet relatively few South Africans know much about the meaning and importance of the rights proclaimed in the Universal Declaration and other documents. This has led frequently to the observation that South Africa lacks a 'human rights culture', by which is meant that South Africans lack a reasonable understanding of the importance of laws which protect human rights — and that state and human conduct must conform to these requirements. For too long the apartheid system has abused people and their property, and often under the authority of the law. It is therefore not surprising that the victims of apartheid, and to some extent the beneficiaries, have had little reason to see law as a protector rather than as a violator of basic rights. Needed now is an appreciation that law which embodies human rights standards is indispensable for a society committed to justice and equality. The publication of this book will have been worthwhile if, even in small measure, it stimulates debate on human rights and broadens an awareness of these crucial issues.

Although the book has been written by 32 people, I have attempted to achieve some consistency in the style and use of language. Many of the authors' contributions were rather more scholarly in their original versions; but, because this is not a book for academics, the text was made simpler and shorter. Some chapters may be more superficial than the authors intended. For this, I take full responsibility.

Debates about human rights are not uncontroversial. Even human rights lawyers differ on important points. It follows that no one contributor agrees with every word in this book. However, we all agree with most of what has been said, and we all believe that human rights have a vital part to play both now and in the future.

Perhaps an example of an issue which elicits differences of opinions is the use in human rights and legal documents of sexist language. In this book, care has been taken to avoid the use of 'he', 'his', and 'him' to denote persons who are not necessarily male. There is one exception: articles of the Universal Declaration itself are reproduced in their original form.

Four important South African human rights documents are reproduced at the end of the book: the ANC's Freedom Charter, Constitutional Guidelines for a Democratic South Africa, and draft Bill of Rights, and the South African Law Commission's draft Bill of Rights.

I express my gratitude to the contributors and other persons who made the book possible. These were assistant editor Megan Seneque, staff at the Centre for Socio-legal Studies, and in particular Rashina Moodley, and Glenda Younge and Sandie Vahl of Oxford University Press. Much is also owed to the institutions which support this Centre. Without their help, our work would be impossible.

Michael Robertson
Centre for Socio-legal Studies, University of Natal
January 1991

Contents

Contributors

Introduction: Lourens Ackermann
SC BA LL B (Stell.) MA (Oxon.); Advocate of the Supreme Court of South Africa; H. F. Oppenheimer Professor of Human Rights Law, University of Stellenbosch; Judge of the Lesotho Court of Appeal; former Judge of the Supreme Court of South Africa.

Chapter 1: John Dugard
BA LL B (Stell.) LL B, Diploma in International Law, LL D (Cantab.), LL D (honoris causa) (Natal); Advocate of the Supreme Court of South Africa; Professor of Law and Director of the Centre for Applied Legal Studies, University of the Witwatersrand.

Chapter 2: Charles Dlamini
B.Proc. LL B LL M LL D (Zululand) LL D (Pretoria); Advocate of the Supreme Court of South Africa; Registrar Academic, University of Zululand.

Chapter 3: Penelope Andrews
BA LL B (Natal) LL M (Columbia); Advocate of the Supreme Court of South Africa; Lecturer in the Department of Legal Studies, La Trobe University, Melbourne, Australia.

Chapters 4 & 5: Cora Hoexter
BA (Natal) BA (Oxon.) LL B (Natal); Advocate of the Supreme Court of South Africa; Senior Lecturer in the School of Law, University of Natal, Pietermaritzburg.

Chapter 6: Dennis Davis
B.Com. LL B (Cape Town) M.Phil. (Cantab.); Advocate of the Supreme Court of South Africa; Professor of Commercial Law, University of Cape Town.

Chapter 7: Christina Murray
BA LL B (Stell.) LL M (Michigan); Senior Lecturer in the Department of Public Law, University of Cape Town.

Chapter 8: Hugh Corder
B.Com. LL B (Cape Town) LL B (Cantab.) D.Phil. (Oxon.); Advocate of the Supreme Court of South Africa; Professor and Head of Department of Public Law, University of Cape Town.

Chapter 9: Michael Cowling
BA (Rhodes) LL B (Natal) M.Phil. (Cantab.); Advocate of the Supreme Court of South Africa; Senior Lecturer in the School of Law, University of Natal, Pietermaritzburg.

Chapter 10: Julia Sloth-Nielsen
BA LL B (Stell.) LL M (Cape Town); Advocate of the Supreme Court of South Africa; Lecturer in the Department of Criminal and Procedural Law, University of Cape Town.

Chapter 11: Nico Steytler
BA LL B (Stell.) LL M (London) Ph.D. (Natal); Advocate of the Supreme Court of South Africa and the High Court of Lesotho; Professor of Law and Chairperson of the Department of Public and Adjective Law, University of the Western Cape.

Chapter 12: Johann van der Westhuizen
BA LL B LL D (Pretoria); Advocate of the Supreme Court of South Africa; Professor and Head of the Department of Legal History, Comparative Law, and Legal Philosophy, University of Pretoria; Director of the Centre for Human Rights Studies, University of Pretoria.

Chapter 13: David McQuoid-Mason
B.Com. LL B (Natal) LL M (London) Ph.D. (Natal); Professor and Dean of the Faculty of Law, University of Natal, Durban.

Chapter 14: Geoff Budlender
BA LL B (Cape Town); Attorney of the Supreme Court of South Africa; Director, Legal Resources Centre, Johannesburg.

Chapter 15: Tanya Woker
BA LL B (Natal); Senior Lecturer in the Department of Business Law, University of Natal, Durban.

Chapter 16: Vincent Mntambo
B.Juris. LL B (Unibo) LL M (Yale); Senior Lecturer in the Department of Public Law, University of Natal, Durban.

Chapter 17: Vinodh Jaichand
BA (UDW) LL B (Natal) LL M (Miami) LL M (Notre Dame); Senior Lecturer in the Department of Private Law, University of Durban-Westville.

Chapter 18: Mike Robertson
BA LL B LL M (Natal) LL M (Warwick); Attorney of the Supreme Court of South Africa; Professor and Director of the Centre for Socio-legal Studies, University of Natal, Durban.

Chapter 19: Paddy Kearney
BA UED (Natal) B.Ed. (Wits) M.Ed. (Toledo Ohio); Director of Diakonia.

Chapter 20: Anthea Jeffrey
BA LL B (Wits) LL M (Cantab.) Ph.D. (London); Research Consultant, South African Institute of Race Relations.

Chapter 21: Chris Albertyn
BA (Hons.) (Wits) B.Proc. (Unisa) LL B (Natal); Attorney of the Supreme Court of South Africa; Co-director, Centre for Socio-legal Studies, University of Natal, Durban.

Chapter 22: Karthy Govender
LL B (London) LL B (Natal) LL M (Michigan); Advocate of the Supreme Court of South Africa; Senior Lecturer in the Department of Public Law, University of Natal, Durban.

Chapter 23: Pieter Le Roux
B.Com. B.Econ. (Hons.) (Stell.) Diploma in Development Economics (Cantab.); Director and Professor, Institute for Social Development, University of the Western Cape.

Chapter 24: Ray Zondo
B.Juris. (UZ) LL B (Natal); Attorney of the Supreme Court of South Africa; formerly part-time Lecturer in the Department of Public Law, University of Natal, Durban.

Chapter 23: Inthiran Moodley
B.Sc. (Hons.) (London); Education Officer, Centre for Socio-legal Studies, University of Natal, Durban.

Chapter 26: Alan Rycroft
BA (Rhodes) LL B (Natal) LL M (London); Attorney of the Supreme Court of South Africa; Professor and Head of the Department of Procedural and Clinical Law, University of Natal, Durban.

Chapter 27: Clive Thompson
BA (Hons.) (Stell.) LL B (Cape Town); Attorney of the Supreme Court of South Africa; Associate Professor and Director of the Labour Law Unit, University of Cape Town.

Chapter 28: Craig Tanner
BA LL B (Natal); Attorney of the Supreme Court of South Africa.

Chapter 29: Ben Parker
BA (Hons.) MA (Rhodes) HDE (Unisa); Co-ordinator, Educational Development Studies, University of Natal, Durban.

Chapter 30: Hilton Staniland
BA (Hons.) LL B (Natal) LL M Ph.D. (Southampton); Professor and Director of the Institute of Maritime Law, University of Natal, Durban.

Chapter 31: John Dugard
BA LL B (Stell.) LL B, Diploma in International Law, LL D (Cantab.), LL D (honoris causa) (Natal); Advocate of the Supreme Court of South

Africa; Professor of Law and Director of the Centre for Applied Legal Studies, University of the Witwatersrand.

Chapter 32: Isobel Konyn
BA LL B (Natal); Senior Lecturer in the Department of Business Law, University of Natal, Durban.

Chapter 33: Kevin Ferguson-Brown
BA LL B LL M (Cape Town) M.Phil. (Cantab.); Senior Lecturer in the Department of Public Law, University of Natal, Durban.

Introduction

The Universal Declaration of Human Rights was adopted and promulgated on 10 December 1948 by the General Assembly of the United Nations. It is the best-known international instrument (document) which formulates fundamental human rights. An ever-increasing number of ordinary women, men, and children throughout the world, of all races, colours, languages, and creeds, regularly appeal to its standards when they feel that they have been unjustly treated or neglected by their governments or societies. Human rights are claims which all human beings have, or ought to have, against their societies as represented by their governments.

The Declaration marks the real beginning of the international recognition of human rights. It also represents the beginning of the end for the idea of absolute state sovereignty, the idea that a state can exist in legal isolation, separate from other states, and that the way it treats its own inhabitants is entirely its own business and no concern of any other state. The Declaration was also a historical response after the Second World War to human tragedy on a global scale and in particular to Hitler's reign of terror.

Of the 56 states which were members of the United Nations in 1948, 48 voted in favour of the adoption of the Declaration, none voted against, while 8 states abstained from voting. The USSR, Czechoslovakia, Poland, Yugoslavia, and the Union of South Africa were amongst the states which abstained. Subsequently six of these abstaining states (including the USSR) have adopted the Declaration as well as more than 100 states which have become members of the United Nations since 1948. Only South Africa and Saudi Arabia, of the original members, have failed to do so.

The United Nations Charter came into force on 24 October 1945. In the Preamble to the Charter, the determination of the United Nations is expressed to 'save succeeding generations from the scourge of war, which twice in our lifetime has brought untold sorrow to mankind', to 'reaffirm faith in fundamental human rights, in the dignity and worth of the human person, in the equal rights of men and women', and to 'promote social progress and better standards of life in larger freedom'. One of the four main objects of the United Nations is stated in Article 1.1 to be the achievement of international co-operation in 'promoting and encouraging respect for human rights and for fundamental freedoms for all without distinction as to race, sex, language or religion'. In Article 55(c) the obligation is assumed by the United Nations to promote 'universal respect for, and observance of, human rights and fundamental freedoms for all without distinction as to race, sex, language or religion'.

The Economic and Social Council, which was established in terms of Article 61 of the Charter, set up a Commission on Human Rights early in 1946 whose task it was to prepare an 'international Bill of Rights' which would comprise a declaration of human rights, a covenant of human rights, and necessary measures of implementation. The first step on this path was the adoption and proclamation of the Declaration in 1948.

The United Nations Commission on Human Rights

Mrs Eleanor Roosevelt was appointed the first chairperson of the Commission which was established in 1946. After much deliberation it was decided that the Commission should consist of 18 members, appointed by governments selected by the Economic and Social Council. The disadvantage of having government representatives on the Commission was and still is that their concern for human rights in other countries may be severely constrained by their own nation's foreign policy objectives. In 1962 the membership of the Commission was increased to 21, in 1966 to 32.

Eleanor Roosevelt was also made chairperson of the drafting committee which was appointed to draft an International Bill of Rights. The eight members of the drafting committee were the representatives of Australia, Chile, China, France, Lebanon, the United Kingdom, the United States (Eleanor Roosevelt), and the USSR. The French delegate, Prof. René Cassin, was awarded the Nobel Peace prize in 1968. Dr. Charles Malik, the Lebanese delegate, took over as chairperson of the Commission in 1951.

When presenting the Declaration to the General Assembly, Eleanor Roosevelt said that the Declaration was 'first and foremost a declaration of the basic principles to serve as a common standard for all nations. It might become the Magna Carta of all mankind'.

The Preamble to the Declaration underscores the fact that, as the first step towards the creation of an international Bill of Rights, the Declaration was not intended to achieve the binding legal effect on states that an international treaty, covenant, or convention would. A declaration is viewed rather as a common expression of opinion and voluntary commitment by the states subscribing to it. Whatever its original status may have been, the passage of time has, in the view of many eminent scholars, changed its binding legal character.

The drafting and acceptance of the envisaged Covenant of Human Rights proceeded neither as swiftly nor as smoothly as many may have hoped. The cold war between east and west had started and ideological differences on several issues (the nature and status of economic rights, the relationship of the individual to the state, the very nature of law and rights themselves) which had been dormant at the time of the Declaration's adoption now surfaced. The realization may also have dawned that all economic rights could not be protected or advanced or enforced in the same way as civil and political rights. The idea of a single covenant was abandoned and work proceeded on two covenants which were simultaneously adopted by the General Assembly on 16 December 1966, the one entitled the International Covenant on Economic, Social, and Cultural Rights (ICOSEC) and the other the International Covenant on Civil and Political Rights (ICCP). States were slow in ratifying these covenants, ICOSEC coming into force only on 3 January 1976 and ICCP on 23 March of the same year.

The ratification and coming into force of these twin covenants has not diminished the standing of the Declaration. If anything, it has achieved greater status because of the delays in formulating the two covenants, which have been ratified by a relatively small number of nations. Moreover, the two covenants are primarily only binding on the states that have ratified them, whereas citizens of the world feel a deep need for a universal human rights instrument to whose terms they can hold governments and societies to account, even when the states in question have not ratified the covenants. The Declaration has become a standard by which to test state constitutions, a weapon in international diplomacy, and a set of principles to which the UN organs refer when confronted by human rights issues. It has served as a guide for constitution makers in the second half of this century and provided them with a ready-made vocabulary for their task. The result has been that most leading international law scholars are today in agreement that the Declaration has been transformed into a source of customary

South Africa and the International Covenant on Civil and Political Rights

Of the 15 human rights outlined in the proposed Covenant, the Nationalist government agreed to 13 in principle, would have liked a change of wording in some, and objected outright to 2.

Prime Minister D. F. Malan (House of assembly Debates, 16 May 1951) outlined why the South African government could not accept the article dealing with freedom of movement and choice of domicile in a territory:

> ... if we are to accept that it means that a number of the Union Acts will be in conflict with this provision, Acts like the Group Areas Act, the Native Urban Areas Act, the Native's Trust and Lands Act, and the Pass Laws. Freedom of movement in a country with a population composed as ours is, is impossible without creating all kinds of undesirable conditions.

To the right of freedom of speech and of opinion he gave the following reasons for not being able to accept it:

> ... these rights are in conflict with the provision of the law dealing with the oppression of communism, and the Native Administration Act. We have a Riotous Assemblies Act. If Natives become agitators, if the non-Europeans are stirred up against the Europeans, then this freedom of speech can be prevented.

Compulsory labour for prisoners and compulsory military service were the two reasons that Malan felt that the government could not accept the right 'Nobody is allowed to do compulsory labour' without qualification.

Malan indicated that the treatment of communists should be made an exception to the right not to be prosecuted for an action that was not punishable at the time it was committed.

To the right of peaceful meeting, Malan outlined the following exception:

> If it is a meeting where the safety of the public and the security of the State are involved, it is self-evident that the State has the right to step in.

Needless to say, South Africa has never adopted the International Covenant on Civil and Political Rights, or any other human rights or anti-discrimination instrument.

international law. Customary international law, very much like customary domestic law, or the 'common law' of a country, comes into existence without covenants, or treaties, or any other specific 'legislative' act, but by the regular observance or recognition of particular rules of conduct by states in their relations with one another.

Although the Declaration gives international standing to a wide range of human rights, it does not legislate or create these rights but rather 'recognizes' their existence and their importance for the well-being of the human family.

The rights referred to in the Declaration are neither new nor foreign concepts (as some South Africans still wrongly believe) introduced by some 'do-gooders' at the end of the Second World War. These rights have in different ways been proclaimed by philosophers for centuries. They have been recognized in major legal systems for almost as long, and since the last decades of the eighteenth century have been incorporated on an ever-increasing scale in state constitutions.

Natural law theories have, despite sporadic attacks on them, continued to provide a theoretical base for universal human rights. The ancient Greek philosophers were concerned about the permanent underlying basis of the law, and the relationship between law and justice. Fundamental to these theories is the idea that law is indispensable for human society and that it is based on the needs of human beings endowed with reason, and not on the arbitrary whims of rulers. The Stoic philosophers exercised a powerful influence on the Roman jurists. They maintained that the law was unchangeable, represented the inner voice of God, and that it provided the only justification for external authority. The idea of the equality of all human beings was universalized and advanced as an important consequence of the recognition that law originated in a higher authority (and not in state authority).

For Cicero, the binding authority of law was dependent upon its being in agreement with reason and the universal attributes of human nature. Ulpian (one of the architects of the Roman Law, and a rich source of South African common law) relied on principles of natural law when he stated that the fundamental principles of justice are to be found in the duty to live honestly, to injure no one, and to let each person have what he or she deserves. The views of Augustine and Aquinus on the law of nature profoundly influenced Western legal thinking, particularly by advancing the idea that eternal legal principles manifested themselves through human 'right reason', and that the only justification for the state's existence was service to the individual. According to Professor H. Lauterpacht, the law of nature ruled supreme in the Middle Ages when the idea that the ruler was under the supremacy of the law was the principal feature of political theory. He points out that the substance of what proved to be the doctrine of the natural rights of human beings was well established.

These values are deeply embedded in our own more recent common law. The great Dutch jurist Hugo de Groot (Grotius) based his famous work on international law, *De Jure Belli ac Pacis*, published in 1625, on the law of nature. In his equally famous introductory work on the Dutch law of his time published in 1631 (his *Inleiding tot die Hollandse Regsgeleerdheid*) he declares that what is prohibited by the law of nature cannot be commanded by the positive law (for example a statute of the lawmaker) and that what is decreed by the law of nature cannot be prohibited by positive law.

It is clear that the idea of a higher law, superior to the state, has been attracting human minds since the beginning of organized society. Philosophers have grappled, for example, with the dilemma of obedience to a tyrannical law. Some of the best minds have focused on the problem of human inability to handle any form of power without being corrupted by and abusing it.

While piecemeal attempts were made in certain countries (notably in England) over a number of centuries to place the rights of the individual on a firm statutory footing, efforts to do so by means of a supreme and comprehensive constitutional document only came about with the work of the American 'founding fathers', who were greatly influenced by the English philosopher John Locke. Locke relied directly and heavily on natural law principles in explaining his fundamental human rights of Life, Liberty, and Estate (which he called the rights of 'man'); his belief that the sole function of government was the better protection of these rights; his concept of limited government; and his proposition that the authority of government rested on the consent of the governed.

The stamp of John Locke on the Virginia Bill of Rights is quite plain. This enactment, which was passed on 12 June 1776, pre-dated the American Declaration of Independence by some three weeks. When Clause 1 of the Virginia Bill of Rights is compared with the Independence Declaration and with the Preamble and Article 1 of the Universal Declaration, the common ancestry of these instruments is apparent. The rights mentioned in Clause 1 of the earliest document are described as follows:

That all men are by nature equally free and independent, and have certain inherent rights, of which, when they enter into a state of society, they cannot, by any compact, deprive or divest their posterity; namely, the enjoyment of life and liberty, with the means of acquiring and possessing property, and pursuing and obtaining happiness and safety.

The idea of limited government, also proclaimed in the Declaration of Independence and which lies at the core of Article 21 of the Universal Declaration, is clearly expressed in Clause 3 of the Virginia Bill:

That government is, or ought to be instituted for the common benefit, protection and security of the people, nation or community ... and that, when any government shall be found inadequate or contrary to these purposes, a majority of the community hath an indubitable, unalienable and indefeasible right to reform, alter or abolish it, in such manner as shall be judged most conducive to the public weal [public good, welfare, or interest].

It was on these concepts of rights, government, and the right of the governed to control their government that the American people justified their revolutionary break with England. These ideas have also found their way into countless state constitutions throughout the world and into regional conventions and charters in Europe, America, South East Asia, and Africa.

There is a growing awareness of the richness of human rights values in African society and custom throughout our continent. Ordinary people desire that human rights be given clear and effective constitutional protection against the actions of governments or other power groupings. The fact that constitutions and Bills of Rights in Africa have often been overturned by political and military powers (as indeed they have elsewhere in the world at various times) in no way detracts from the ever-increasing legitimacy which human rights are gaining as a universal concept for all humankind.

It is important to appreciate the strong theological support that fundamental human rights receive in the world's religions. In the Judaeo-Christian tradition human beings are seen as created in the image of God. They represent the crown of creation and enjoy equal human worth. So that people can fulfil their destiny of having been created in this image, their fundamental rights have to be fully acknowledged and exercised. It must be noted, however, that human rights are not demands made on God, but claims which people make on their organized societies. The theological commitment to universal human rights is also evidenced by the work done by, for example, the World Council of Churches and the Commission of the Churches for International Affairs, the World Alliance of Reformed Churches, the Lutheran World Federation, and the Roman Synod of Bishops. The idea of fundamental human rights also finds support in Islam and in the Hindu value system.

The Declaration consists of a Preamble and 30 articles. It proclaims, on the one hand, civil and political rights (sometimes referred to as the 'first generation' rights) and, on the other hand, economic, social, and cultural rights (sometimes referred to as the 'second generation' rights). These terms are descriptive and do not imply superiority of the one 'generation' over the other. The two generations are interdependent. As President Roosevelt remarked 'a necessitous man is not a free man'. It is indeed obscene to point out to starving people that they are free. On the other hand a well-fed prisoner of conscience still remains a prisoner. Both generations of rights address wrongs associated with oppression and exploitation in society. The first combats physical and political oppression and exploitation, while the second opposes economic, social, and cultural oppression and exploitation.

While the two generations of rights are interdependent, all the rights in the two generations are not necessarily of the same nature. They cannot be enforced or protected in precisely the same way. This is particularly so in the case of certain second generation rights (like the right to social security) which cannot be protected in the same way as first generation rights, like the right to free speech. Certain second generation rights require positive state action and in particular state expenditure. The realization of these rights may therefore be limited. This was appreciated by the drafters of the Declaration who, in Article 22, made the realization of these second generation rights dependent, amongst other things, on the 'resources' of each state.

The phrases 'affirmative action' and 'group rights', which are much used in the current South African human rights and constitutional debate, are not to be found in the Declaration. In essence, affirmative action is a remedial or compensatory principle. It is a response to the fact that the multiple harmful effects (political, educational, economic, and social) of past discrimination on various levels, particularly statutory and other state-enforced discrimination, do not cease the moment these statutory and other formal discriminatory measures come to an end. The effects are ongoing, unless remedial or compensatory measures are approved and applied by the state.

Although there is substantial agreement that affirmative action is essential to remedy the effects of past discrimination, there is disagreement regarding the methods to be employed. Should affirmative action be planned to achieve genuine equality of opportunity, or must it go further and bring about equality of result? Opponents of the latter goal would argue that any programme to achieve such a goal would have all the potential dangers of other large-scale social engineering schemes, such as unpredictability, uncontrollability, and bureaucratic inefficiency. There is no easy answer to this problem, for the concept of affirmative action exists in tension with another important human right, namely equality before the law or equal treatment under the law.

Equality before the law does not, of course, mean that all people are to be treated identically in all situations. Where education is made compulsory by the state the law applies only to a limited age group. Military conscription in the majority of countries applies only to males of a certain age. People are prevented from practising a wide variety of professions unless they hold certain statutorily-defined qualifications. Such treatment is not seen as unjust, although there may be disagreement, for example, as to what the minimum qualifications ought to be in order to practise medicine or law, or what acts fall within the definition of practising medicine or law. These distinctions are made on the grounds of overriding considerations of legitimate public policy or state or community objectives. However, certain distinctions (particularly those made on the grounds, for example, of race, ethnicity, or language) are immediately viewed with suspicion and are hardly ever allowed in a system which tries genuinely to apply equality before the law. Where the object of affirmative action is to compensate past victims of race discrimination for the continuing effects of such discrimination, then differential treatment is seen as just and fair and serving important objects of society generally. Affirmative action principles are contained, for example, in the constitutions of Canada, India, and Namibia.

A discussion of 'group rights' is clouded by the fact that almost every person has a different definition of the phrase. If 'group rights' are understood to mean what could be called 'associational rights' then they do not conflict with the Declaration. In fact the Declaration gives protection (albeit sometimes indirectly) to associational rights. Article 20 protects freedom of assembly and association, Article 23(4) the right to form and to join trade unions, Article 26(3) the right of parents to choose the kind of education that must be given to their children, and Article 27 the right of everyone freely to participate in the cultural life of the community. The ICCP expressly protects associational rights. Article 18 includes in its right to freedom of religion the freedom to manifest such religion 'or belief' either individually or 'in community with others'. Article 27 expressly provides, in respect of those states in which ethnic, religious, or linguistic minorities exist, that persons belonging to such minorities shall not be denied the right 'in community with the other members of their group' to 'enjoy their own culture, to profess and practise their own religion, or to use their own language'.

The Declaration does not prescribe what form of government a state must have, save that Article 21(3) prescribes that 'the will of the people shall be the basis of the authority of government' and that such will must be expressed in periodic, genuine, and free elections by 'universal and equal suffrage'. If a 'group right' means the right of a constituent state to be represented in a second chamber of a national legislature by the same number of representatives as any other constituent state, even though the former state has half the number (or even considerably less) of registered voters of the latter state, such right would not conflict with the Declaration.

A constitution which makes it impossible to amend certain of its provisions, or requires very substantial majorities to amend it, does not offend the terms of the Declaration. Proportional representation is quite compatible with the Declaration, which does not prescribe any particular voting system. However, if a right is given to a minority group (whether it is defined by territorial residence, ethnicity, race, or even party membership) to elect representatives to a parliament and the number of representatives is grossly disproportionate to the voting strength of the majority, this might well conflict with the Declaration. Similarly, there will probably be a conflict with the Declaration if minority representatives are given a veto right which enables them to block ordinary legislation. One would in every case have to ask whether the effect of such a right (whatever one chooses to call it) is such that it can still genuinely be said that the 'will of the people' forms 'the basis of the authority of government' and that such will has been expressed by 'equal suffrage'.

Confusion in this debate would be avoided if the expression 'group rights' was not used at all and if, instead, the enquiry was focused on the particular 'rights' and 'interests' which are of concern to minorities and which they fear losing under majority rule. Some of these rights and interests deserve protection and can be protected under a constitution based on the Declaration. Others do not deserve protection and would conflict with the Declaration.

The various rights and freedoms in the Declaration are explained by the contributors in the chapters that follow. Article 1 explains the philosophy on which the Declaration is based and Article 2 emphasizes the basic principle of equality and non-discrimination in the enjoyment of human rights. Article 3 declares the right to life, liberty, and security of person, an indispensable right for the enjoyment of all other rights. The civil and political rights are set out in Articles 4 to 21. Article 22 introduces the economic, social, and cultural rights which are detailed in Articles 23 to 27. The concluding articles, Articles 28 to 30, emphasize the fact that human rights can only be exercised in a social and international order receptive to such rights and that individuals also have duties to the community. In Article 30 a militant attitude is adopted in defence of the rights and freedoms set forth in the Declaration against attack by any state, group, or person.

The rights and freedoms are interdependent. The common denominator is the dignity, autonomy, and equality of all people.

1
The Preamble of the Universal Declaration of Human Rights

Whereas *recognition of the inherent dignity and of the equal and inalienable rights of all members of the human family is the foundation of freedom, justice and peace in the world,*

Whereas *disregard and contempt for human rights have resulted in barbarous acts which have outraged the conscience of mankind, and the advent of a world in which human beings shall enjoy freedom of speech and belief and freedom from fear and want has been proclaimed as the highest aspiration of the common people,*

Whereas *it is essential, if man is not to be compelled to have recourse, as a last resort, to rebellion against tyranny and oppression, that human rights should be protected by the rule of law,*

Whereas *it is essential to promote the development of friendly relations between nations,*

Whereas *the peoples of the United Nations have in the Charter reaffirmed their faith in fundamental human rights, in the dignity and worth of the human person and in the equal rights of men and women and have determined to promote social progress and better standards of life in a larger freedom,*

Whereas *Members States have pledged themselves to achieve, in co-operation with the United Nations, the promotion of universal respect for and observance of human rights and fundamental freedoms,*

Whereas *a common understanding of these rights and freedoms is of the greatest importance for the full realization of this pledge.*

Now, therefore, *the General Assembly* **proclaims**

This universal declaration of human rights *as a common standard of achievement for all peoples and all nations, to the end that every individual and every organ of society, keeping this Declaration constantly in mind, shall strive by teaching and education to promote respect for these rights and freedoms and by* *progressive measures, national and international, to secure their universal and effective recognition and observance, both among the peoples of Members States themselves and among the peoples of territories under their jurisdiction.*

Background to the Preamble

The Preamble of the Declaration sets out the philosophical ideas and historical factors that prompted the adoption of the Declaration and calls upon peoples and nations to promote the rights it enshrines.

The idea that every person has certain inherent and inalienable human rights, irrespective of whether they are recognized and enforced by the law of the state in which they live, stems from the teachings of natural law. This doctrine has had a profound effect on the course of history. (See the discussion in the Introduction.) It provided, for example, the inspiration for both the American and the French Revolutions.

In the nineteenth and early twentieth centuries, however, natural law fell into disfavour. The view that law was simply the will of the sovereign power in each state became the dominant view. The idea that certain inalienable rights attached to every person simply because he or she was a person was rejected as absurd. During the 1930s Nazi leaders and other dictators took the new philosophy to its logical conclusion. If law was the unrestrained will of the state, and notions of equality before the law and respect for human rights were irrelevant, there was no reason why the state could not use the law as a weapon to brutalize its own people and those of conquered countries. It took the horror of the holocaust to demonstrate the invalidity of this notion of law and to bring home to political leaders the need for a different approach to law.

In the Declaration the leaders of the world returned to the tradition of natural law. The Declaration recognizes that the principle of equality and the inalienability of the rights of all persons forms the foundation of freedom, peace, and justice (the first paragraph). It recalls the barbarous acts that the world had so recently experienced and warns that people will rise in rebellion against their rulers if their basic human rights are not protected by the rule of law (the second and third paragraphs). Here the Declaration reminds governments, as did the natural law philosophers, that they hold their offices in trust for the people as part of a social compact (the third paragraph).

The Declaration emphasizes the need for governments to fulfil this trust by protecting human rights by means of 'the rule of law'. This phrase is misunderstood by many. In South Africa the National Party government has equated the 'rule of law' with 'rule *by* law' or 'the rule of law and order'. Consequently it has sought to justify repressive security laws as compatible with the rule of law. This shows a complete lack of understanding for this concept. According to the notion of the rule of law the individual enjoys certain basic human rights, including equality before the law, which are to be protected by independent courts employing fair procedures. The exercise of arbitrary power by officials is completely contrary to the dictates of the rule of law. The natural law roots of the rule of law are obvious. In essence the rule of law asserts that natural rights and the social contract between governor and governed are to be protected by the law and its institutions.

Natural law and the rule of law are principally concerned with the civil and political rights of the individual. Socialism is more concerned with the obligation of the state to provide economic and social rights to its people. The Declaration seeks to achieve a synthesis between these two categories of rights — today known as first and second generation rights respectively. Thus, in its second paragraph, it lists 'freedom from want' (a phrase coined by President Roosevelt during the Second World War) along with the traditional first generation freedoms of speech and belief and the freedom from fear.

A theme running through the Preamble is the connection between respect for human rights and international peace (fourth paragraph). Traditionally international law permitted a state to treat its own citizens as it pleased. The 'domestic jurisdiction' of a state was its own domain in which other states might not interfere. The result of this was that during the 1930s the democracies of the world refused to intervene in the affairs of the dictatorships in the West and East, until it was too late. Had the democracies adopted a firmer stance against the suppression of human rights in Germany, Russia, Spain, Italy, and Japan in the 1930s, they might have prevented the Second World War. The evidence of the close connection between the suppression of human rights, dictatorship, and war made the drafters of both the United Nations Charter and the Universal Declaration determined to create a world order in which international peace would be preserved through the protection of human rights in individual states.

The new order is reflected in Articles 55 and 56 of the United Nations Charter in which member states reaffirm their faith in fundamental human rights and pledge themselves to promote universal respect for human rights without distinction based on race, gender, language, or religion. The fifth and sixth paragraphs of the Preamble reiterate this commitment and pledge. Articles 55 and 56 of the Charter do not describe the human rights to be respected in any detail. This is left to the Declaration, which describes the basic civil, political, economic, and social rights that states are expected to respect and promote.

In its final paragraph the Preamble proclaims the Universal Declaration 'as a common standard of achievement for all peoples and all nations' and calls upon individuals and governments to promote respect for the rights contained in the Declaration, both within their own countries and abroad, by means of public education and the introduction of progressive laws. This paragraph serves to emphasize an obvious truth: the Declaration, as a recommendatory resolution of the General Assembly of the United Nations, does not itself impose legal obligations upon states. Instead it is a clarion call to them and to their citizens, backed by powerful moral and political authority, to observe and to promote these rights.

The two main sources of international law are treaties (written agreements between states) and custom (those rules of practice between states that are widely accepted and are felt by states to impose legal obligations upon them). A resolution of the General Assembly does not create a rule of international law because it is neither treaty nor custom. However, if sufficiently repeated and translated into the practice of states, a resolution may acquire force of law as a customary rule of law. Today it is convincingly argued that many of the rights and freedoms enunciated in the Declaration are part of customary law on the grounds that they have been reaffirmed in numerous resolutions of the General Assembly and Security Council, embodied in many human rights treaties, and endorsed by many domestic constitutions. In 1968 a United Nations Conference on human rights attended by 84 members met in Teheran, Iran, to review the progress made in the 20 years since the adoption of the Universal Declaration. It proclaimed:

The Universal Declaration of Human Rights states a common understanding of the peoples of the world concerning the inalienable and inviolable rights of all members of the human family and constitutes an obligation for the members of the international community.

South Africa's response to the new world order

South Africa's common law, with its roots in Roman-Dutch law of the seventeenth to eighteenth centuries and English law, is strongly influenced by natural law. The great Roman-Dutch jurists, such as Hugo de Groot (1583–1645) and Johannes Voet (1647–1713), who shaped the development of Roman-Dutch law, belonged to the school of natural law; and the English common law is founded on the principles of equity and fairness inherent in the rule of law. After the Second World War South Africa was a respected member of the international community. In 1945, the Prime Minister of South Africa, General Smuts, played a leading role in the drafting of the Preamble to the United Nations Charter, which reaffirms the faith of 'the peoples of the United Nations' in fundamental human rights. South Africa was therefore well placed to become a leading member of the new world order.

But it was not to be. In May 1948 the National Party came to power. It repudiated any suggestion that law was an autonomous institution committed to the advancement of human rights and principles of fairness. Instead, law became the weapon in the hands of the National Party to achieve a legal order premised on white racial superiority and political repression. Natural law and the rule of law were discarded: law was simply the will of the National Party.

South Africa, together with the Soviet bloc and Saudi Arabia, abstained from voting on the Universal Declaration. It rejected the argument that South Africa was in law obliged to respect human rights by reason of South Africa's ratification of the United Nations Charter, including Articles 55 and 56. Instead it claimed that in terms of the Charter and traditional international law there were no restraints on the manner in which it treated its own citizens. It could do what it liked in its own domestic jurisdiction.

Initially there was support for this approach from some colonial powers. But as the imperial powers decolonized their empires, and human rights became a more pervasive theme in international relations, South Africa became increasingly isolated. South Africa's Western allies rejected the argument that apartheid was a domestic affair beyond the concern of the United Nations, and in 1971 the International Court of Justice, in an advisory opinion on Namibia, held that Articles 55 and 56 of the United Nations Charter imposed binding obligations on South Africa in the field of human rights.

The political organs of the United Nations imposed economic sanctions on South Africa. The Commonwealth, the European

Countries which have adopted the Declaration

Afghanistan*
Albania
Algeria
Angola
Antigua & Barbuda
Argentina*
Australia*
Austria
Bahamas
Bahrain
Bangladesh
Barbados
Belgium*
Belize
Benin
Bhutan
Bolivia*
Botswana
Brazil*
Brunei
Bulgaria
Burkina Faso
Burma
Burundi
Byelorussian SSR*†
Cameroon
Canada*
Cape Verde
Central African Rep.
Chad
Chile*
China*
Colombia*
Comoros
Congo
Costa Rica*
Cuba*
Cyprus
Czechoslovakia*†
Denmark*
Djibouti
Dominica
Dominican Republic*
Ecuador*
Egypt*
El Salvador*
Equatorial Guinea
Ethiopia*
Fiji
Finland
France*
Gabon
Gambia

Germany
Ghana
Greece*
Grenada
Guatemala*
Guinea
Guinea-Bissau
Guyana
Haiti*
Honduras*
Hungary
Iceland*
India*
Indonesia
Iran*
Iraq*
Ireland, Rep. of
Israel
Italy
Ivory Coast
Jamaica
Japan
Jordan
Kampuchea
Kenya
Kuwait
Laos
Lebanon*
Lesotho
Liberia*
Libya
Luxembourg*
Madagascar
Malawi
Malaysia
Maldives, Rep. of
Mali
Malta
Mauritania
Mauritius
Mexico*
Mongolian PR
Morocco
Mozambique
Nepal
Netherlands*
New Zealand*
Nicaragua*
Niger
Nigeria
Norway*
Oman

Pakistan*
Panama*
Papua New Guinea
Paraguay*
Peru*
Philippines*
Poland*†
Portugal
Qatar
Romania
Rwanda
St. Kitts-Nevis
St. Lucia
St. Vincent &
    the Grenadines
São Tome e Principe
Senegal
Seychelles
Sierra Leone
Singapore
Solomon Islands
Somali Republic
Spain
Sri Lanka
Sudan
Surinam
Swaziland
Sweden*
Syria*
Tanzania
Thailand*
Togo
Trinidad & Tobago
Tunisia
Turkey*
Uganda
Ukrainian SSR*†
USSR*†
United Arab Emirates
United Kingdom*
United States*
Uruguay*
Vanuatu
Venezuela*
Vietnam
Western Samoa
Yemen Arab Republic
Yemen PDR
Yugoslavia*†
Zaire
Zambia
Zimbabwe

* Members of the United Nations in 1948.
† Members of the Soviet bloc, 6 of 8 countries that abstained from voting in 1948, claimed that the Declaration did not put enough emphasis on economic, social, and cultural rights. Saudi Arabia and South Africa have never adopted the Declaration: Saudi Arabia as it believed that the article on religious freedom is contrary to the Koran; South Africa, while hoping to give South Africans basic human rights, believed that the Declaration 'went too far'.

Economic Community, and individual states, notably the United States of America, followed suit. South Africa was excluded from a host of international organizations and denied participation in the General Assembly of the United Nations. Sporting and cultural ties were severed by other countries. All this action was taken by reason of South Africa's failure to comply with its legal obligations under both the Charter and the customary law of human rights.

Over the years the South African government has changed its attitude towards human rights. At first it attempted to argue that apartheid in the guise of separate development did not violate the principal human rights norms proclaimed in the Declaration. More recently it has abandoned this approach and now it accepts the need to bring South African law into line with international standards. Hence its support for a Bill of Rights, which contains many of the rights proclaimed in the Declaration.

2
The right to human dignity

Article 1 All human beings are born free and equal in dignity and rights. They are endowed with reason and conscience and should act towards one another in a spirit of brotherhood.

What this article means

This article means that human beings are free and have the same dignity and rights. No one has a claim to more freedom, more dignity, or more rights than another. All people have special gifts of reason and conscience which set them apart from animals. For this reason they can distinguish between right and wrong and act accordingly. It follows that they should always treat one another like sisters or brothers; they should treat one another on the basis of equality.

Equality of treatment does not mean that people should be treated equally whatever their position. Because social, economic, or political conditions of people vary, this might merit different treatment. For example, poor people cannot be expected to pay the same tax as rich people. In this case it would be unfair to treat them the same way. What equality of treatment means is that if there has to be a difference of treatment, it should not be based on unjustifiable grounds, such as colour and religion.

Divisions between people have been created in the course of history by the more powerful, in order to justify more privileges. Although no person can claim to be superior to another on the grounds of blood, race, or colour, distinctions on the basis of social class and race have developed. Power enables certain groups or individuals to decide on the distribution of the resources of the country, and they often claim a greater share on the basis of supposed noble descent, colour, class, or race.

Those who are discriminated against usually resent this treatment. As a result, they clamour for the same rights and privileges as their rulers, who resist. Quite frequently, conflict results. The intensity of the conflict depends on the prevailing circumstances.

After the Second World War, it was recognized (through documents such as the Universal Declaration) that one of the guarantees against future world wars was international respect for and protection of human rights. Human rights require that people should be treated as human beings and not otherwise. Even the ruler or state must respect the rights of the individual. There must be an area of freedom for the individual in which, simply, the state must not interfere.

Major religions, philosophies, and poetic traditions have long asserted the freedom and equality of human beings. One example is the Holy Bible in which, in the book of Genesis, the common ancestry of people and the common parenthood of God is emphasized.

Influential philosophers have asserted that human beings are born free and equal. Jean Jacques Rousseau's ideas inspired the French Revolution; John Locke had a considerable influence on English philosophical and political thinking. Their ideas influenced the American Revolution and the declarations which followed. The ideas in these documents also contributed to the development of the concept of human rights. The American Declaration of Independence contains the following famous lines:

> We hold these truths to be self-evident, that all men are created equal, that they are endowed by their Creator, with certain unalienable rights, that among these are life, liberty and the pursuit of happiness. That to secure these rights, governments are instituted among men, deriving their just powers from the consent of the governed, that ... it is the right of the people to institute new government laying its foundation on such principles, and organizing its power in such form, as to them shall seem most likely to effect their safety and happiness.

The Virginia Declaration of Rights contains similar claims.

Despite this tradition of respect for freedom and equality, history is full of cases of people being treated harshly. Slavery, which has been practised in various societies, denies the freedom and equality of all people. A slave has no freedom and no dignity. Slaves are the property of their owners.

Those who are enslaved, oppressed, or discriminated against often find ways of rising up against their position of servitude. Freedom is the greatest desire of all people. People resent unequal treatment because it is discriminatory, unjust, and oppressive. Wars of liberation have been fought as a result of oppression and discrimination. The purpose of Article 1 is to guarantee freedom, equality, and dignity so that oppressed people do not have to turn to conflict to gain liberation.

The article in South African law

It is well known that since 1948 the South African government has violated Article 1 through its policy of apartheid, which is based on racial separation and discrimination. Admittedly, when the National Party took over power in 1948 it did not invent racial segregation; it had existed long before. From the earliest contact between white and black people in South Africa the policy of whites was one of no equality between the races. Attempts at integration was one of the factors which led to the Great Trek. The Boers were looking for a place where they could be free to pursue this policy of no equality. In the Boer republics which were later established, this policy of inequality between the races was restored. This does not mean that the English colonists in Natal believed in integration and respected the black people. They did not. The roots of segregation are found in Natal as well.

When the Union of South Africa was formed in 1910, racial separation continued. Although South Africa is not unique in practising racial discrimination, this country has enforced apartheid through a carefully-constructed legal order.

The cornerstone of the government's policy of apartheid is the Population Registration Act of 1950 which provides for the classification of people as whites, 'coloureds', or Africans (with subdivisions within the African and 'coloured' groups). The Indian group (a sub-group of 'coloureds') became an effective fourth statutory group. The criteria for classifying people are appearance, social acceptance, and descent. In other words, in order to be classified white, you must obviously look like a white person; you must socialize with and be accepted by the whites as a white person; and you must be born of white parents. If one of your parents is not white, it means you are not white but 'coloured'.

The application of this act has been extremely harsh and humiliating. It has brought about untold suffering, misery, and broken hearts for black people of this country, and especially to 'coloureds'. Families have been torn apart when husbands and wives, parents and children, brothers and sisters have been classified as belonging to different 'race' groups.

To reinforce racial separation, the government prohibited people of different 'races' from marrying one another or having sexual relationships with one another. This was decreed in the Prohibition of Mixed Marriages Act of 1950. Although the act has been abolished, it has left a trail of destruction and misery behind it. And although 'mixed marriages' are now allowed, there is still little provision for the residence of mixed couples.

In terms of the Group Areas Act of 1950, separate residential areas for different racial groups were created in every city, town, or village. Hundreds of 'coloureds' and Indians were uprooted. Property was expropriated. Many white speculators were enriched while Indian and 'coloured' owners were moved. In some areas Africans also experienced forced removals.

There are many other pieces of legislation which authorized invidious discrimination against black people. Examples include legislation creating separate amenities for different race groups; the influx-control laws which severely restricted the freedom of movement of African people; the labour legislation which curtailed collective bargaining by African labour; education legislation which created separate educational institutions for whites and blacks; and political legislation which created separate structures for the black people of this country. The final solution was that ultimately there would be no African South Africans. Africans would be citizens of one or other 'independent homeland'.

These discriminatory laws were reinforced by security legislation. These lead to detention without trial, restriction, and silencing and banning of organizations and individuals who dared to criticize or attempted to frustrate the government's policy of apartheid. Many people were imprisoned and others died in prison under suspicious circumstances.

The government has, however, paid a very high price for its policy of apartheid. It has created a crisis of legitimacy for the whole legal system. Black people have revolted against this policy and the laws based on it. This violence has led in the past to the declaration of a state of emergency.

One of the effects of the violation of Article 1 has been the entrenchment of racism. It has created divisions and suspicions which will be difficult to eliminate. It has also bred bitterness and resentment in the hearts of black people, who have been dehumanized by the system. The hostility which this treatment has created has sometimes been suppressed because blacks have been unable to retaliate against their source of oppression.

When people have been treated harshly, they tend to do the same to others. If people learn that they are not cared about, they in turn do not care about others. The endemic violence which has engulfed the country recently is evidence of this development. The destruction of life and burning of property has become commonplace. Some of the most violent actions have been directed against those who have been identified as collaborators in the system. People have been 'necklaced' and houses have been petrol-bombed. Sometimes the perpetrators have danced and clapped their hands in satisfaction.

The consequences of apartheid mean international isolation, economic sanctions, an ailing rand, a weak economy, massive unemployment, and excruciating poverty. The government is now reaping the fruits of what it has sown over the years. In the light of this crisis South Africans need to reassert the freedom and equality of all human beings. They need to treat one another in a spirit of brotherhood and sisterhood.

The law of the future

There is no doubt that just as the violation of Article 1 has led to certain consequences, the recognition of the article will have certain effects. Violation led to discrimination and consequent anger, frustration, bitterness, hate, racial conflict, and brutality. Recognition could result in racial harmony and healthy relations across the country.

The observance of this article would lead to the restoration of the dignity of black people as equal citizens of South Africa. It would restore their full humanity and respect. The fostering of healthy race relations would facilitate freedom and ensure that the resources of the country are used more profitably to promote human welfare and development rather than to enforce a wicked political system. Resources would be used to improve education and workers' skills. This would lead to greater productivity, more employment opportunities, and less poverty. Violence would also diminish.

In order to achieve this, all racially-discriminatory laws must be repealed and all forms of racial discrimination should be prohibited. Although racial discrimination is based on deep-seated racial attitudes, there is no doubt that when legal discrimination has been abolished it may lead to the altering of racial attitudes. The outlawing of discrimination encourages those who are against it to fight it. It provides a support system for developing non-racial attitudes. It is obviously easier to change one's actions than one's attitude. Yet if the law discourages any practice, one is ultimately forced to change one's attitude.

There are certain areas which are less responsive to change than others. However, it is possible to drum up support for the change of racial attitudes on the grounds that it is in the national interest to be non-racial. Racial discrimination has been the major reason for the international isolation of South Africa. Many black leaders have fought for the dismantling of apartheid through international pressure. The removal of apartheid would mean that a non-racial democratic dispensation will be established in South Africa. This will mean that South Africa will be on its way to being restored to its place in the community of nations.

All this will take time and effort, requiring compromises and sacrifices. Yet it will be well worth the effort; any attempt to cling to the old order would be suicidal.

The recognition of Article 1 requires all South Africans to realize that it is ultimately in their interests to respect the human dignity and liberty of all, and to treat each other as fellow human beings. To do otherwise only leads to conflict, violence, and destruction. The price to be paid for observing the provisions of the article is far lower than the cost of disregarding it.

The repeal of the laws that discriminate, not only on the basis of race but also on the basis of gender, will improve people's attitudes towards South African law. This will lead to the creation of a legal system that enjoys the support of the majority of the people. Law does not simply depend on punishments for its enforcement, but also on the belief on the part of the people that the law protects and furthers their interests.

3
Freedom from discrimination

Article 2 Everyone is entitled to all the rights and freedoms set forth in this Declaration, without distinction of any kind, such as race, colour, sex, language, religion, political or other opinion, national or social origin, property, birth or other status.

Furthermore, no distinction shall be made on the basis of the political, jurisdictional or international status of the country or territory to which a person belongs, whether it be independent, trust, non-self-governing or under any other limitation of sovereignty.

What this article means

Article 2 consists of two sections: the principle of non-discrimination, and its territorial application. For reasons of clarity they will be discussed separately.

Because of the multiracial, multi-cultural, and multi-ethnic nature of South African society, the first section of Article 2 deserves more attention, although this does not mean that the second section is unimportant.

1. No discrimination

The Universal Declaration sets out different kinds of rights and freedoms to which human beings are entitled. For example, all have the right to a nationality (Article 15), and a right to equal pay for equal work (Article 23). Article 2 states that *everybody* is subject to all the rights and freedoms set out in the Declaration, and that the race, colour, or gender of the person should play no part in determining whether he or she may enjoy those rights and freedoms. For example, the right to own property (Article 17) means that any individual has the right to buy land anywhere, and that right should not be interfered with because the persons wishing to buy the land are not of the 'right colour'. Nor should the right to participate in the government (Article 21), whether it be at the national or local level, be restricted to any section of the population because of their race. Furthermore, an individual's status in marriage should not be weaker on account of the individual's gender (Article 16).

In the same way the 'religion, political or other opinion, the national or social origin, property, birth or other status' of a person should not determine whether he or she should enjoy the rights set out in the Declaration. For example, the right to marry (Article 16) should not be interfered with because the persons wishing to marry are not of the same religion. Nor should the right to life (Article 3) or the right to be equal before the law (Article 7) be less seriously asserted because people are poor, or not of the 'right class'. The underlying principle is that one's birth or status, over which one has no control, ought never to be held against one. This applies no matter what family one is born into, whether one's parents are rich or poor, whether one is black or white, male or female, Muslim, Christian or Hindu. *All* are entitled to certain fundamental rights.

The issue of discrimination based on race, gender, colour, religion, or language is one that has concerned the international community for decades. The experience of Nazism during the Second World War has shown the world the evils of racism, and what destruction can be done in the name of racial purity. The extent of the concern of the world community about this issue is clear from the wording of Article 2.

The United Nations has gone even further in an attempt to give Article 2 more teeth. Since the Declaration was passed in 1948, other important anti-discrimination instruments have been passed. These include the Racial Discrimination Convention, the Discrimination against Women Convention, and the Declaration on the Elimination of All Forms of Intolerance and of Discrimination Based on Religion or Belief. In short, the world community views discrimination as morally wrong, as fundamentally unjust, and an evil which ought to be eradicated.

2. Territorial application of non-discrimination

This part of the article attempts to overcome a particular problem. It tries to ensure that the rights and freedoms in the Declaration are not denied to citizens of certain countries or territories. For example, a citizen of a small island or country, which becomes part of and is administered by a larger neighbouring country, is entitled to the rights and freedoms enjoyed by the citizens of the larger country. If education is provided to all the citizens of the larger country, then education should also be provided to the inhabitants of the dependent territory.

In essence, the idea behind this clause is that people who have rights of residence in a particular country must be able to enjoy all the rights and freedoms which the citizens of that country enjoy. There must not be any discrimination on the grounds that an individual is associated with another territory.

The article in South African law

1. No discrimination

South Africa's contribution to discrimination can be illustrated by means of a short story.

Mr. and Mrs. Mabaso live in a two-roomed house in KwaMashu with their three children, Mojalifa, Thulani, and Thandi and their two grandchildren, Nomsa and Siphiwe. Mr. and Mrs. Mabaso were lucky to obtain their house in 1954 when they were married, because there was such a big housing shortage in the township, as well as a long waiting list. Because Mr. Mabaso had a lodger's permit in the house when the registered tenant died, he was able to persuade the local council to let him take over as the registered tenant.

Mrs. Mabaso works in a florist shop in Westville, and she travels there by bus every day. Mr. Mabaso is employed as an order clerk in a Durban library. Mr. Mabaso is due to retire in a year or two, and he is expecting a big pension payout.

Mr. and Mrs. Mabaso intend to buy a house when he receives his pension, as their family wish to remain together, and their two-roomed house in KwaMashu is no longer adequate. Their children have offered financial assistance to obtain the house, because they wish to continue living with their parents.

On her way to and from work Mrs. Mabaso regularly sees beautiful houses for sale in Westville. She knows that even if she and her husband could afford them, those houses cannot be sold to them. In terms of the Group Areas Act of 1966 (which sets aside separate areas for different race groups, e.g. whites, 'coloureds', and Indians) they are not by law allowed to own or occupy a house there. Houses in most of Westville are reserved for ownership and occupation by whites only.

Thandi Mabaso has worked as a clerk for a small clothing business in Clairwood for the past five years. She is told by the supervisor that he will be moving to Johannesburg at the end of the year, and because she is such a diligent and good worker, she should apply for his position. In the past she has done his job whenever he was away and she feels she is qualified to be a supervisor. She approaches her manager, and asks to be considered for the position of supervisor. Her manager informs her that even though she is an excellent worker, she cannot be placed in the position of supervisor because the other workers will not take her seriously. He feels that a man would carry more authority.

Thandi wishes to enrol her son, Siphiwe, for school the following year, but there are not enough schools in KwaMashu close to where she lives. Most schools in the township, even those further away, are already full. She decides to enrol her son at a local primary school in Clairwood. When she goes to see the principal, he explains to her that the school caters only for children of the Indian community, and that she cannot enrol her son there, because he is not classified as an Indian.

One day, on her way home from work, Mrs. Mabaso notices a group of children, including her two grandchildren, milling around a shop at a street corner. They are all bending over an old man who looks as if he has fallen. Mrs. Mabaso then sees that the old man is in pain, and that he desperately needs a doctor. She goes to the shop and asks the shopkeeper to telephone for an ambulance immediately. The shopkeeper makes the call while Mrs. Mabaso goes back to the injured man. A few minutes later the shopkeeper runs out the shop and tells Mrs. Mabaso that the white ambulance cannot come to KwaMashu, and that it might take the black ambulance about half an hour to get there.

Mrs. Mabaso calls a local doctor who treats the injured man. Later it is discovered that the old man's injuries are permanent. The doctor advises him to apply for social welfare benefits, and the injured man sends his daughter along to a government department to get the necessary forms. She is handed a form for 'non-white' recipients, and is given a schedule of payments for the different racial groups.

Unfortunately, the story does not end here. But it does highlight some aspects of life in South Africa. It also shows how often Article 2 is violated:

❏ not allowing certain racial groups to own property in a particular residential area amounts to racial discrimination;

❏ making distinctions on the basis of a person's gender is discriminatory;

❏ setting aside different schools for different racial groups is in direct contradiction to the requirements of Article 2;

❒ providing medical care and social services along racial or ethnic lines is discriminatory.

2. Territorial application of non-discrimination

South Africa's 'homelands' system persistently violates the rights contained in Article 2. For example, when 'homelands' become 'independent' many people lose their rights to South African citizenship and all the benefits flowing from citizenship.

Much more could be said about these forms of discrimination. See, for example, the chapters dealing with questions of nationality and freedom of movement (Chapters 16 and 14).

The law of the future

Article 2, in insisting that all the rights and freedoms set out in the Declaration are provided *without discrimination*, implicitly recognizes the link between discrimination and peace. In order for good relations and harmony to exist between the citizens of a country, all citizens must have equal access to the benefits which that society has to offer. If any kind of discrimination exists, and it is officially approved in the laws, there can never be peace. To a large extent the turmoil and conflict in South Africa has its roots in the discriminatory apartheid system.

Furthermore, the principle of non-discrimination is important for peace between the different nations of the world. The spirit of the Universal Declaration is that nations of the world will exist as peaceful neighbours, and that within the international community the fundamental rights and freedoms will be respected without discrimination. South Africa has been strongly condemned by the international community through the United Nations. The International Convention on the Suppression and Punishment of the Crime of Apartheid, passed in 1973, is the most obvious example of this condemnation.

South Africa needs to take seriously the rights and freedoms set out in the Declaration. The entrenchment of these rights and freedoms would be best achieved in a Bill of Rights. This would go a long way to ensuring that equality and justice become part of the culture of this country.

If Article 2 were to be applied in South Africa, then all people who were born within the borders of this country would have the same rights and freedoms. The borders of this country are those that were in place when the Union of South Africa was formed in 1910. The 'homeland' borders are artificial, and need to be swept away.

Article 2 provides the umbrella, the framework, for all the rights and freedoms stated in the Declaration. It attempts to set the tone as to how the Declaration ought to be looked at. The underlying idea of Article 2 is that discrimination, and unfair or arbitrary distinctions, have no part to play in a decent society. Nor should an 'accident of birth', such as race, ethnicity, or gender, be a liability. Article 2 also attempts to ensure that people's nationality is not used unfairly against them; that the status of the territory or country into which they were born is not used to deprive them of fundamental rights.

Without the discrimination of apartheid, all South Africans can be more optimistic about a peaceful and prosperous future.

4
The right to life, liberty, and security

Article 3   *Everyone has the right to life, liberty and security of person.*

What this article means

1. Life

The right to life is an essential prerequisite for all the other rights listed in the Universal Declaration, and this makes it the most fundamental right of all. Without life, none of the other rights is of any use.

Because of its basic importance, the right to life appears in virtually every international and regional human rights instrument, including the European Convention on Human Rights. On the other hand, it is equally true that a right to life is useless on its own. Life without any other benefits (guarantees of freedom, security, and so on) would be a miserable thing indeed. Other, more specific rights are needed to give significance to the condition of being alive.

A problem common to all instruments containing a right to life is its abstract character. Because 'life' is such a general concept, it is difficult to translate it into concrete terms or to give it specific meaning. One thing is clear, however: since death is a certainty for every human being, there can be no unqualified or absolute right to life. With the best will in the world, no government can prevent the natural death of every one of its citizens; and what is the point of having a right which is impossible to enforce?

It would be more realistic, therefore, to speak of a right not to be deprived of one's life, and of corresponding duties on the government to take all the necessary steps to prevent untimely death. But what does this actually mean? On a very narrow interpretation, it might mean that the state should not take one's life 'arbitrarily', or without lawful authority. On a wider interpretation, it might mean that the state should abolish the death penalty and make abortion (bringing about the death of an unborn baby) illegal. On the widest possible interpretation, it might mean that the state should take steps to reduce the incidence of death by preventable causes; for instance, by improving its health and welfare services, prohibiting or limiting the sale of alcohol, cigarettes, and firearms, and by educating its citizens against the spread of AIDS and other fatal diseases.

This third interpretation is certainly a pipe-dream, and is not upheld anywhere in the world. One reason is that positive action of this kind tends to be expressed in vague terms. At what point will the health services comply with the required standard? How many hospitals must the government build — one, ten, or fifty? Another reason is the expense involved in programmes for social reform. Many of the world's governments simply could not afford to implement such reform, even if they wanted to. A third reason arises out of the problem of enforcement by the courts, what lawyers call the problem of 'justiciability'. It is one thing for judges to support the right to life by sentencing a murderer, but quite another for a judge to make an order that health services should be improved. The decision to put more money into health services is regarded as a political decision rather than a legal one, and politics is a game traditionally played by the government, and not by the courts.

The second, more practicable interpretation of what a government must do to prevent untimely death avoids these problems. But even it is unrealistic: nearly all the countries which supported the Universal Declaration in 1948 continue to impose the death penalty in the case of serious crimes such as murder. The reason for keeping the death penalty is often said to be its value as an effective deterrent to other would-be murderers; and, therefore, that the death penalty actually helps to uphold the right to life. In many of those countries abortion is also practised legally. Here it can be argued that an abortion performed in the early stages of pregnancy does not conflict with the right to life, on the basis that the baby's 'life' has not yet begun. It can also be argued that it is right to terminate the life of an unborn baby where continued pregnancy is a danger to the mother's life. But note that these arguments do not justify abortion 'on demand', or even abortion where the pregnancy has resulted from a rape. Both these grounds of abortion are permitted by law in some countries which support the Declaration.

For these reasons, the most widely supported interpretation of the government's duty to protect life is the first and narrowest one: that the right to life merely prohibits the 'arbitrary' or 'unlawful' deprivation of life. Again, one has to ask what this means. If it means that the government is free to kill its citizens as long as there is a law saying so, the right to life becomes valueless. For the right to have significance, then, it must mean that the laws which allow people to be killed (such as a law which provides for a death penalty) must comply with some minimum standard of justice or fairness. That minimum standard will, of course, vary from society to society, and it will partly be shaped by the other rights officially recognized by the society. In a country supporting the Universal Declaration, for example, a compulsory death penalty applying only to light-skinned, blue-eyed rapists would conflict with Articles 1 and 2. These promote the equality of human beings and prohibit discrimination on the grounds of race and colour. A death penalty for all convicted rapists, on the other hand, might well be thought acceptable.

Euthanasia (mercy killing to put an end to suffering) poses great difficulties in relation to the right to life. Though it seems that involuntary euthanasia (without the consent of the ill person) is clearly contrary to the right to life, the same is not necessarily true of voluntary euthanasia, where the ill person agrees to the act. It can be argued, for instance, that the right to life includes a right to die with dignity, when and how one chooses. On this argument, one would permit voluntary euthanasia and one would not punish attempted suicides. There is no clear answer, however. It is worth noting that international law seems to regard euthanasia, abortion, and the death penalty as matters of 'legitimate diversity'; that is, issues on which different communities are bound to disagree.

2. Liberty

Liberty means freedom. Together with 'life', liberty is a classic political right which is protected in every major human rights instrument; but liberty (like 'life') is such a broad concept that it is virtually meaningless. Being free sounds like a good idea, but what does it promise? Does it mean freedom from slavery, freedom of speech, freedom of association, or freedom of religion — or all of those things?

The most common interpretation is probably that of physical freedom, or freedom of body and movement; the idea that no one may be held in slavery or otherwise be confined to a place without his or her consent. Since this and many other forms of freedom are specifically conferred in later articles of the Universal Declaration, the reference to liberty in Article 3 may seem to be superfluous. However, the general right to liberty could be a useful aid to interpretation in the case of doubt about the existence of a particular freedom.

Most human rights documents contain articles against the arbitrary deprivation of liberty, or denial which is not authorized by law. This means that it is quite possible to have laws which allow for the deprivation of liberty even though one has a Bill of Rights. Throughout the world, exceptions to the right to liberty are commonly made for the imprisonment of persons convicted of a crime; for keeping in custody persons who are to be tried or deported; and for detaining persons on the grounds of mental illness or contagious disease.

3. Security of the person

Security of the person is generally thought to refer to freedom from physical harm or pain such as torture and inhuman punishment — matters which are dealt with specifically in Article 5 of the Declaration. In order to comply with the right, a government would have to take steps to protect its citizens from harm. As with the rights to life and liberty, though, there is a limit to what governments can be made to do.

The right could reasonably imply freedom from unlawful assault, arrest, and many other forms of physical interference or restriction, including interference with one's privacy; but it could hardly include freedom from all kinds of pain. Thus, a government would probably be complying with the right if it merely discouraged assault and torture by means of legislation, and if the system provided remedies (such as money damages) for those who suffered breaches of the law.

The freedoms implied by this provision are already guaranteed in other articles of the Declaration, so 'security of the person' seems to fulfil a similar function to the other rights in Article 3; this is to reinforce the specific guarantees, and to provide a guide to the interpretation of the law.

The article in South African law

1. Life

In South African law, the right to life is already protected by legislation which makes it a criminal offence to perform or obtain an abortion. The Abortion and Sterilization Act of 1975 does, however, allow for legal abortion in certain cases; for example, where the pregnancy was the result of incest or rape, and where continued pregnancy would endanger the life or the physical or mental health of the mother. Euthanasia, whether voluntary or involuntary, is also illegal. But the punishment of mercy-killers has often been nominal: in a 1975 case, a medical doctor who gave a fatal dose of drugs to his aged and suffering father was imprisoned for less than a day.

South African law is in apparent conflict with the right to life in that it allows for the imposition of the death penalty. This penalty is reserved for the most serious crimes, such as murder, treason, and rape. As stated above, it is a penalty which continues to be imposed in most of the countries which recognize the right to life, so South African law is by no means an exception. Until recently the number of people executed in South Africa was extremely high. In 1987, for example, hangings averaged almost one every two days.

2. Liberty

The right to liberty receives very little protection in our law. While arrest with or without a warrant is a feature common to the law of every country, South African law is exceptional in that it allows arrested persons to be detained for long periods without being charged with an offence, and without being brought to trial. The Internal Security Act of 1982 is full of provisions allowing for detention without trial, and the Emergency Regulations have prohibited family members, friends, and lawyers from visiting detainees without official permission. The Internal Security Act also permits people to be 'banned', which prevents them from moving about freely or from exercising rights to freedom of speech, association, and assembly. Though our common law contains an important and valued remedy for freeing a person who has been illegally deprived of his or her liberty, virtually every piece of South African statute law which allows detention also contains a provision preventing the courts from taking up the matter. Fortunately, these provisions (called 'ouster clauses') are sometimes ignored by the courts.

Many other forms of liberty are restricted under South African law. The discussion of these (below) will show that our law authorizes violations of liberty which would never be tolerated in democratic countries.

3. Security of the person

It is a crime in our law to assault a person, or even to threaten harm, unless one is acting in self-defence or with lawful authority (for example, a policeman may have to use force to arrest a person). The law regards torture as a form of unlawful assault, but there is strong evidence to suggest that it is used extensively by the police to force confessions (see Chapter 6). As far as privacy is concerned, South African law permits considerable interference both with the private lives of its citizens and with their dignity (see Chapter 13).

The law of the future

1. Life

Many aspects of the right to life are regarded as issues of 'legitimate diversity' which means that they are highly subjective matters on which people and their governments easily disagree. This makes it difficult to speculate about the changes that might occur if South Africa ever committed itself to the right to life. Abortion and euthanasia would probably remain illegal, since the existing position would tend to gain support from an official recognition of the right to life. In relation to the death penalty, the most realistic scenario is probably that provided by the South African Law Commission in its working paper on group and human rights. The working paper recognizes the right to life, but recommends that the right should be limited to allow the death penalty to be imposed for the most serious crimes. However, the Law Commission may yet have reason to change its proposals. There have been signs of renewed interest in the abolition of the death penalty, and South African attitudes may well change as a result of the abolitionists' campaign.

2. Liberty

A commitment to liberty would undoubtedly bring about important changes, both to the law and to thousands of South Africans who have had to live with the threat — or the reality — of indefinite detention, banning orders, and the like. In particular, the infamous system of detention without trial would be in conflict with even the narrowest interpretations of the right to liberty. This is borne out by the South African Law Commission's proposals, which limit detention to the following (internationally-accepted) forms: the admission of mentally ill or drug-dependent persons into institutions; the detention of persons awaiting trial, extradition, or deportation; the imprisonment of convicted offenders; and detention in order to prevent the spread of infectious diseases.

3. Security of the person

As already mentioned, freedom from unlawful arrest, assault, torture, invasion of privacy, and inhumane punishment are specifically dealt with in other articles of the Declaration. Their implications for South African law are discussed in other chapters.

5
The right not to be held in slavery or servitude

Article 4 No one shall be held in slavery or servitude; slavery and the slave trade shall be prohibited in all their forms.

What this article means

Article 4 is a more concrete expression of the general provision that 'All human beings are born free and equal in dignity and rights' (Article 1). Because slavery involves the oppression of a person or a class of people, it is based upon the idea of the *inequality* of human beings. Slavery (or servitude such as forced labour) robs people of their dignity and reduces their human status by denying them freedom to live and work where and how they choose.

The word 'slavery' conjures up the practices of bygone eras; one tends to think of Roman slaves or of Negroes working on the plantations of the old American South, where people were treated as 'chattels' or things: they were bought and sold, kept in chains, made to work for little or no wages, and were often brutally punished for disobedience. Partly as a result of the International Slavery Convention of 1926, this extreme form of slavery has certainly been abolished all over the world, and the slave trade would probably be regarded as illegal even in countries with the poorest record of respecting human rights.

But there are less extreme forms of slavery which are regularly practised in many countries of the world: for example, the temporary sale of children for their work, and the system of debt bondage, in which a debtor pays off his or her debt by becoming the 'slave' of the creditor. These practices amount to forced or compulsory labour, which, though not expressly referred to in the Universal Declaration, is outlawed as a form of slavery in many other international human rights conventions.

But what is forced labour? Compulsory military service, or

conscription, can be regarded as forced labour, as can compulsory civil service of any sort. For this reason many human rights instruments make exceptions for conscription and other forms of compulsory service to the state, most obviously the compulsory work done by convicts. By contrast, the African Charter places a duty on *every* citizen to put his or her intellectual and physical abilities at the service of the national community.

Forced labour is not the only modern form of slavery. For example, arranged marriages are regarded by some as slavery in that they take away one's freedom to marry the person of one's choice. Furthermore, laws or customs which are racially discriminatory, or which reduce the status of adult women below that of adult men, so injure the ideals of human equality and dignity that they may well be thought to amount to slavery. Whether or not this is so, such laws or customs would in any event be contrary to Articles 1 and 2 of the Declaration, which proclaim the equality of all human beings and which prohibit discrimination on the grounds of gender and race.

The article in South African law

Though our law contains no explicit right not to be held in slavery, there is a special legal remedy to challenge the unlawful deprivation of liberty. This remedy was originally used in Roman law to obtain the liberty of a freeman who was being held as a slave.

As in most countries, forced labour is not uncommon for South African convicts. Detainees, however, are exempt from this kind of labour. On the other hand, our system of compulsory military service and annual 'camps' is one of the world's most demanding. Conscripts who refuse to do military service may be (and frequently are) sentenced to a maximum of six years' imprisonment, which would be regarded as cruel and inhumane punishment in most of the countries which support the Declaration.

As for forms of 'economic slavery', these are rife in South Africa. There is no national minimum wage, and many workers who are not protected by labour legislation receive 'slave' wages or no money wages at all. Domestic workers and farmworkers are particularly disadvantaged. Farmworkers sometimes work in return only for food and accommodation. Though the old system of 'labour tenancy' was legally abolished 20 years ago, it continues to be practised on many farms where labourers (or their families) are obliged to work in exchange for the right to live on the farm.

The law of the future

The abolition of slavery means increased respect for human freedom and dignity, and an increased concern with the equality of all people. This kind of concern is foreign to many South Africans brought up under the apartheid regime. The abolition of slavery in *all* its forms is highly unlikely, but even the slightest reform in this area would bring about radical changes to South African attitudes.

In relation to forced labour, the South African Law Commission's proposals provide a possible picture of the future. The Commission's proposed Bill of Rights includes the right not to be held in slavery or to be subjected to forced labour. However, it makes exceptions for forced labour during imprisonment and 'such compulsory military or civil service as may reasonably be acceptable in a democratic state'. This formula is used in many other human rights instruments. Unfortunately, it is by no means clear what *would* be regarded as acceptable. Would two years in the army (or in the civil service) be 'reasonable'? One year? Six months?

As far as other forms of 'slavery' are concerned, the Law Commission has made a number of important proposals. For instance, its Bill proclaims the right to freedom of movement and residence, freedom of marriage, racial and sexual equality, and the right to participate in economic activity 'freely and on an equal footing'. There is no reference to fair or minimum wages, however. Such provisions could turn out to be essential to the abolition of economic slavery in its less obvious or indirect forms.

6
Freedom from torture and ill-treatment

Article 5 *No one shall be subjected to torture or to cruel, inhuman or degrading treatment or punishment.*

What this article means

This article prohibits torture and cruel, inhuman, or degrading treatment or punishment. Torture describes treatment which has a purpose such as the obtaining of information or confessions. For these reasons it is considered to be a severe form of cruel and inhuman or degrading treatment. The definition of torture also includes non-physical treatment such as the causing of mental suffering. This produces anguish and stress in the victim.

Inhuman treatment can be defined as causing pain or suffering for its own sake. Therefore, deliberately causing physical or mental pain or suffering against the will of the victim is an example of inhuman treatment. So is causing pain or suffering as part of criminal punishment where that punishment is out of proportion to the offence.

Degrading has been defined as lowering in rank, reputation, or character; therefore degrading treatment amounts to acts designed to lower the victim in the eyes of other people or of himself or herself. It has been pointed out by a number of international courts that all forms of judicial punishment are degrading but some further degrading treatment must be present to bring it into conflict with this article. In other words, the humiliation or debasement of the victim must be far beyond the usual element of humiliation experienced in the ordinary operation of the criminal justice system.

In the interpretation of the Eighth Amendment to the United States (US) Constitution, which prohibits the infliction of 'cruel and unusual punishments', the US Supreme Court has recognized that the meaning of this prohibition is 'highly elastic' and that its meaning will be determined by 'evolving standards of decency that mark the progress of a maturing society'.

For this reason it can be said that the meaning of Article 5 cannot be defined precisely, but, to a large extent, will depend upon the development of standards of decency and morality amongst humankind.

The commonly-accepted meaning of Article 5 (or similar articles in other documents) can be seen in court interpretations. The following forms of treatment have been held to fall within the scope of the article:

❏ sterilization without consent;

❏ ill-treatment of persons serving sentence, such as lack of adequate or correct medical treatment, flogging, confinement in isolation if it is harmful to the physical or mental health of the prisoner;

❏ ill-treatment of detainees (In the context of Article 3 of the European Convention on Human Rights, the European Court of Human Rights held that five methods used by the security forces in Northern Ireland to interrogate detainees, namely wall standing, hooding, subjection to noise, deprivation of sleep, and reduction of diet, did not, even cumulatively, amount to torture but did constitute inhuman and degrading treatment.);

❏ forms of punishment such as beatings of the feet, electric shock treatment, the administration of drugs, and flogging (It has also been argued that corporal punishment is a form of cruel and inhuman treatment.);

❏ deportation and extradition to countries where the prisoner can expect ill-treatment (The US Supreme Court has held that depriving a citizen of his nationality on the basis of a court-martial conviction for his desertion in time of war — when he had been absent from his duty for less than a day and had willingly surrendered — was 'cruel and unusual punishment' and hence in violation of the Eighth Amendment. In general, it has been argued that denationalization as a form of punishment is neither necessary nor appropriate.); and

❏ a number of organizations and legal authorities have argued that the death penalty is a cruel and inhuman punishment within the meaning of Article 5. (Amnesty International, in their report on the death penalty, argue that the death penalty, like torture, constitutes an extreme physical and mental assault on a person who has already been made helpless by government authority.)

The article in South African law

The extent of South Africa's adherence to the standards of Article 5 can be measured by analysing the forms of treatment mentioned above.

1. Prisons

There are certain punishments which a commissioned officer has the power to impose on a prisoner which conflict with the standards contained in Article 5. Corporal punishment not exceeding six strokes may be given provided that the prisoner is a convicted male under the age of 40 years. Solitary confinement in an isolation cell may be ordered for a period not exceeding 30 days, and this can be combined with the punishment of spare diet. (Spare diet consists of 200 g of maize meal, twice daily, boiled in water without salt, and 15 g of protein soup powder boiled in 570 ml of water, once daily.) As far back as 1945 Mr. Justice Krause in the case of *R v Kumbana* described this punishment as follows: 'the sentence of solitary confinement with spare diet, is a form of cruelty reminiscent of the middle ages'.

Whipping is still imposed by the prison authorities. In a recent Supreme Court case of *S v November*, two prisoners were sentenced by the prison authorities to be whipped because they had refused to put their thumb print on a register after the completion of an official search. Mr. Justice Tebbutt said that 'whipping is a drastic punishment. It is also humiliating and demoralizing. It has repeatedly been held by our courts that it must be imposed with circumspection.' The court found that the prison authorities had not acted with the necessary circumspection and decided that the whipping should not be carried out.

2. Ill-treatment of detainees

Since the introduction of detention without trial in 1963 there have been persistent allegations of ill-treatment of detainees by the police. Between 1963 and 1988, 64 persons died whilst in detention. As a result, a number of official inquiries have been held, including the Biko and Aggett inquests which attracted massive public attention. André Brink also wrote a novel, *A Dry White Season*, which was later made into a film which dealt in graphic detail with torture of detainees.

Although the system of detention without trial was examined by a judicial commission of inquiry, the Rabie Commission, the report contained no examination of the methods of interrogation employed by the security police. Unfortunately no official commission has been appointed since the Rabie Commission. However, reports and studies published during the past five years provide clear indication of violations of Article 5.

A study of detention based upon interviews with 176 ex-detainees published in 1987 claimed that 83 per cent of these detainees reported some form of physical torture during detention. Forms of torture frequently used were beatings, forced standing, maintaining abnormal body positions, forced gymnasium-type exercises, electric shock treatment, and strangulation either by hand or by means of a cloth or towel.

All of the detainees interviewed claimed to have suffered some form of psychological torture. This included solitary confinement, verbal abuse, false accusations, threatened violence, threats of execution of the detainees or family, misleading information, and constant interrogation.

The Minister of Law and Order at the time, Mr. Louis Le Grange, together with some academics criticized the study as being unscientific and politically biased. However, there have been other studies which support evidence of torture. In 1987 a group of doctors published a study alleging that 72 per cent of 40 detainees interviewed had claimed that they were assaulted; that 97 per cent of these had shown signs of physical abuse; 78 per cent claimed to have been subject to mental abuse through interrogation, threats of physical violence, and having to take off their clothes; 32 per cent had been detained in solitary confinement; and 84 per cent suffered psychological problems after their release.

In terms of the government's own figures given in parliament in 1987, 253 persons detained after the declaration of the state of emergency in June 1986 were hospitalized between August 1986 and February 1987.

. In recent times, less systematic information has been published about detention without trial owing to the prohibition in the Media Emergency Regulations. These made it an offence to publish information about conditions of detainees.

However, sufficient evidence has been published over the years to show that the system of detention without trial in South Africa constitutes a cruel, inhuman, and degrading form of punishment and that systematic torture of detainees has taken place since the introduction of the so-called 90-day detention clause in 1963.

Detainees have no legal rights to see doctors of their choice, nor to consult with lawyers. Although the Minister of Law and Order has published directives which provide that 'a detainee shall at all times be treated in a humane manner with proper regard to the rules of decency and shall not in any way be assaulted or otherwise ill-treated or subjected to any form of torture or inhuman or degrading treatment', no provision has been made for the external and independent supervision of detainees. In short, once detained, a person is isolated from the outside world and is completely at the mercy of his or her captors. As Breyten Breytenbach has written:

> There's nothing, there's nobody, no power anywhere in the world that has any say over them. They can keep you forever. They can put their heavy hands on you. They can break you down. They may even go red in the face and really let rip.

3. Denationalization

It has been estimated that as a result of the government's 'homeland' policy more than eight million Africans lost their South African nationality, and became foreigners in South Africa and citizens of an 'independent homeland'.

Citizens of 'independent homelands' became aliens in South Africa and were prohibited by law from entering or remaining in the Republic for the purpose of permanent residence, or from temporarily visiting South Africa without possessing a temporary residence permit. Some exemptions have been given but are subject to ministerial power to cancel them. Furthermore, since 1 July 1986, certain citizens of 'independent homelands' have become entitled to the restoration of South African citizenship which they lost upon 'independence' of their 'homeland'.

The Minister of Home Affairs has the power to deprive any South African of his or her citizenship if it was obtained by means of registration or naturalization. The Minister may do this on the grounds that the person has been disloyal. This amounts to a breach of Article 5.

4. Capital punishment

South Africa has one of the highest records of judicial executions in the world. Over the period 1979–89 the annual total of executions exceeded 100 in every year except for 1983. Allegations of racial bias in sentencing practices in capital cases have been made, most prominently by the late Prof. Barend Van Niekerk, whose research suggested that black defendants stand a greater chance than white defendants of receiving the death penalty, particularly when the victim is white. Although Prof. Van Niekerk's study has been criticized for being unscientific, differences in capital sentences between the races continue to exist and are difficult to explain.

There is also evidence to show that there are significant differences in sentencing practices of different judges. A retired Supreme Court judge and a retired magistrate have both confirmed recently that judges do have different philosophies regarding punishment and that some judges go out of their way to find reasons which will allow them to impose a punishment other than death. The fact that a person's life can depend upon the philosophy of the judge might in itself constitute a breach of Article 5.

Once sentenced to death a person is imprisoned on 'death row'. The rigid conditions on death row and the fact that all the prisoners there are waiting to be executed creates a traumatic, terrifying environment which causes terrible anguish and pain. Such a penal system, which has been described as a 'factory which produces corpses', is arguably one which creates conditions of inhuman punishment.

Finally, the execution itself is a barbaric event. It is described by Prof. Chris Barnard as follows:

> The man's spinal cord will rupture at the point where it enters the skull, electrochemical discharges will send his limbs flailing in a grotesque dance, eyes and tongue will start from the facial apertures under the assault of the rope and his bowels and bladder may simultaneously void themselves to soil the legs and drip onto the floor.

The law of the future

If the provisions of Article 5 are to become law in South Africa this would probably happen by means of a Bill of Rights which would include a provision similar to Article 5.

At the time of writing there is considerable interest concerning the applicability of a Bill of Rights for South Africa. The South African Law Commission has proposed the introduction of a Bill which includes a prohibition against torture, assault, or cruel, inhuman, or degrading treatment of any person accused or convicted of a crime. Although the Constitutional Guidelines of the African National Congress are silent on the issue, provision is made in the Guidelines for the introduction of a Bill of Rights based on the Freedom Charter. The Charter provides that imprisonment shall aim at re-education and not vengeance. Although it does not deal with capital punishment, the criminal justice system it calls for would be in conflict with the death penalty.

Some organizations and writers have referred to the African Charter on Human and Peoples' Rights as a document to be considered seriously for South Africa. It contains a specific provision prohibiting torture and cruel and inhuman punishment.

There is apparent agreement on the need to have a provision similar to Article 5 as part of the law of a future South Africa. Whether such a provision would protect the people effectively would depend more on the mechanisms set up to enforce a Bill of Rights than on the written provisions themselves. In this respect the attitude of the courts will be important. The courts themselves will be influenced by the prevailing political and social environment. Consequently there is no guarantee that a court would prohibit capital punishment or the practice of detention in solitary confinement. Much would depend on the structure and nature of the political system in a future South Africa. Obviously, if there existed a political climate more receptive to rights than there is at present, the courts will be more likely to interpret a Bill's provisions extensively, so as to maximize its protection of human rights. In this case, a provision similar to Article 5 would reduce extensive use of detention without trial, 'Middle Ages' prison conditions, and the excessive use of the death penalty. Possibly, the death penalty would go completely.

7
The right to recognition before the law

Article 6 *Everyone has the right to recognition everywhere as a person before the law.*

What this article means

At first glance Article 6 seems straightforward. Of course everyone should be recognized as a person before the law. But what does this mean practically? Articles 1 and 2 of the Declaration assert the equality of all, outlawing discrimination based on race, colour, sex, language, religion, political or other opinion, national or social origin, property, birth, or other status. Article 7 is specific about equality before the law. Does Article 6 say anything that is not more clearly covered in these and other provisions of the Declaration?

Opinion is divided on this question. There are those who say that Article 6 has rhetorical force but no real content; that it is vague and meaningless. Others disagree, basing their interpretation of the article on an examination of the proceedings at which the Declaration was drafted and adopted. The records show, they argue, that Article 6 has a very specific, distinct meaning. It is intended to guarantee to everyone what lawyers call 'legal capacity'. This includes the right to enter transactions, to buy and sell things, and conclude contracts of employment, for example, and the right to litigate, which is necessary to enforce these rights. In short, on this interpretation, Article 6 seeks to protect legal integrity — the ability to conduct one's affairs and fulfil one's needs — in much the same way as other articles protect physical integrity (by outlawing torture, for instance).

The second interpretation seems by far the better one. It gives meaning to the article and ensures the protection of rights which are important, although not as glamorous as many others in the Declaration. But it also raises some very difficult social and legal issues. There are some exceptions to the idea that everyone should be recognized as a person before law. These are generally accepted as obvious and inevitable. Children and mentally disabled people, for example, are deprived of the right to legal recognition to varying degrees and this is seldom controversial. We tend to perceive laws which limit a child or insane person's ability to enter contracts as *protective* laws, rather than as laws which withhold basic human rights. Married women have been similarly 'protected' for centuries.

This second interpretation of Article 6, which ensures everyone's legal capacity, requires us to look again at such protective legislation. It would require us to withhold rights such as the right to contract and the right to sue only when it is absolutely necessary. It might require us to reconsider the arbitrary cut-off points (like the age of 21) which we often use to determine these rights. It may also invite us to scrutinize a broader field. Does our law relating to people who are in institutions (such as prisons and mental hospitals) not perhaps limit their right to recognition as people before the law more than is needed?

International human rights law requires any exceptions to human rights standards to be as narrow as possible. For this reason all deviations from Article 6 need to be examined to ensure that they limit the right only where limitation is absolutely necessary.

The article in South African law

With one important exception the South African legal system is not very different from most other Western ones in its observation of Article 6. Factors affecting legal status in South Africa include nationality, domicile, age, illegitimacy, adoption, mental disability, insolvency, marriage, and 'population group'. It is the inclusion of population group (or 'race' as it is commonly known) on this list that particularly sets South Africa apart from other countries.

The fact that South Africans are all classified according to their race or ethnic group has many well-known implications. This classification is a means of limiting people's political rights and their access to property. It affects their personal lives by determining where they should live and which schools their children may attend, for instance. However, the significance of population group as a factor affecting legal capacity in particular may not be immediately apparent. For instance, no law states that black people have limited legal capacity or that, like children, they may not enter contracts without special supervision. However, the mesh of laws that constitute apartheid South Africa has this effect. Both white and black South Africans are restricted in the free exercise of their right to full legal capacity by legislation such as the Group Areas Act of 1966 and the Black Land Act of 1913 which limit the right of people to own, occupy, or use land by setting aside areas for particular population groups. The Mixed Marriages Act of 1949 which limited a person's right to marry is no longer in force but, for instance, the 'ethnic grouping' of parents and child is a factor to be taken into account in granting an adoption order, and the indications are that ethnic matching is often (mistakenly) considered to be required. In addition, separate education systems exist for people classified into different racial groups. These matters are discussed in other chapters.

It is because of distinctions in legal capacity based on race that South Africa is different from other countries. However, its treatment of women constitutes as serious a departure from the principle enshrined in Article 6. On the face of it the law in South Africa discriminates against women very occasionally. Nevertheless, women are disadvantaged in South African society. To protect women adequately, legislation needs to affirm women's rights and create equality of participation. These issues rise squarely under Article 2 which secures the rights and freedoms of the Declaration for all, and Article 23 which deals with employment, for instance. Article 6, however, alerts one to an instance of express legal discrimination against women: the retention of what is known as the marital power in certain marriages.

In marriages in which the marital power is retained, the law does not treat spouses as equals. Instead the husband has full legal capacity and the wife is in a position similar to that of a child. She is unable to sue or be sued in her own name but must be assisted by her husband; she cannot enter contracts without his authorization. In such marriages the husband has wide powers over the joint property of the spouses. Although, if the marriage is in community of property half the joint estate belongs to the wife, the husband may administer it for his own benefit, subject only to limited protection that the wife is given under the Matrimonial Affairs Act of 1953. If the marital power is retained in a marriage that is not in community of property, the husband controls both his and his wife's separate property.

The existence of the marital power can have a major effect on a woman's life. Say, for example, that Mrs. X, whose husband deserted her 20 years ago, wishes to buy a house in the township in which she is living under the freehold scheme introduced in 1986. She is likely to be told by the township authorities that her husband must sign the papers; that she has no contractual capacity because, in terms of her long-forgotten marriage, her husband still has the marital power to make these decisions. (Divorce may be the only practical solution in a case like this, but it could be a very expensive one.)

The Matrimonial Property Act of 1984 excluded the marital power from all marriages between whites, 'coloureds', and Indians concluded after 1 November 1984 and, in 1988, the exclusion was extended to civil marriages entered into by Africans. These changes mean that over the years fewer and fewer civil marriages with the marital power will remain. Nevertheless, the South African law of marriage still fails to live up to Article 6 in two ways. It has not eradicated the marital power where it exists in marriages concluded before the legislation was passed, and the position of women in so-called customary unions is unchanged.

Many Africans are party to these customary unions which are not generally recognized as true marriages (because they are potentially polygamous — see Chapter 17) but which have significant consequences for the status of the wife. In terms of customary law, on her marriage, guardianship over a woman moves from her father (or his heir) to her husband. She is thus regarded as a minor and in the position of a child, under the guardianship of her husband. She has few rights of property ownership and, like women married under the old civil 'marital power' system, limited capacity to conclude contracts.

Children are another group of people deprived of full legal status. Like mentally disabled people, children have limited legal capacity to enter into commercial transactions and to be involved in litigation, for instance. Instead, their parents or guardians must act on their behalf. It is usually only when people turn 21 that they acquire full legal capacity, but for some matters legal capacity is acquired earlier. After turning 7, children become responsible for their criminal and civil wrongs, and once they are 16 they can make their own wills. At 18 they can consent to medical treatment and operations without the assistance of their parents or guardians.

There are other exceptions to the principle that full legal capacity is acquired only at the age of 21, but what is important to note here is that it is seldom controversial to deny young people full 'recognition as people before the law'. The law is perceived as offering protection to children, guarding them against their own immature judgment rather than depriving them of rights.

Nevertheless, there may be situations in which the limitations on a child's legal capacity are not simply protective. A controversial issue in this context is whether a doctor can prescribe contraceptives for people under 18 without their parents' consent. Article 6 may require the answer to this question to be 'yes', provided that the teenager concerned has an adequate understanding of the issues involved.

Article 6 requires us to limit legal power only when it is absolutely necessary to do so. Whether or not a particular limitation is justified will always be a value judgment in which conflicting interests and concerns are weighed up. However, under this article the starting point must be that as few limits should be placed on legal integrity or power as possible.

The law of the future

If the Declaration were applied in South Africa, race would have no place in the legal system, married men and women would be equals, and the law would strive to enable children and disabled people to participate in society to their full ability.

But aside from requiring this, the open-ended and even vague character of Article 6 may make it a creative tool for tackling new issues and refining existing rights. The imaginative development of the idea of the right to recognition as a person before the law may require us to examine children's rights from a perspective broader than that initially encompassed by the concept of legal capacity. For instance, does Article 6 not perhaps require us to implement some of the provisions of the 1989 Convention on the Rights of the Child? It may already challenge our treatment of prisoners. Do we recognize prisoners as people before the law as fully as possible? Are prison conditions as humane as they should be? Our treatment of the mentally ill may come under scrutiny. Does the process by which the mentally ill may be confined to institutions without their consent contain adequate safeguards?

Most importantly then, Article 6 could give us the flexibility to offer protection to people in ways in which and in situations where the need for protection has not yet occurred to us. The implementation of Article 6 may allow the law to keep up with evolving concepts of human rights.

8
The right to equality before the law

Article 7 *All are equal before the law and are entitled without any discrimination to equal protection of the law. All are entitled to equal protection against any discrimination in violation of this Declaration and against any incitement to such discrimination.*

What this article means

This Article fits together logically with Articles 6, 8, 9, 10, and 11 to provide a procedural safety-net. These procedures specify basic minimum requirements for the political and legal systems of every state. The articles are intended to protect the individual from threats to his or her safety and welfare, whether these dangers come from the organized power of the government, private bodies, or other individuals within that state. The law plays a crucial role in these procedures because it is regarded as one of the most effective ways of ensuring fair and impartial treatment and of providing limits to power, even though it is sometimes abused and used as a tool to oppress ordinary people. These articles therefore overlap to a certain degree, and they must be read together to form a single set of procedural guarantees.

Article 7 in particular embodies several interdependent ideas whose common theme is 'equality before the law'. There are at least four aspects of this underlying theme which need more detailed discussion.

1. 'All are equal before the law ...'

This means that every single legal subject (whether a human being or a commercial company, a trade union or a sports club, a police officer or a cabinet minister, and so on) is subordinate to the law. This idea became established in most of the developed world only about 200 years ago, and many of the political struggles and revolutions in Europe in the 1800s were concerned with making the government, at least in theory, subject to the law. That no one should be above the law is an idea which is also often expressed in the principle that the law rules, 'the rule of law', rather than the rule of human beings. This part of Article 7 also means that every legal subject has equal weight in the eyes of the law. Here again we see that the Declaration of the Rights of Man and of the Citizen of 1789, which was an important symbol of the French Revolution, demands that the law 'should be the same for all, whether it protects or punishes'. In other words, the law must treat rich and poor, man and woman, black and white, Jew and Hindu, president and private individual *equally*.

The achievement of the rule of law idea as a basic requirement of modern government is a considerable triumph for ordinary people. However, many practical steps are needed before it can be said that true legal equality exists. This is because inequality of resources (such as wealth and education) in everyday life is usually not overcome by equal treatment in the eyes of the law. What is certain, however, is that the law itself must not create *inequality* by treating similar groups or classes of people in different ways.

At this point it is important to note that in our legal system there is a distinction between the common law and statute law. The common law is a body of rules which has acquired the status of law through customary use by the people, or by judicial approval in a court of law. Statute law consists of legal rules made by the various law-makers in a particular country, such as central, provincial, and local government bodies. Statute law usually overrides common law when their rules conflict.

2. '... and are entitled without any discrimination to equal protection of the law.'

This aspect of Article 7 follows on directly from the 'equal weight' provision just discussed — the law must protect all people equally. The most famous use of the words 'equal protection of the law' occurs in the Fourteenth Amendment of the United States Constitution (part of its Bill of Rights), which was enacted in 1868 after the American Civil War and the abolition of slavery. Similar provisions occur in the Indian Constitution and in the Canadian Bill of Rights.

There has been much argument about the meaning of 'equal protection of the law'. It seems that what is unacceptable here is not the classification of people by law on reasonable grounds of distinction (such as that those who earn less should pay less tax, which may discriminate against the wealthy), but rather 'class legislation'. This type of law makes certain rules applicable only to people of a particular race, ethnic group, religion, or gender, etc. The distinctions between people must be based on intelligible features and must be rational.

In other words, even though the law will on occasion differentiate between people or even groups of people, all persons subject to such a law must be treated alike under like circumstances. Therefore, what is intended here is equality in the *application* of the laws which exist.

3. '... equal protection against any discrimination in violation of this Declaration ...'

This aspect of Article 7 further emphasizes equality in seeking and obtaining a remedy to overcome discrimination. In other words, it constitutes a right not to be discriminated against on any of the grounds mentioned in the Declaration, particularly those in Article 2, and this right must be equally available to all those who suffer discrimination.

Not only do people have this right in a negative sense, in that they can complain (through the law) against any violation of this right, it is arguable that the state (and possibly all individuals within it) has a *duty* to take steps to prevent discrimination from occurring (by outlawing it), and also to improve the position of those who have been victims of discrimination. This is often known as 'affirmative action'. It involves special steps to discriminate in favour of certain groups of people because of previous disadvantages they have suffered. This sort of discrimination is not normally regarded as a violation of the Declaration.

4. '... equal protection ... against any incitement to such discrimination.'

This aspect of Article 7 obviously contemplates a duty on the state authorities to prohibit by law any call or action which is intended or will have the effect of discriminating against people in ways which violate the rights protected in the Declaration. This step in itself amounts to a restriction on the rights to freedom of opinion and expression (Article 19) and to freedom of peaceful assembly (Article 20), which clearly shows that few rights are unlimited in effect.

The article in South African law

It will come as no surprise to anyone to be told that Article 7 rights and protections have had a tough time in South African law. Equal protection and non-discrimination laws are not the characteristics which most people associate with the South African legal system. The situation is not quite as simple as this, however, and it is necessary to take a deeper look at the law as a whole.

The common law of South Africa, based primarily on the Roman-Dutch and English legal systems which were imposed on this country by European settler governments, proceeds from the point of view that all people are subject to the law and equal before it. Famous Dutch legal writers such as De Groot and Voet, who have deeply influenced our private law, and equally famous English lawyers such as Dicey and Blackstone, whose work has shaped much of our public law, have all stressed the rule of law and the equality of the individual in the face of the law.

On the other hand, critics have maintained that our common law is rooted in the period in European history which saw the triumph of capitalism over feudalism, which gives it a basically capitalist flavour and a concentration on the individual, which has been said to favour the possessors of wealth. It has also been argued that the supremacy and equality of the law has remained theoretical and has not been put into practice by the courts. A further point of criticism is that our law, being based upon the isolated individual, fails to pay sufficient attention to that individual in his or her socio-economic or cultural context. Despite these criticisms, this historical foundation of our common law in the principle of equality provides an important argument for those who plead for non-discrimination and the rule of law in our *statutes*.

For it is in the area of statute law that the main attack on legal supremacy and equality has occurred. This has happened since the earliest colonial times and has been intensified since apartheid became the chief component of government policy in 1948. Much of the groundwork was laid before that date, however. Notable early laws were the Glen Grey Act of the Cape Colony of 1894 and the segregation policy of Shepstone in Natal (both of which acted as building blocks for the system of land dispossession and segregation), and the openly racist (and sexist) constitutions and practices of the Republic of the Orange Free State and the Zuid-Afrikaansche Republiek before 1900.

The Constitution of the Union of South Africa (in 1910) denied the vote to the vast majority of South Africans merely on the ground of race, and discrimination was further entrenched by the industrial laws of the mid 1920s, which favoured white workers, and also the two statutes which set aside the land which eventually became the 'homelands' (the Land Act of 1913 and the Development Trust and Land Act of 1936).

The cornerstone of the most widespread, official, and prolonged programme of discrimination was laid in 1950, with the adoption of the Population Registration Act. This act attempted to 'systematize' racial classification as the basis for the apartheid system. Compulsory classification and inevitable imprecision on the border-lines between the 'groups', as defined in the statute, led to untold hardship and cruelty. Two further early statutes, the Reservation of Separate Amenities Act and the Group Areas Act, facilitated far-reaching race-segregation measures in almost every walk of life. A series of acts of parliament created the detailed structures and mechanisms which both excluded Africans from the urban areas and attempted to channel their political and economic needs to the 'homelands'.

While only one statute specifically declared blacks to be unequal to whites, all this racially-exclusive 'class legislation' effectively locked black South Africans into a status of substantial legal inequality. (The single statute referred to was the Blacks (Prohibition of Interdicts) Act of 1956 which denied Africans the right to approach the courts to attempt to delay or halt the implementation of apartheid measures.) In this context, it must certainly also be remembered that the 'security' laws of the 1950s and 1960s often removed all rights of a detained or arrested person, and that these laws were most often used against blacks. As a result, the statute law of the country very deliberately and consistently created inequality on the basis of an often vague and sometimes arbitrary classification by 'race group'.

Poor socio-economic conditions worsened this legislative inequality: the position of blacks as workers, peasants, or the unemployed was such that, for all *practical* purposes, the legal process was unavailable to them as a remedy. To make matters worse, most blacks who found themselves before a court experienced a legal process which was alien and intimidating to them. As regards Africans in particular, their customary laws were largely disregarded, and many of them had to rely for their understanding of the proceedings on the court interpreter, as they were unfamiliar with both official languages (let alone the peculiar language which all lawyers seem to use).

As far as law enforcement was concerned, the 'protection of the law' in Article 7 was hardly satisfied. Policing in black areas concentrated more on trapping offenders against apartheid regulations than on ordinary crime prevention and investigation. Judicial officers, whether in the Supreme or magistrates' courts, showed very little understanding of the harsh injustice of the laws which they enforced.

South African statute law nevertheless appears to go some way towards meeting the requirement of Article 7 as regards a prohibition of incitement to discriminate. For the past 60 years or so there has been legislation making it a criminal offence to say or do anything with the intention of promoting feelings of hostility between whites and blacks. Indications are, however, that these laws have been used mainly against those who have pointed out that power and wealth lie almost exclusively in the hands of whites. These laws have never been used against the government of the day.

The law of the future

There can be no doubt that the full or even partial implementation of the requirements of Article 7 would substantially, possibly radically, improve the position of every South African, and our social welfare in general. What are the chances of such a beneficial development?

Many South Africans pay at least lip service to the ideas of equality before the law and equal protection of the law in the future. The ruling National Party has included these provisions both in its election propaganda and the Preamble to the 1983 Constitution Act. The South African Law Commission (a statutory body set up by parliament to investigate problem areas and recommend changes in the law) has proposed that the government implement far-reaching procedural protections in a Bill of Rights, which would collectively achieve much of what is intended by Article 7. The Bill of Rights proposed by the KwaZulu-Natal Indaba proposes in Article 1(2) that 'everyone is equal before the law, and shall be entitled to equal protection of the law'.

As far back as 1955, the 'Congress of the People' meeting near Johannesburg adopted the Freedom Charter which provides that:

> All people shall be equal before the law ... All laws which discriminate on grounds of race, colour or belief shall be

repealed. The preaching and practice of national, race or colour discrimination and contempt shall be a punishable crime.

More recently, the major participant in that Congress, the African National Congress (ANC), has issued its Constitutional Guidelines (1988), which state that:

There shall be equal rights for all individuals, irrespective of race, colour, sex or creed. ... The constitution shall include a Bill of Rights based on the Freedom Charter. Such a Bill of Rights shall guarantee the fundamental human rights of all citizens. ... The state and all social institutions shall be under a constitutional duty to take active steps to eradicate, speedily, the economic and social inequalities produced by racial discrimination. The advocacy or practice of racism, fascism, nazism or the incitement of ethnic or regional exclusiveness shall be outlawed.

Elsewhere on this continent, the African Charter of Human and Peoples' Rights provides (in Article 3):

1. Every individual shall be equal before the law.

2. Every individual shall be entitled to equal protection of the law.

Internationally, this type of article has appeared in many charters of rights, so much so that it has probably now become part of customary international law, with strong persuasive value in domestic courts. It is quite clear, therefore, that equality before the law and non-discrimination are likely at least to be part of the rhetoric of any future South African government.

Whether the propaganda will become reality will depend on many factors, the most important of which is the nature of the process of transition to majority rule (which is inevitable in the medium term). If this process is marked by stubborn dogmatism and widespread violence on all sides, it is likely that the noble sentiments contained in Article 7 will perish in the cross-fire, more particularly because any new government will have to exercise strong central control in the period of reconstruction. If the transfer of power is characterized by a measure of flexibility and a negotiating spirit, with violence at a fairly low level, it might be that a rights-based solution will have a greater chance of emerging.

The challenge which faces all those who seek the protection of basic rights, one of the most important of which is contained in

Article 7, is to place the issue firmly on the agenda for negotiating South Africa's future immediately, to fight for its observance in all circumstances, and to ensure that it becomes part of the consciousness of every South African, both now and for all time.

9
The right to effective remedies

Article 8 *Everyone has the right to an effective remedy by the competent national tribunals for acts violating the fundamental rights granted him by the constitution or by law.*

What this article means

This article emphasizes the fact that in any legal system there can be no rights without effective remedies. There is no point in providing basic human rights if people cannot enforce them. For example, it is meaningless for laws to say that you enjoy a right to privacy if the police (or anyone else for that matter) can enter your home whenever they please, and you are powerless to do anything about it. One can only talk in terms of human rights if they are backed by enforceable remedies.

Each state must ensure not only that its legal system contains all the rights and guarantees that are set out in the Declaration, but also that 'an effective remedy by the competent national tribunals' is available for each one of those rights. This may seem logical enough but it is remarkable how many legal systems and constitutions make reference to rights and freedoms without specifying how they will be protected and enforced.

Article 8 attempts to ensure that remedies do exist. These remedies must operate against any person who attempts to violate another's rights. There should be no difference whether the violator is a private person (such as your neighbour) or a public official (such as a policeman or a soldier). This means that under normal circumstances no one should be allowed to deprive you of your rights. If this does happen, you are entitled to ask for help in the courts.

The courts play a particularly important role in the process of human rights protection. They must be considered to be the watchdogs over basic human rights and must guard against violations and abuses. To do this, courts must operate in an impartial manner, which means that they must exist independently of the other branches of government. It is the court's function to monitor and limit the powers of government to an even greater extent than it limits and monitors the actions of private individuals. This is commonly referred to as the judicial role.

A sound legal and constitutional system consists of a legislature (parliament) that is elected by the people on the basis of universal suffrage (see Chapter 22). In this way the legislature is answerable to the people and should therefore not make laws that would deny, violate, or undermine fundamental rights and freedoms. But it is also necessary to place additional controls on the legislature and the executive (the branch of government which carries out the laws).

The best way to exercise control is to separate legislative, executive, and judicial powers. Where all these powers are given to a single person (or body of persons) there can be no effective controls. This is because the ruler would not only make the laws, but would also be empowered to carry them out and to interpret them. It is necessary, therefore, to have impartial and independent courts which can control the exercise of power by the legislature and executive. This is probably the only way to ensure that these two branches of government do not encroach upon the fundamental rights and freedoms of citizens.

If citizens are able to approach courts for an effective remedy when human rights are threatened or harmed, this is a clear indication that Article 8 of the Declaration has been complied with. Remedies would usually take one of three forms: an interdict which prevents another from carrying out an unlawful threat or from continuing with unlawful action; an order which compels the person who has done wrong to do something to rectify the situation (e.g. hand back property which has been unlawfully taken); and an order for damages (in the form of financial compensation) for an unlawful act (e.g. an assault).

The article in South African law

In South Africa fundamental rights and freedoms are supposed to be protected by a mechanism known as the rule of law. In its most basic form the rule of law requires that the courts ensure that all the powers exercised by the legislature and the executive are properly authorized. This means that the exercise of any power by a government official (especially where it results in a denial of fundamental rights to a citizen) will be carefully scrutinized by the courts. If the official's action is not backed up by law it will be declared unlawful and overturned by the court.

It has been argued that in this way effective remedies have been built into the constitution which ensure that fundamental human rights and freedoms are protected. In this view, therefore, the provisions of Article 8 are complied with by the South African legal and constitutional system.

However, South Africa has one of the worst human rights records in the world, especially in the post Second World War period. One of the reasons for this lies in the fact that parliament is supreme. This means that the legislature can enact any legislation it pleases. It follows that, if the legislature makes laws which deprive individuals of their fundamental rights and freedoms, the courts have no alternative but to apply that legislation.

To a large extent, this has been the case in South Africa. Instead of democratic government, legislative power has been concentrated in the white minority. This means in practical terms that there is nothing to prevent parliament from making laws which violate the fundamental rights and liberties of the black majority. The legislature has relied exclusively on the support of the white group and has entrenched the privileges and domination of whites to the detriment of the rest of the community. To take an obvious example, the Land Acts of 1913 and 1936 — which allow Africans (80 per cent of the population) to occupy 13 per cent of the land — would never have been passed if blacks had had proper parliamentary representation.

The vital political element of a truly representative legislature (which provides the basis for the operation of the rule of law in other countries) is missing in South Africa. Furthermore, the South African legal system does not have an effective mechanism that can ensure that the rights and freedoms contained in the Universal Declaration will not be undermined. Although the courts can be described as 'competent national tribunals' they are powerless to prevent the legislature from denying basic rights. For this reason it can be argued that effective remedies are not available to the ordinary citizen in South Africa.

The law of the future

Part of the solution to South Africa's political and constitutional crisis lies in ensuring democratic participation of all people on the basis of universal suffrage. A future parliament that is responsible to the majority of South Africans will be more likely to protect fundamental human rights and freedoms. The apartheid legal order will disappear.

But an important question remains. Will democratic rule be sufficient to ensure effective and adequate remedies with regard to all the various fundamental rights and freedoms contained in the Universal Declaration? As long as there are no restraints on the content of laws which may be enacted, parliament will be free to do what it pleases. For this reason it can be argued that the best way to ensure that South Africans have proper remedies is to introduce a Bill of Rights into the constitution.

A Bill of Rights is a document which sets out fundamental human rights and freedoms (similar to those contained in the Universal Declaration) that need to be protected from violations by government and other citizens. Therefore, a Bill must be entrenched in the constitution. In this way it could only be amended by special procedures. Furthermore, it must contain a provision which empowers the courts to set aside any executive action, or strike down any legislation, that violates the fundamental rights. This power to strike down legislation is known as a 'testing right'.

The existence of a Bill of Rights would not mean the abolition of legislative supremacy. The legislature would still be free to make any laws it pleases provided that human rights were unaffected. In this way both the legislature and the courts would be supreme in their own areas. This would mean a real and effective separation of powers.

It must be borne in mind, however, that South Africans view a Bill of Rights in a suspicious light. This view is justifiable in the case of blacks, who for so long have been the pawns of unchecked legislative supremacy of the white legislature. To black South Africans it must seem ironic that as soon as white political supremacy is under threat, the introduction of a Bill of Rights suddenly looks attractive to whites. It has been suggested that a Bill of Rights will only help to preserve existing white privilege.

This argument is partly understandable. However, it is necessary to take an objective view of the long-term problems of human rights protection in South Africa. Justice and democracy should not be tempered by feelings of revenge. Thus injustices of the past are not automatically cured by changing the roles of the oppressors and the oppressed or, for that matter, replacing tyranny of the minority with tyranny of the majority.

To argue that politicians in a new, democratic system should have exclusive powers to decide the content of legislation is to take a very narrow view of democracy. Politicians are always answerable to particular constituencies and interest groups. Given the nature of South African society there is always the possibility of conflicts between various interest groups. This could very easily result in certain people's fundamental rights and freedoms being ignored.

The principle in Article 8 is an extremely important feature of any legal system. Not only must it apply to situations where fundamental human rights and freedoms of one individual are violated by another but, more importantly, Article 8 is vital in cases where the government infringes or violates these rights. Violations can occur when the government ignores the laws protecting basic rights. They can also occur when parliament passes laws interfering with these rights. In all cases courts must be able to provide an effective remedy, so that all human rights continue to be taken seriously.

10
Freedom from arbitrary arrest and detention

Article 9 *No one shall be subjected to arbitrary arrest [or] detention ...*

What this article means

This article is closely connected with Article 3 which establishes not only the right to life, but also the right to liberty and security of person. The idea that the liberty and freedom of individuals should be protected by law was recognized in the Magna Carta of 1216, and today many constitutions protect their citizens from arbitrary arrest and detention.

The people who drafted the Universal Declaration considered the protection of the individual's liberty so important that it warranted separate mention in Article 9. Perhaps the most important human right of all is the protection against arbitrary arrest and detention. As Arnold Brecht has said 'the other features of the most generous bill of rights may stand destitute of meaning, as long as individuals can be detained indefinitely by police action without appeal'.

The power of state officials to arrest and to detain individuals inevitably infringes upon the freedom and liberty of citizens. However, the arrest and detention of people who are charged with, or convicted of, a crime is justified when it is necessary to protect society. But because history has shown that the procedures and penalties of the criminal process can easily be abused, it is necessary to have laws to limit the exercise of arbitrary power over the freedom of ordinary people. In the United States of America these principles are described as 'due process' requirements. In the South African legal system, the same notion is expressed in the concept 'the rule of law'.

The Declaration prohibits the arbitrary use of powers of arrest and detention. This prohibition was spelt out further in the International Covenant on Civil and Political Rights which was adopted on

16 December 1966. Article 9 of the Covenant specifies when a state may deprive a person of his or her liberty. It also details the rights that should be granted to a person who has been arrested or detained. Some guarantees are applicable in the case of any arrest or detention (for example, of a mentally ill person, an AIDS carrier, or a vagrant) while extra guarantees are provided when a person is arrested or detained on a criminal charge. Since most of the provisions of Article 9 of the Covenant have been internationally accepted, they will be discussed here.

1. *'No one shall be deprived of his liberty except on such grounds and in accordance with such procedures as are established by law.'*

The aim of this provision is to require all states to stipulate in legislation the circumstances in which an individual's liberty may be limited. This means that rules and procedures must be laid down to define the powers of public officials. For example, the police should not be entitled to decide, at their own discretion, who can be arrested, how, and why. This article does not allow laws to be written too widely.

Commentators have also pointed out that the intention of those who drafted the original clause in the Declaration was to protect individuals from despotic legislation such as that which was used in Nazi Germany, to authorize mass arrests of political opponents. 'Arbitrary' in this sense also means 'unjust'. Any law allowing for arrest and detention can therefore be tested against international principles of justice. The Declaration does not permit unjust detention even if it has been authorized in another law.

2. *'Anyone who is arrested shall be informed, at the time of arrest, of the reasons for his arrest and shall be promptly informed of any charges against him.'*

The purpose of this requirement is to give the detained person enough information so as to judge whether the detention is legal. Only with sufficient knowledge of the reasons for the arrest can the detained person decide whether or not to challenge the detention.

3. *'Anyone who is deprived of his liberty by arrest or detention shall be entitled to take proceedings before a court, in order that the court may decide without delay on the lawfulness of his detention and order his release if the detention is not lawful.'*

It is crucial to counterbalance the drastic nature of an arrest and detention with the right of an individual to challenge the correctness of the removal of his or her liberty. The remedy in these circumstances is an application to bring the detained person to court, together with a demand to know why he or she has been arrested.

When this application is made the judge must investigate the circumstances surrounding the arrest and detention, and decide whether there are reasons to justify continued detention. If there are no acceptable legal reasons for the detention, the court will order the person's release. The court's scrutiny of arrest and detention is a practical example of the influence of the rule of law principle. It means that an independent judiciary can exercise control over the actions of government officials.

4. *'Anyone arrested or detained on a criminal charge shall be brought promptly before a judge or other officer authorized by law to exercise judicial power and shall be entitled to trial within a reasonable time or to release. It shall not be the general rule that persons awaiting trial shall be detained in custody, but release may be subject to guarantees to appear for trial, at any other stage of the judicial proceedings and, should occasion arise, for execution of the judgment.'*

This provision ensures special guarantees for persons who have been arrested or detained on a criminal charge. Interpreting this provision, the Human Rights Committee of the United Nations has said that to bring a person before a judge a month after arrest, after being held in solitary confinement and without access to a lawyer, is a clear violation of this provision.

Other rights given to people accused of criminal offences include the right to be put on trial within a reasonable time and the right to be released on bail (unless there is the danger that the accused will disappear or it is likely that the offence will be repeated).

The article in South African law

The spirit of the prohibition in Article 9 of the Declaration has not been respected in South Africa over the last 30 years. In fact, deviations from the article have become notorious. Detention without trial, in particular, has come to symbolize the repressive legal order that has prevailed in South Africa. This is so despite the fact that the Criminal Procedure Act of 1977, which regulates ordinary criminal arrests, by and large complies with the minimum human rights standards in international documents.

For example, the Criminal Procedure Act specifies that a person may be arrested on a criminal charge if a warrant of arrest is issued by a magistrate. A magistrate can authorize a warrant only when there is a reasonable suspicion, on the available evidence, that a person has committed a crime. The police are entitled to arrest without a warrant only in certain clearly defined circumstances, such as where they see a crime in progress. The act also provides that any person who is arrested must be informed of the reasons for the arrest and be brought to court within 48 hours. Rules such as these normally ensure that judicial control is exercised over arrest and detention.

South African law also has a specific remedy to compel judicial inquiry into the legality of an arrest or detention. In one famous case the Appeal Court interpreted this remedy very widely. Not only detainees themselves, but their family, friends, church leaders, or local politicians have the right to apply to have the detained person brought to court.

But all these laws have been overshadowed by harsh security measures, allowing what amounts to arbitrary arrest, unlimited by judicial control, and indefinite detention. The slide down this slippery slope began with the passing of the infamous 90-day detention law in 1963. In terms of this, political activists could be detained for interrogation until they had satisfactorily answered all questions put to them by the police, or for a maximum period of 90 days. (After 90 days, they could be re-arrested for a further period.) No court was allowed to order their release. In 1965, this provision was replaced with a 180-day detention law, which also prohibited any access to a detained person. This included visits by lawyers.

By 1967 the public was accustomed to detention without trial and there were few protests when the Terrorism Act was passed. This allowed *indefinite* detention without trial. Any member of the police force above a specified rank could arrest any person suspected of being a terrorist or of having any information about terrorists. Effectively this gave the police a free hand to decide who to arrest, why, and for how long, because access to the courts to test the correctness of the arrest or detention was forbidden.

Present-day security laws also depart fundamentally from the principles of due process. The Internal Security Act of 1982 consolidated previous security laws. It now authorizes three forms of detention: preventive detention, pre-trial detention, and the detention of witnesses. Preventive detention is designed to remove people from public life if they are regarded as a threat to society. The purpose of pre-trial detention is quite different, since it is usually used to obtain information or evidence from the detainee. Prof. Tony Mathews maintains that the current pre-trial detention provisions:

> create a situation in which police officials have under their absolute power a defenceless detainee from whom they are usually determined to extract information ... Indefinite detention for the purposes of interrogation without adequate safeguards is a legal invitation or incentive to the ill-treatment and abuse of detainees.

The long list of South Africans who have died in detention is evidence of Prof. Mathews' concern.

The section which allows witnesses to be detained (for six months or until they have given their evidence in court) is in direct violation of international standards. Like other detainees, witnesses can be held in isolation without access to lawyers or courts. What is worse is that these laws allow people to be arrested on the basis of opinion rather than fact. The police have been given an almost uncontrolled licence to act in what they think is 'the interests of national security'.

This bleak picture has been worsened by the declaration of five successive states of emergency in South Africa. The Emergency Regulations gave even wider powers to the security forces, and allowed even the most junior 'kitskonstabel' wide discretion to imprison people. Repeated attempts by civil rights lawyers to challenge the conditions under which thousands of detainees were being held and to force the state to account for unjustifiable arrests were unsuccessful. Judges generally failed to give judgments in favour of the liberty of the individual, even when there were opportunities for them to do so.

According to international law a state is allowed to deviate from Article 9 in times of emergency. But strict criteria have been laid down to determine when so drastic a step may be taken. South African emergency laws have failed in all respects to meet these requirements.

There have been recent encouraging signs that political detentions will decrease, and the government has gone a little way towards meeting international demands about the plight of detainees. The State President has announced that detention will in future be limited to six-month periods and that detainees may have access to lawyers and medical advisers of their choice. What then are the prospects of a return to the position when the freedoms protected by Article 9 of the Declaration were guaranteed in South Africa?

The law of the future

There can be no question that the implementation of the guarantees contained in Article 9 would significantly benefit South Africans. It would also signal an improvement in the image of the legal system as a whole. It is no secret that the legitimacy of the legal system has suffered enormously because the law has failed to protect citizens from arbitrary arrest and detention. There has also been widespread torture of detainees.

At the present time there are many debates about the possibility of introducing a Bill of Rights in South Africa. Universally, the type of protection given by Article 9 would ordinarily be included in a Bill. The South African Law Commission has endorsed the introduction of a clause which gives effect to the intention behind Article 9. The Commission recommends that 'no person shall be arbitrarily arrested or detained and any person who is apprehended shall as soon as possible be informed of the charge against him and brought before a court of law'.

In Constitutional Guidelines published in 1988, the African National Congress proposed that a Bill of Rights should be enacted to guarantee the fundamental human rights of all citizens. Although no mention is made of specific procedural protections against arbitrary arrest and detention in this document, it is noteworthy that the Freedom Charter of 1955 declares that 'no one shall be imprisoned, deported or restricted without a fair trail'. The Freedom Charter is widely regarded as the forerunner of the ANC's Guidelines. It seems therefore that a return to the principles of due process and the rule of law is being considered by important participants in the debate about South Africa's constitutional future.

But there is still room for much caution. One of South Africa's most respected human rights lawyers, Sydney Kentridge, has warned that:

> One day where will be a change in South Africa. Those who then come to rule may have seen the process of law in their country not as protection against power but as no more than its convenient instrument, to be manipulated at will. It would

then not be surprising if they failed to appreciate the value of an independent judiciary and of due process of law. If so, then it may be said of those who now govern that they destroyed better than they knew.

In spite of the possible introduction of a Bill of Rights in South Africa, there is a danger that a future South African government may reform the system of detention without trial, rather than implementing all the individual protections that Article 9 envisages. It should be insisted, however, that a future South African government should re-introduce human rights standards by condemning all arbitrary interference with individual liberty. The protection of citizens from arbitrary arrest and detention should be of paramount concern, never to be traded for other gains. In Zimbabwe, for example, the government that was elected after independence retained and used detention without trial provisions. But these laws have recently been abolished, and Zimbabwean law no longer permits detention without trial.

There is another benefit to be derived from the implementation of Article 9 guarantees. It would encourage the application of numerous international human rights decisions in criminal cases. This would ensure an enlightened approach to issues like the speedy disposal of criminal trials, the granting of bail, and compensation for wrongful arrests. The principles derived from this body of international law would be of considerable benefit to the administration of justice in South Africa.

The introduction of a provision like Article 9 would overcome some of the iniquities of the South African legal system, providing an opportunity to develop a criminal justice system that values international standards.

11
The right to a fair trial

Article 10 Everyone is entitled in full equality to a fair and public hearing by an independent and impartial tribunal, in the determination of his rights and obligations and of any criminal charge against him.

What this article means

This article is about access to justice. Access to justice deals with the ability of every person to use courts of law to solve legal disputes. The courts as dispute-resolving institutions are valuable only if, first, they can dispense justice and, second, they are accessible to every member of the public. There are important aspects to court-room justice. They will be looked at separately.

1. Independent and impartial courts

The judicial officer (a judge or a magistrate) should be impartial. This means that he or she should not be prejudiced against one of the parties. The judicial officer should therefore not take sides in favour of one of the parties before hearing all the evidence.

One of the most important factors contributing to an impartial judicial officer is that he or she should be independent from outside pressures, whether direct or indirect. Of particular importance is that the judicial officer should be independent from the government. In other words, the government should not be able to tell a judge or magistrate how to decide a case. A judicial officer should also not fear what may happen if a decision is given against the government.

The type of person who should be appointed as a judicial officer should ideally have a legal qualification, experience in all aspects of the administration of justice, and not be closely associated with the state. It would therefore be wrong to appoint judges or magistrates only from the ranks of state prosecutors because they may be biased in favour of the prosecution.

Once appointed, judicial officers should be granted tenure. This means that they cannot be removed from office by government officials if a judgment is given which is unfavourable to the government. A judicial officer should only be removed from office on the grounds of incapacity or misbehaviour. Further, a judicial officer should not be transferred without his or her consent.

2. Fair hearing

For justice to be done in any particular case, every party to a dispute should be given a fair hearing. There are two important principles about a fair hearing which need mention here.

Firstly, every party to a dispute should have the right to participate fully in every stage of the trial, and before any decision is made by the judicial officer. To participate in a trial means that each party may lead evidence on any issue and address the court before any decision is made. In this way each party has an opportunity to influence the judicial officer's decision.

Effective communication is essential to be able to participate properly in a trial. A person will not be able to participate if he or she is not able to speak the language used in court. It is the duty of the judicial officer to appoint an interpreter on behalf of a litigant (person before court) where he or she does not have a proper command of the language being used.

Secondly, because one of the primary functions of a court is the settlement of factual disputes, it is essential that the truth is established. This can only happen if all relevant evidence is placed truthfully before the court. Any party should have the right to call any witness who may favour his or her case. A party should also be able to compel an opponent to disclose information which may be of assistance in the conduct of his or her case.

All evidence should be given orally in court. This enables a party to confront the other side's witnesses. A party should be able to question such witnesses in order to test whether they speak the truth.

3. Justice seen to be done

Justice must not only be done, but must clearly be *seen* to be done. The administration of justice should therefore be done in public. This has two functions. First, the public has a right to know what is done in the name of justice, and the court must be able to justify its decisions to the general public. Second, the courts should play an important educational role because they determine, amongst other things, what is socially acceptable behaviour. Furthermore, so that the criminal courts can have a deterrent effect, the consequences of criminal conduct — the punishments — must be communicated to the public at large.

4. Equality

It is essential that all people have equal access to a fair and public hearing. This means that the right and capacity to participate fully in a trial should not be determined by irrelevant criteria such as a party's race, gender, religion, language, or social and economic status.

5. Access to lawyers

Rights are useless unless the people who have those rights are aware of them, their significance, and how to use them effectively. It is in this regard that lawyers play an important role: to make access to justice possible. With their legal training, knowledge, and skills they are able to participate effectively on behalf of a litigant. But, because lawyers are organized in a private profession and ask high fees for their services, most people cannot really afford them. A person who cannot afford the services of a lawyer will be at a disadvantage in asserting his or her rights, particularly if the opponent is represented by a lawyer. Because the absence of a lawyer in a case could result in injustice, an important question is: whose responsibility should it be to pay for the services of a lawyer? It is now widely accepted that the state should carry the financial burden to provide this social service.

The article in South African law

Access to justice is very uneven in South Africa. Often justice is not done because courts are not impartial and independent. Sometimes the principles of a fair trial are inadequate to overcome injustices which have taken place before the matter came to court. Furthermore, the justice that the courts can dispense is most often only accessible to a small section of the population who can afford the services of lawyers.

The majority of judges of the Supreme Court are regarded as being impartial. They are appointed by the State President, usually from the ranks of practising senior advocates. Advocates are regarded as independent-minded because they practise on their own. Although they are paid for their services, they do not receive a salary from a single employer. They receive work from both the state and private persons.

On a few occasions senior state advocates (attorneys-general) have been appointed as judges. Because they have been prosecutors for the government throughout their careers, they are said to display a bias in favour of the prosecution.

Another factor that may affect the impartiality of the Supreme Court is the fact that no black person has ever been appointed as a judge in South Africa. A white judge, without an understanding and knowledge of indigenous languages or culture, may not be able to do justice to black litigants. Particular judges have, over the years, been criticized for racial and political bias in their judgments.

Judges are given independence by their conditions of service. They may only be removed from office by the State President at the request of parliament on grounds of gross misbehaviour or incapacity. Furthermore, their salary is fixed by an act of parliament. The government therefore cannot dismiss a judge or withhold his or her salary.

It has often been said that magistrates, who sit in the lower courts, are not impartial or independent. Criminal magistrates are appointed solely from the ranks of the prosecutors. All magistrates are civil servants. Their dismissal, promotion, transfer, and salary are determined by the government. Their status as civil servants is sometimes seen to make them susceptible to undue influence from the government.

In general, the court proceedings in South Africa adhere to the established principles of a fair trial. A party is allowed to participate fully in the proceedings in order to influence the court in its decision. With regard to language problems, the state provides an interpreter for persons who are not familiar with the language used in court. A magistrate, for example, is under a duty to call for a competent interpreter if the accused person does not properly understand the language in which evidence is given. English and Afrikaans are the official court languages.

There are rules of evidence which try to ensure that all relevant evidence is placed before court and that its truthfulness can be tested. Any party to a dispute may call and compel any witnesses to appear in court. Witnesses' evidence can be tested under cross-examination.

However, keeping to the principles of a fair trial may mean very little where a conviction has effectively been obtained before the trial itself begins. In South African law an accused person may be convicted by a judicial officer on the basis of a prior confession made to a police officer. Through various methods such as torture, police may get (and have done so on many occasions in the past) accused persons to incriminate themselves falsely. When the individual appears in court, the circumstances surrounding the confession are denied by the police, and the accused person is found guilty on the basis of the confession.

It is a principle of South African law that all court proceedings are open to the public. However, in criminal cases there are some exceptions to this principle. If it is in the interests of the security of the state, good order, public morals, or the administration of justice that proceedings should be held behind closed doors, then the court may order that the public or certain people should not be present. Court cases may also be closed to the public if there is a likelihood that harm might result to a witness. The court may order that a witness should give evidence behind closed doors and that his or her identity should not be disclosed. This has often been done in political trials where persons employed by the security police have given evidence for the state.

Where a closed hearing is ordered so as to protect a witness, it is still essential that the public be informed about the evidence. Even where the public is excluded from the case, the media should still be able to report on the evidence, provided that the witness remains properly protected.

Where an accused person is under the age of 18 years, the case must be held behind closed doors. The aim of this rule is to protect the identity of the juvenile in the interests of encouraging the rehabilitation of the young criminal.

In South Africa there has been a long struggle to gain equal protection before the law. Until 1986 there were separate courts for blacks, called commissioners' courts. They dealt with all civil cases and also criminal cases which involved pass and influx control offences. Now, the latter offences have been removed from the law and the magistrates' courts deal with all civil cases irrespective of the 'race' of the parties.

Despite these changes, unequal justice is still dispensed. This is because much depends on a person's economic position. Although the Legal Aid Board provides some free legal assistance to poor persons in both civil and criminal cases, the amount of money the government makes available for this purpose is far too small. In the Supreme Court, advocates are appointed by the state to represent poor persons who face a charge which may result in the death penalty. In the magistrates' courts, the vast majority of accused persons are poor and therefore have to fend for themselves, without the benefit of lawyers. Because they do not have the same legal skills as prosecutors, undefended accused persons are prejudiced by their own ignorance and incompetence. It cannot therefore be said that there is equal access to justice for all in the criminal courts.

Much the same applies to civil cases. Only a small number of litigants receive legal aid. To lessen this problem, the small-claims court has been established. Here, parties may not be represented by lawyers and claims may not be more than R1 500. The judicial officer, called a commissioner, gives a decision which is just in the circumstances of the case. By dispensing with the need for lawyers, this court has made justice much more accessible to people who cannot afford expensive lawyers' fees.

The law of the future

If the principles of Article 10 are adopted in South Africa, access to and the quality of justice will be greatly improved. First, if the lower courts are given greater independence from the government, and persons other than prosecutors are appointed as magistrates, the impartiality and the quality of justice in those courts will be greatly enhanced.

Second, although the principles of a fair trial are on the whole observed, the pre-trial procedures in criminal cases have effectively undermined these principles. To give effect to the principles of participation and the search for the truth, the police powers should be drastically limited so that the courts can determine the guilt or innocence of accused persons on the evidence produced in court.

Thirdly, the realization of the principle of equal access to court will, more than any of the other principles, benefit the general public. Independent and impartial judicial officers together with fair and public hearings mean nothing to people who, because of low income, cannot afford access to the legal process. Making courts accessible by providing free legal assistance to persons who cannot afford the services of a lawyer should be of overriding concern.

12
Rights of people accused of crimes

Article 11 (1) Everyone charged with a penal offence has the right to be presumed innocent until proved guilty according to law in a public trial at which he has had all the guarantees necessary for his defence.

(2) No one shall be held guilty of any penal offence on account of any act or omission which did not constitute a penal offence, under national or international law, at the time when it was committed. Nor shall a heavier penalty be imposed than the one that was applicable at the time the penal offence was committed.

What this article means

Article 11 (like Articles 5 and 10) deals with human rights in the administration of justice and, more specifically, with criminal law and procedure. Criminal law is viewed as a part of public law (as opposed to private law), which has traditionally been described as a body of rules regulating relationships between the state and its subjects and between different branches of state authority. Whereas the state obviously needs power in order to maintain order and security and to pursue its policies, all individuals need the protection of the law against the abuse of state power.

The criminal law determines which actions are punishable as criminal offences. The elements or requirements of specific crimes are to be found both in common law rules, accepted and applied over a long period, and statutes made by the legislature. To illustrate this point, murder, assault, and theft are examples of common law crimes, whereas the possession of a firearm without a valid licence, the failure to submit income tax returns, and exceeding the speed limit are examples of statutory offences.

When someone is suspected of having committed a crime, he or she is prosecuted by the state in a criminal court. The rules of criminal procedure then apply. These rules are important not only for the sake of the smooth and disciplined running of a criminal process, but also to guarantee a fair and just decision and sentence. They also protect basic human rights to freedom, dignity, and equality. Human rights protected in this way are often referred to as 'procedural rights'. In any legal system these are extremely important.

1. The presumption of innocence

When someone is charged with a criminal offence, the state has to prove the accused's guilt *beyond a reasonable doubt*. An accused person is not expected to prove his or her innocence. If at the end of the trial there is a reasonable doubt, a finding of 'not guilty' should be made.

Any person accused of committing a crime is therefore presumed to be innocent until proven guilty. The reason for this rests on the assumption that human beings are free and have basic rights as to life and personal property. Any infringement of these rights, such as imprisonment, corporal punishment, execution, or the imposition of a fine, may only follow from a fair trial, in which an accused is properly confronted with charges and is in a position to present a defence.

Another reason for the presumption of innocence is the fact that officials of the state, such as police officers, are responsible for the investigation of crimes and can therefore be expected to be in possession of the relevant facts and in a position to put forward the necessary evidence. An accused who is innocent could find it impossible to prove his or her own innocence without the required knowledge as to the facts concerning the crime. Accepting that mistakes can occur, and that court findings are not necessarily always correct, it is often said that it is better that several guilty people be acquitted (found not guilty), than that one innocent person should be punished.

2. The need for a public trial and guarantees necessary for an accused's defence

The guarantees include the right to be told, in detail, what one is charged with, to be given adequate time and facilities to prepare one's defence, and to defend oneself in person, or to be defended by a lawyer of one's own choice, to be provided at state expense if necessary. It also includes the right to examine all state witnesses and to have one's own witnesses heard, as well as to have a free interpreter when necessary. An accused has the right to testify (give evidence), but cannot be compelled to do so. This is often referred to as 'the right to remain silent' or 'the right against self-incrimination'. The guarantees include, furthermore, the right to appeal to a higher court against a conviction and the right not to be tried again for the same offence after being either convicted or acquitted.

3. Retrospectivity, or the concept of legality

In determining whether a person is criminally liable, the first question is obviously whether the alleged conduct is a crime. The fact that certain conduct may be regarded as morally wrong, socially unacceptable, or sinful from a religious point of view does not mean that it is prohibited by law. There cannot be a crime without a legal provision and state officials are prevented from punishing people in an arbitrary fashion.

This principle also implies that the conduct must have been prohibited as a crime at the time it was committed. Article 11(2) recognizes this as a basic human right, as it also does the principle that a heavier penalty than the one applicable at the time the offence was committed must not be imposed.

People must therefore know as accurately as possible what conduct is criminally punishable and also how severe the punishment is likely to be. In 1939 this principle was suspended in Nazi Germany when courts were given the power to punish any conduct 'which ought to be punished according to the fundamental ideas of criminal law and popular feeling'. Thus the courts proceeded to punish conduct which even the drafters of the law that gave the courts this power may not have foreseen!

The article in South African law

1. The presumption of innocence and the guarantees necessary for an accused's defence

The presumption of innocence is generally recognized in the South African law of evidence. It is a general rule of policy, which requires that the prosecution should ordinarily bear the onus of proof on all issues. Thus the prosecution has the burden to prove all the elements or requirements of a crime. The prosecution also has to negate all the usual defences which an accused may raise, such as provocation, drunkenness, self-defence, necessity, consent, compulsion, alibi, and lack of capacity because of youth.

In South African law parliament is regarded as sovereign. This means that no South African court has the power to declare parliament's laws invalid. Therefore parliament can direct that the burden of proof is on the accused rather than the prosecution, and has done so with serious political crimes. In terms of the Internal Security Act of 1982, the crime of terrorism consists of the commission of a certain violent act accompanied by intent, such as the intent to overthrow or endanger state authority. In terms of the act the accused has the burden of demonstrating that he or she did not have such an intent! In a number of decisions the Appellate Division of the Supreme Court has succeeded in placing some restrictions upon these provisions.

In 1963 an amendment to the old Internal Security Act of 1950 made it a capital offence to undergo training anywhere, or to obtain information, which could be of use in furthering the achievement of any of the objects of communism or any unlawful organization. The prosecution only had to establish that the accused had received training, or obtained information, in order to oblige the accused to prove that his or her intent had not been to use the information to further the achievement of any of the goals of communism, or of an unlawful organization. Someone who studied abroad and obtained information about communism could therefore be charged and would have had to prove his or her innocence.

The detention of people without trial has also resulted in a violation of accepted rules of evidence. In terms of section 217 of the Criminal Procedure Act of 1977 an admission or confession by an accused, which was made voluntarily and without duress or undue influence, may be used as evidence against him or her. An apparently voluntary admission or confession, which is reduced to writing by or in the presence of a magistrate, is regarded as voluntary, unless the contrary is established by the person who made it.

It can be accepted that people detained without trial, often in isolation, who are interrogated and perhaps assaulted or tortured, would be prone to making confessions which are not voluntary. To prove that they were made involuntarily, under such circumstances, is extremely difficult. In the case of *Christie* in 1982, for example, the Appellate Division decided that being held in detention did not in itself mean that a statement was not made voluntarily. This was despite the fact that Christie claimed that he believed that he was being held under indefinite detention, and despite the power of the police to detain him indefinitely (and that it seemed certain that he would have been held indefinitely if he did not co-operate). Christie was convicted because of his own statements in detention.

In one case evidence was accepted under circumstances when an accused person, allegedly under duress, pointed out certain things and places to the police (in terms of the Criminal Procedure Act). In another, statements made by a witness who had been detained for over 500 days were accepted. Sections of the Internal Security Act of 1982 still provide for detention without trial and oblige the detainee to furnish information against himself or herself in order to obtain release. Provisions such as these, together with a number of court decisions, have resulted in a substantial erosion of the basic presumption of innocence.

Apart from laws made by the legislature, the socio-economic situation in South Africa often results in a miscarriage of justice. Because of poverty and a lack of education, many people do not have access to legal aid and effective legal representation, or a proper understanding of legal procedures. Inadequate communication, often through interpreters or inexperienced *pro deo* counsel, can directly or indirectly result in decisions which amount to a disregard or violation of the rights contained in Article 11(1).

2. Retrospectivity

It is generally accepted that South African courts are not allowed to create crimes by declaring immoral or anti-social behaviour to be offences. The legislature furthermore ought not to create crimes with a retrospective effect, and newly-created crimes must apply to future acts only.

In some ways South African criminal law theory is more liberal than most other systems in the world. The Appellate Division ruled in 1977 that ignorance of the law is a valid defence and that a person who did not know that his or her conduct was criminally punishable (even though this ignorance was unreasonable) must be found not guilty.

However, because parliament is regarded as sovereign it can create crimes as it deems fit. The South African legislature is therefore free to enact statutes with a retrospective effect and has in fact done so, for example, with regard to the offence of terrorism mentioned above. Unless a statute specifically states that it operates retrospectively, a court will not readily accept that it has a retrospective effect.

If the punishment for a crime is increased by statute, it may not operate retrospectively with regard to someone who committed the crime before the punishment was increased. The appeal court once set aside the death penalty imposed for robbery with aggravating circumstances, because the robbery had been committed before the act providing for the heavier sentence was passed.

The principle of legality, upon which all these protections are based, also means that the legislature ought not to create crimes with a vague content. However, nothing prevents the South African parliament from defining crimes vaguely, and it has often done so. In terms of Section 54(1) of the Internal Security Act the crime of 'terrorism' is committed by any person who, with intent to promote any social change, performs any act which is aimed at promoting an act or a threat of violence. This could mean any act committed with intent to endanger the safety, health, or interests of the public at any place in the Republic. Therefore, throwing an empty beer can into the Vaal Dam with the intention to endanger the health or interests of the public could amount to a crime.

There is a further aspect to retrospectivity which is directly relevant to the South African situation. When Nazi war criminals were prosecuted in Nuremberg after the Second World War, many lawyers wanted them to be punished for their deeds, but felt uneasy about the fact that the 'crimes against humanity', of which they were accused, were not recognized as punishable offences at the time the actions were committed. In 1973 the United Nations declared apartheid to be a crime against humanity under international law. Therefore, if people or organizations are later charged with the crime of practising apartheid, they would not be able to rely on the rule against retrospectivity.

The law of the future

Any credible Bill of Rights for South Africans should explicitly protect the rights recognized in Article 11 of the Declaration. The unequivocal protection of these rights is not controversial in the constitutional and human rights debates. How to guarantee that they are respected and upheld in *practice* is more difficult. The Bill of Rights must be constitutionally entrenched and it must be justiciable. The courts must have the power to enforce the provisions of the Bill, and to be the final arbiters as far as individual freedom is concerned. The doctrine of parliamentary sovereignty will have to be replaced by constitutionalism. Acts of parliament violating these basic rights could then be declared invalid by the courts.

Under a new dispensation the courts will also be in a position to break away from judicial precedents, which have substantially eroded principles such as the presumption of innocence. This will have to be done and should, despite technical arguments as to the authority of precedents, not be difficult in practice. Much will depend, however, on the willingness of the courts to interpret statutes and previous judgments in a way which is sympathetic to human rights. Such an approach should not follow only from a Bill of Rights, but from the basic attitude and philosophy of the courts.

Every legal system has to grapple with a tension between respect for individual freedom and the urgent need to combat crime effectively. A society in which dangerous criminals mostly go free because of procedural technicalities will be neither safe, nor just. Therefore, the tendency to water down the presumption of innocence in practice occurs in many legal systems. Solutions should be sought through innovative thinking and the development of a rich jurisprudence, rather than unsophisticated legislation which brutally violates basic human rights.

It has become a cliché to call for the growth of a human rights culture. However, without an awareness of the value and importance of human rights and the strong will to preserve them amongst judges, the legal profession, and the public, any Bill of Rights will be worth little more than the paper on which it is written. With a human rights culture and the desire continually to strive for democracy, South Africa may have a legal system respected by its citizens and by all civilized people.

13
The right to privacy, honour, and reputation

Article 12 No one shall be subjected to arbitrary interference with his privacy, family, home or correspondence, or to attacks upon his honour and reputation. Everyone has the right to the protection of the law against such interference or attacks.

What this article means

The article uses the phrase 'arbitrary interference'. This means interferences that have not been approved by the law or that occur without people having the opportunity to challenge them. It is necessary to examine the words 'privacy', 'family', 'home', 'correspondence', 'honour', and 'reputation' separately.

1. Privacy

Article 12 protects the 'right to privacy' which is the right not to have one's private life interfered with. Invasions of privacy include intrusions; public disclosures of private facts; placing people in a 'false light'; or using a person's name or likeness without consent.

❒ *Intrusions:* An intrusion happens when a person's private life is interfered with for no good reason. The following are examples: (a) people being continually watched by others; (b) illegal searches by the police; (c) the tapping of telephones; (d) unlawful videoing, photographing, or tape recording of people and their conversations; (e) continual telephone calls that disturb people; (f) unlawful following about of people by the police or private detectives; (g) harassment of people by the police or debt collectors; (h) laws requiring information about a person's religion or race; (i) blood tests to decide if people have been drinking; and (j) the watching of people held in prison or detention.

❒ *Public disclosure of private facts:* This happens when a person tells somebody about the private life of another person. It will be an invasion of privacy if the person who is talked about is not a well-known figure who likes publicity. These types of invasion happen when a person tells another about somebody else's: (a) debts, or how much they owe; (b) illnesses, or deformities, and the public does not need to know; (c) private life, where the person is not a well-known figure; (d) childhood or family life; (e) past activities and history; (f) embarrassing experiences; or (g) relationship with a doctor, or lawyer. It can also be a disclosure to publish facts about a person where the information has been kept in computers.

❐ *Placing a person in a false light:* This type of invasion of privacy happens if somebody publishes untrue information about another person; for example, if an advertisement says that a married woman is looking for boyfriends, and it is not true.

❐ *Using a person's name or likeness without consent:* This is also an invasion of privacy. It would occur, for example, where a person's image or likeness is used in advertisements, films, books, magazines, newspapers, or on radio or television without his or her consent. People are not allowed to make profits out of other people's names or likenesses without their consent.

2. Family

Article 12 protects the right of people not to have their family life disrupted. People in a family usually live together and have a close relationship (husbands and wives, parents and children, people who share a home). People are protected from interferences with their family life. They have the right to marry, or to live together, or to start a family, and not to have their family broken up. For example, people should not: (a) be separated from their families by immigration laws; (b) be denied access to their children after divorce, except if there is a good reason to protect the children from them; (c) have to send their children away to schools far from where their family lives; (e) be prevented from living with people of the same, or different, sexes; (f) have their authority as parents interfered with, unless it is in the best interests of their children.

3. Home

Article 12 regards a person's home as his or her 'castle'. Usually people are entitled not to have their homes interfered with unless it is done by people or authorities who have followed the necessary legal procedures. For example, the police may search a home only if they have a search warrant. In most countries it is also unlawful to break into a person's house, damage property, or to trespass on property.

If the interference is in the interests of 'national security', 'public safety', the prevention of disorder or crime, or the protection of health or morals, it will usually be allowed if it does not conflict with a country's constitution or Bill of Rights.

4. Correspondence

'Correspondence' refers to things in writing that are sent or received. These include letters, telegrams, postcards, and other written documents. People should not be allowed to interfere with other people's mail unless the law allows them to do so. Many countries, however, allow the authorities to censor the mail of prisoners and people doing military service.

Even though telegrams are read by the post office staff who send them, they should not be read by other people. Postcards should also not be read by others, including post office staff. Telegrams and postcards should only be read by the people to whom they are addressed.

5. Honour

A person's 'honour' refers to his or her good character and dignity. People are entitled to have their dignity respected in their social and individual life. They should not be exposed to rude and hurtful treatment, or to ill-will, hatred, or ridicule. They should also not be insulted or humiliated. Examples of when a person's honour will be attacked are when he or she is subjected to: (a) insulting words or signs; (b) unlawful dismissal from a school or university; (c) unreasonable police interrogation; (d) rude language (e.g. being called a 'kaffir' or a 'bitch'); (e) having to walk around naked; or (f) insulting words in a letter.

Sometimes the honour of one person is injured when the honour of another person is attacked. For example, if a husband's wife is called a 'prostitute', or someone's child is called a 'bastard', the husband or parents would also have an action for insult to their honour.

6. Reputation

A person's 'reputation' is what other people think about that person's character. If people are 'defamed', their reputation is lowered in the eyes of others. For example, people are entitled not to have their reputations attacked by being accused of being: (a) criminals; (b) dishonest; (c) immoral; (d) cowards; (e) Nazis; (f) traitors; (g) bastards; (h) mad; or (i) unfit for their work or business.

The article in South African law

South Africa's common law protects people against arbitrary interferences with privacy, family, home, correspondence, and attacks upon honour and reputation. However, the introduction of apartheid laws has resulted in many of these rights being taken away.

1. Privacy

The right to privacy in South Africa has been undermined by the wide powers of the police under the Internal Security Act of 1982, the Criminal Procedure Act of 1977, and the Public Safety Act of 1953.

Security laws give the police wide powers to intrude into people's private lives. People who actively oppose apartheid have sometimes had their bodies and homes searched without good reason. It has been claimed that their telephones have been tapped, and that they have been subjected to nuisance calls and threats made over the telephone. Opponents of apartheid have been harassed and intimidated by the police or their agents. The same has happened to families of political prisoners detained without trial under the Emergency Regulations or the security laws.

The police have also been accused of releasing embarrassing information about the private lives of people, and of having files on many citizens who are actively opposed to the state. There is also talk of a 'dirty tricks' unit that spreads embarrassing and false information about people opposed to the state's policies. Most of these activities would be unlawful if South Africa had a Bill of Rights that included an article like Article 12.

2. Family

Apartheid laws have severely disrupted family life in South Africa. Under the influx control and pass laws families were forced to live apart. Husbands were separated from their wives and children when they went to seek work in the cities. Families whose members look as if they belong to different 'race groups' have had to live in different areas. In the past, apartheid laws also prevented people of different races from having sexual intercourse with, or marrying, each other.

Laws based on racial discrimination are outlawed by most countries in the world. If South Africa had possessed a Bill of Rights with an article like Article 12, the courts would have refused to recognize apartheid laws that disrupted family life.

3. Home

Apartheid laws in South Africa have also affected people's homes. More than three million people have been moved from areas where they lived, in the process of implementing apartheid. As mentioned, people of different 'races' who belong to the same family may be forced to live in different areas.

In democratic societies it is generally recognized that in the interests of national security, public safety, the prevention of crime, or the protection of health and morals, certain restrictions may be imposed on citizens. However, many of the interferences with people's homes in South Africa would be unacceptable in a democratic society.

4. Correspondence

It has been claimed that opponents of apartheid have had their correspondence interfered with in terms of the security and post office laws. In these cases the security police work with the post office. The post office may intercept postal articles if it is necessary 'in the interests of state security'.

The authorities may also intercept articles suspected of being obscene or indecent or related to lotteries and sports pools. Many democratic countries require a court order before a person's mail can be intercepted.

5. Honour

The security laws give the police wide powers to detain people without trial, and without access to lawyers, friends, family or private doctors. Some detainees have claimed that they have suffered degrading and humiliating treatment in detention. There have been claims of torture, unreasonable police interrogation, and of detainees being sworn at and insulted. Some detainees have given evidence that they were not allowed proper medical treatment, clothing, sleep, exercise, and toilet facilities.

Under South African common law these sorts of police activities are unlawful. However, it is very difficult for a detainee to prove that he or she has been the victim of unlawful conduct by the police. There are usually no independent witnesses.

6. Reputation

Apartheid laws have led to some strange defamation judgments by our courts. For example, for many years it was said that to call a white person 'African' was defamatory. The courts have said that it is defamatory to call a person a 'communist', although many people in South Africa may approve of communism. As in many other countries, it is defamatory to call a person a 'Nazi'. Sometimes people who have been opposed to apartheid have been accused of being 'traitors' and 'communists'. These people would have been entitled to recover damages for such accusations.

Generally, the law of defamation in South Africa is in line with that in most democratic countries, and a person's reputation is protected.

The law of the future

If a Bill of Rights based upon the Universal Declaration of Human Rights were part of South African law, there would be a considerable improvement in the rights and liberties of its citizens. Many of these exist in the common law, but can only be revived if apartheid legislation is repealed. It will also be necessary to remove the wide powers of the police under the security laws. If this were done South African citizens would share the same benefits as those in other democratic countries.

The common law protects people against arbitrary interferences with their privacy, family, home, or correspondence, and attacks upon their honour and reputation. These rights would be strengthened by an article like Article 12 in a South African Bill of Rights.

The biggest challenge to a future South African legal system is to ensure that one repressive system is not replaced by another. Therefore, when limitations are placed on the right to privacy, family, home, or correspondence, and to attacks upon honour and reputation, they should be the same as those recognized in other democratic countries. These rights should be enshrined in a Bill of Rights that has been negotiated by the majority of people in South Africa. They will be meaningless, however, if South Africa fails to develop a 'rights culture'.

14
Freedom of movement

Article 13 *(1) Everyone has the right to freedom of movement and residence within the borders of each state.*

(2) Everyone has the right to leave any country, including his own, and to return to his country.

Article 9 *No one shall be subjected to arbitrary ... exile.*

What these articles mean

These articles guarantee freedom of movement. Freedom of movement has both 'internal' and 'external' elements. The 'internal' elements are contained in Articles 13(1) and 9. They deal with the right of individuals to move freely inside the country, to live where they wish, and to remain in the country. The 'external' elements are contained in Article 13(2), and deal with the right to leave the country and to return to it.

Freedom of movement actually consists of five separate freedoms. With one exception, these freedoms are not restricted to citizens of the state concerned. The first three freedoms deal with 'internal' movement, and the last two with 'external' movement.

1. Freedom of movement within a state

No person should be prevented from moving freely within a state. Laws or policies which say people must have permission to be in any part of the country are contrary to the article. Article 13 does not allow a person to be placed under an order of 'internal exile', banishment, or restriction.

2. Freedom of residence within a state

Every person living within a state should be free to live wherever he or she chooses. It is important to note that this right is not limited to citizens. Sometimes governments give aliens permission to enter the country, but say that they may not live in a particular area. This is contrary to Article 13.

3. Freedom from exile

A state may not force its citizens to leave the country. In addition some scholars believe that the freedom from exile provision prohibits the state from forcing part of the population to become refugees by other means. This would happen where laws discriminate harshly against part of the population and make their lives intolerable or unsafe.

4. Freedom to leave a country

Every person has the right to leave a country. Can a government prevent one of its citizens from leaving the country by refusing to issue a passport? This certainly does happen in many countries, but it is probably contrary to Article 13.

5. Freedom to return to a state

Every person has the right to enter his or her country. This is the only one of the freedoms contained in Article 13 which is not granted to aliens. States have always retained the right to refuse entry to aliens.

The articles in South African law

The South African law on freedom of movement has changed a great deal in the past few years. Most of these changes have been for the better, in the sense that they have removed some of the restrictions on freedom of movement. Citizenship also affects freedom of movement, and particularly in South Africa. The question of citizenship is discussed in Chapter 16 but some aspects will be mentioned here.

1. Freedom of movement

As is well known, the pass laws very severely restricted the movement of Africans. These laws stated that no African could remain in the towns outside the 'homelands' for longer than 72 hours except under particular circumstances. This was obviously contrary to Article 13. In 1986 the pass laws were repealed together with laws preventing Indians from being in the Orange Free State.

There is no longer any general restriction on freedom of movement in South African law. However, the law still allows specific restrictions such as those under the Internal Security Act of 1982 which gives the Minister of Law and Order the power to restrict the freedom of movement of individuals. 'Restriction orders' under the state of emergency prevented people from moving freely. In addition, the Black Administration Act of 1927 gives the Minister of Education and Development Aid the power to banish people who have been convicted of promoting hostility between Africans and whites.

2. Freedom of residence

There is no freedom of residence in South Africa. Every person is classified in a particular racial group, and all land in the country has been allocated to one or other group. It is a crime to live in an area which has been allocated to another group. As is well known, the major law which has this effect is the Group Areas Act of 1966. Other land acts also prevent freedom of residence. These are the Black Land Act of 1913 and the Development Trust and Land Act of 1936.

There have been many attempts to challenge the Group Areas Act in the courts. In 1960 a Mr. Lockhat challenged the validity of the Governor-General's proclamation which described and allocated the various group areas. The basis of his challenge was that the effects of the proclamation were highly discriminatory and unequal, and that the Group Areas Act did not authorize the Governor-General to discriminate in this way. The Appellate Division of the Supreme Court decided that although the act did not actually say that the Governor-General could discriminate, it was clear that the act intended to give him this power.

Years later, in 1979, another attempt was made to challenge the validity of the group areas proclamations, on similar grounds. This was done in the cases of Mr. Werner and Mr. Adams, who had been prosecuted for living illegally in 'white' areas of Johannesburg. Again, the Appellate Division rejected the challenge.

Despite these laws, a growing number of people live in areas where they are not supposed to live. There are many reasons for this, such as the shortage of land near the city centres for occupation by people who are not classified as white. The government has not been successful in its efforts to evict people who are living in the wrong area. Today, there are so many people living in the 'wrong' area, that it would be difficult to prosecute all of them. The courts would become clogged up with these cases, many of which would probably be defended. The Govender case of 1982 has also reduced the usefulness of prosecutions to the government in its attempts to ensure that people live only in the 'correct' area. In that case, the Supreme Court decided that before ordering the eviction of a person convicted under the Group Areas Act, the court first had to consider a number of factors. One of these factors is whether other accommodation is available for the person who has been convicted. Because there is a tremendous shortage of accommodation for people who are not classified as white, it seems unlikely that the courts will often order eviction. There is therefore no purpose for the government in prosecuting people, if the court will not evict them.

During 1988 the Free Settlement Areas Act was passed. Once the government declares a free settlement area it means that anyone, whatever his or her racial classification, will have the right to live in that area. There will therefore be freedom of residence in these areas. At the moment it seems likely that only very few areas will be declared free settlement areas. This will cause great problems, because these areas are likely to become overcrowded as a result of the housing shortage.

Any discussion of freedom of residence would be incomplete without reference to the many forced removals which have taken place in the past. The government has now stated that it is no longer in favour of forced removals. Some of the laws which created the power of forced removal have been repealed.

3. Freedom from exile

Exile usually means expelling an individual from the country where he or she lives, and forcing him or her to go and live elsewhere. South African law does not give the government the power to force a South African citizen to leave South Africa. In this sense, South African law respects the freedom from exile.

However, in practice people have been exiled through the establishment of 'independent homelands' which has resulted in changes to the borders of South Africa. People who had lived in South Africa all their lives suddenly found that legally they were living in another 'country', when the 'homeland' in which they lived was declared 'independent'.

Even after Transkei, Bophuthatswana, Venda, and Ciskei became constitutionally independent, the process of exiling people continued. Parts of South Africa have from time to time been incorporated into the 'independent homelands'. One example is Braklaagte in the Western Transvaal but there are many others, particularly in the Eastern Cape and Western Transvaal. Braklaagte had always been part of South Africa but on 30 December 1988 the government announced that Braklaagte was no longer part of South

Africa, and that it had become part of Bophuthatswana. The people of Braklaagte suddenly found that they were no longer living in South Africa; they were now living in another country. This is a form of exile.

4. Freedom to leave a country

Before 1955 it was not illegal for South African citizens to leave South Africa without a passport. If they left without a passport, they could also not be prevented from returning to South Africa.

In 1955 the Departure from the Union Regulation Act was passed which made it a crime to leave South Africa without a passport. The government was also given the power to refuse to issue a passport. (In 1988, for example, 210 people were refused passports.) The result is that the government has the power to refuse to allow South Africans to leave the country. This is contrary to Article 13.

The act also says that the government is obliged to issue a permit to leave the country to any person who satisfies the Department of Home Affairs that he or she intends to leave the country permanently. This is known as an 'exit permit'. It means that the person may leave South Africa, but may not return. However, this right to leave the country with an exit permit is also limited, as the case of Mr. Robert Sobukwe demonstrates.

Mr. Sobukwe was a 'banned' person who had been restricted to the magisterial district of Kimberley. During 1970 he applied for an exit permit to study and to teach at an American university. Although a permit was issued, he had a problem: he could not leave Kimberley to get to the airport. He therefore asked the Minister of Justice for permission to leave, which was refused. Mr. Sobukwe challenged this refusal in court, but the Appellate Division decided that the refusal was lawful. The result was that although Mr. Sobukwe theoretically had the right to leave South Africa, he was prevented from doing so.

5. Freedom to return to a state

South Africans who leave the country using a passport have the right to return. However, a significant number of South Africans have left the country by means of exit permits because they were refused passports. The result is that they have lost the right to return to South Africa. They are now exiles.

The right of return has also been limited by the constitutional independence of Transkei, Bophuthatswana, Venda, and Ciskei, which deprived millions of South Africans of their citizenship. The

South African government has recently decided to allow the citizens of these territories to enter and live in South Africa without obtaining any permission. As a result, their freedom of movement has not been restricted. However, the government has the power at any time to require citizens of these territories to have permits to enter or live in South Africa.

This has happened in a number of cases. An example is the case of Mr. Steve Tshwete, a South African who lost his citizenship when Ciskei became constitutionally independent. The government decided that he would have to have a visa (permit) in order to enter South Africa, and a residence permit in order to live in South Africa. Mr. Tshwete took the matter to court. The Appellate Division decided that because of a provision in the Aliens Act, Mr. Tshwete had the right to live in South Africa without obtaining a residence permit. If he left South Africa, however, he would not be permitted to return unless he had a visa issued by the South African government. Mr. Tshwete lived in the Eastern Cape. The road which he used to travel to his work at King William's Town went into Ciskei, and then re-entered South Africa. The result was that he needed a visa to go to work, because by travelling along this road he would be leaving and then re-entering South Africa; and, once he went to work, he needed a visa to return home!

The law of the future

If freedom of movement as defined in Articles 9 and 13 became part of South African law, the lives of many South Africans would improve greatly. People would be allowed to buy land and live wherever they wanted. Individuals could no longer be restricted to a particular area by administrative decision of the Minister of Law and Order. People could no longer be exiled by the declaration that the land where they live is no longer part of South Africa. All South Africans would be free to travel outside the country, and to return home to South Africa.

It would be necessary to consider whether these changes would be retrospective in their effect: in other words, where people had already lost their freedom, would it be restored to them? For example, one can look at the case of exiles who left South Africa on exit permits, and lost their right to live in South Africa. Would they have the right to return? And what of those people who lost their South African citizenship and therefore their right to live in, and return to, South Africa? Would their citizenship be returned to them? These questions also apply to people whose land was incorporated into a 'homeland'.

What this demonstrates is that it is not enough to decide that, in future, South Africans will have the freedoms contained in the Universal Declaration of Human Rights. We have a history of centuries of deprivation of human rights. Any attempt to bring human rights into South African law has to take account of the results of this history.

In some cases, it would be relatively simple to reverse the results of past laws and practices. For example, a law could be passed declaring that all people who lost their South African citizenship will be entitled to recover it. But other problems are more complex, and are more difficult to reverse. For example, what is to be done about people who were removed from their homes decades ago as a result of the Group Areas Act? After they were removed, other people bought those houses. Is there any way in which the effects of this denial of human rights can be remedied, or do we have to turn our backs on the effects of history and start afresh? This question is of the greatest importance. It has been estimated that from 1960 to 1983 approximately 3,5 million South Africans were subjected to forced removals under various laws.

Francis Wilson has pointed out that apartheid legislation is like the scaffolding of a building. When the building is being erected, it is necessary to have the scaffolding around the building. When the building has been completed, the scaffolding can be removed, and the building does not fall down. In the same way, apartheid laws (particularly with regard to freedom of residence) have created apartheid structures in South Africa. If the laws were removed, many of those structures would remain in place. People would remain dispossessed, and the practical results of generations of human rights deprivations would continue to live on with us. The great challenge, therefore, is not only to apply human rights in South Africa, but also to find ways of reversing and redressing the human rights deprivations which will otherwise not only be part of our history, but also a part of our future.

15
The right to asylum

Article 14 *(1) Everyone has the right to seek and to enjoy in other countries asylum from persecution.*

(2) This right may not be invoked in the case of prosecutions genuinely arising from non-political crimes or from acts contrary to the purposes and principles of the United Nations.

What this article means

This article establishes the right of individuals, who face persecution in their own countries, to seek refuge in another country. These people are termed refugees and can be distinguished from aliens or immigrants in that they have been forced through fear to leave their country of origin. For this reason they do not wish to return. In seeking asylum they are in fact looking for somewhere else to live on a permanent basis, and not just for temporary protection.

The problem of refugees goes back a long way. However, it was only after the First World War that international organizations began to treat the problem as an international concern. At that stage there were no written rules regarding refugees and each state had the right to decide how to deal with them. Accordingly, each state had the right to decide who should be allowed to stay and who should be returned to their country.

After the war the newly-formed League of Nations was faced with the problem of the plight of 800 000 Russian refugees. In February 1921 the Council for the League passed its first Resolution on Refugees and from that time on the problem of refugees has frequently been on the agenda of organizations, like the United Nations and the Organization of African Unity.

The problem has escalated since the Second World War. Many international human rights documents which refer to refugees, like the Declaration, have been adopted by various countries at different times.

In December 1950 the General Assembly of the United Nations adopted a statute which established a United Nations Office of High

Commissioner for Refugees. This office is the international body which deals with refugees. It was established to provide legal protection for refugees and to seek solutions to the problems. Its work was to be humanitarian and social, and not of a political nature.

In Africa, for example, rapid decolonization has been followed by social upheaval, leading to great refugee problems in some countries. In response, the Organization of African Unity adopted a Convention in 1969 in an attempt to alleviate the difficulties.

1. Who is a refugee?

A limited definition of the term 'refugee' is to be found in United Nations documents. To qualify as a refugee an individual must prove:

1. 'a well-founded fear of persecution by reason of his race, religion, nationality, political opinion or membership of a particular social group'; and
2. 'that his own government will not protect him'.

Once this has been established, the appropriate international bodies will attempt to protect the refugee's basic human rights such as the right to life, liberty, and security. They will also attempt to ensure that the refugee is not returned to the country in which he or she will be in danger. It is a fundamental principle of refugee law (known as the principle of non-refoulment) that no refugee should be returned to a state in which he or she is likely to face persecution.

A broader definition of a refugee is to be found in the Organization of African Unity Convention. This includes in its definition, people compelled to leave their home country owing to external aggression, occupation, foreign domination, or events seriously disturbing public order.

2. Who does not qualify as a refugee?

In terms of Article 14(2) of the Declaration, an individual does not have the right to seek asylum where he or she is being prosecuted for a non-political crime or where an act was committed which is contrary to the purposes and principles of the United Nations.

There are four categories in which refugee status may be lost or denied. These are:

1. where there is a voluntary act by the individual, for example to return to his or her country of origin;

2. where there are fundamental changes in the country which remove the basis for any fear of persecution;
3. where the individual is already receiving the protection of another state or United Nations Organization;
4. and where certain crimes are committed, for example non-political crimes.

3. The meaning of the term persecution

'Persecution' does not have a single meaning. It includes the threat of death or imprisonment and also less harsh measures which have the effect of harming people's dignity and interests in a way considered unacceptable under international standards. Persecution might therefore include the denial of employment or education, or the imposition of restrictions on freedoms which are traditionally guaranteed in a democratic society such as the freedom of speech, assembly, worship, and movement.

4. The right to be granted asylum

Are refugees entitled to demand that they be granted permanent residence and protection? States have been reluctant to commit themselves to the principle that a refugee is entitled to lasting protection. Each state has the discretion whether to grant asylum or not, and to decide on the nature of the asylum.

5. The principle of non-refoulment

This principle states that no refugee should be forced to return to the country in which he or she faces persecution. This means that while states still have the right to decide whether to accept refugees as permanent members of their community, they may not send them back to countries in which they face persecution. All states are therefore obliged to grant temporary protection to refugees. This principle has become so fundamental that it is even accepted in situations where there is a mass influx of people into areas which do not have the resources to cope with them.

The article in South African law

South Africa is not a party to any of the regional or international instruments concerning refugees which means that it is not bound by any treaty. People who do not enter South Africa at a designated port of entry with satisfactory travel documents are treated as illegal immigrants. Officials are entitled to detain and repatriate them.

In the 1970s thousands of refugees migrated into what was then South West Africa during the civil strife in Angola. These people (who were regarded as aliens) were granted provisional asylum and were provided with basic humanitarian assistance. Many had close links with Portugal and were returned to their country of origin. They were not penalized for their illegal entry into South Africa and there were no reported cases of people being forced to return to Angola.

The response of the South African authorities has been very different with regard to the thousands of black Mozambican refugees who have entered South Africa over the last decade. Mozambique has been torn by conflict and it is clear that the government is unable to protect its people. Villagers and farmers have been caught in the middle of a war. They have been forced to provide assistance to both sides in the conflict and have faced terrible recriminations on being found out. The nature of the persecution that these people face qualifies them for refugee status.

In 1985 the then Minister of Home Affairs, Mr. Stoffel Botha, stated that his department was repatriating about 1 500 Mozambicans a month. It was made clear that these people would not be treated as refugees but as illegal immigrants and that they would be repatriated to Mozambique. This indicates a complete lack of respect for the principle of non-refoulment.

The law of the future

As long as civil strife continues in Southern African countries the refugee problem will continue. Thousands of people could eventually find their way to South Africa. By refusing to assist them, the South African authorities refuse to recognize a problem which other communities are trying to solve. Sending people who are in fear of their lives back to the country from which they have fled will not solve the problem. In all probability they will be forced to flee again and the problem will intensify. Other African countries, despite their more fragile economies, have been able to assist refugees and provide temporary asylum to them.

The refugee problem is a world-wide issue which South Africa does not have to deal with on its own. International bodies have been set up to deal with these issues. Many other countries have specific legislation dealing with the status and rights of refugees. Organizations have also been set up to deal with requests for asylum. In most of these countries the United Nations High

Commissioner of Refugees has a role to play, even if it is in an advisory capacity.

In their treatment of refugees the South African authorities are influenced by the fact that masses of individuals have flooded into areas which are already experiencing serious economic difficulties. This problem is not unique to South Africa and is one which is recognized by the United Nations and other organizations. The granting of asylum may place heavy burdens on certain countries but satisfactory solutions depend upon international co-operation.

While South Africa refuses to recognize refugees and repatriates them to countries where they will continue to face serious personal danger, solutions cannot be found.

Recognizing the refugee problem for what it is and providing relevant legislation to deal with it will only go part of the way to solving the problem. But at least South Africa will be playing its part in the international community towards seeking solutions.

16
The right to a nationality

Article 15 *(1)* *Everyone has the right to a nationality.*

(2) *No one shall be arbitrarily deprived of his nationality nor denied the right to change his nationality.*

What this article means

The right to nationality refers to the right of every person to be a member of a state and therefore its citizen. The importance of this right lies in the fact that it is only through state membership that certain rights and privileges are available to an individual. These include the right to own property and to live within a state; the right to participate in the decision-making processes through voting or being elected to public office; and the right to be issued with a passport and to be allowed to travel beyond the borders of one's state.

The purpose of the right to nationality is to protect people from statelessness. The condition of statelessness, or lack of nationality, often results in suffering and hardship offensive to the dignity of human beings. It means the absence of a state or community willing and able to guarantee rights to the stateless person.

Because of the widespread and strict requirements for travel documents in the modern world, stateless persons find it very difficult to find states willing to receive them and to grant them nationality. A stateless person has no claim on any state for essentials such as a birth certificate, a passport, and state social welfare services, etc. In short, a stateless person is not recognized as a person with rights.

The right to change one's nationality is also regarded as a fundamental human right. Although the right to nationality is an important and sometimes crucial human right, being a national of a state may sometimes impose certain obligations which an individual finds burdensome. In such cases the only option open to such a person may be to change nationality. States are, however, generally reluctant to allow people to change their nationality voluntarily. This reluctance is usually greater in the case of individuals who possess certain skills, or during times of war or threats of war against the state.

The terms 'nationality' and 'citizenship' are often used interchangeably to refer to the legal relationship which exists between a state and an individual in terms of which the individual enjoys certain rights and privileges as a member of the state. Within this relationship the citizen or national has corresponding obligations, such as to protect the existence of the state and to refrain from acts which may harm the integrity of the state, by, for example, committing acts of treason against the state.

There are two principal ways in which nationality can be acquired in most states of the world today. Some states grant nationality to all persons who are born within their territory; others grant nationality to descendants of their nationals. Nationality can also be acquired through naturalization or registration.

A person can acquire the nationality of the state in which he or she was born and also be regarded as a national of another state, such as the national state of the parents. In such a case the person is said to have dual nationality. Although dual nationality has a number of definite advantages it can lead to problems where, for example, one of the states requires the person to perform activities that are regarded as treasonable by the other state, especially in times of war.

For example the case of *Kawakita v United States*, decided by the US Supreme Court in 1952, involved a charge of treason against Kawakita, who was a national of both the United States and Japan. The case against Kawakita was that he had, while in Japan during the Second World War, engaged in various activities including acting as interpreter of communications between the Japanese and the American prisoners of war. It was alleged that these acts amounted to acts of treason against the United States. Kawakita's defence was that he had voluntarily surrendered his United States nationality, but this was rejected by the court and he was convicted of treason.

The rules of acquisition and loss of nationality have, in recent years, become very complex in many states. In general, nationality gained through birth or descent is more enduring (i.e. not easily lost) as compared with nationality acquired by registration or naturalization. Most countries have strict residence requirements which, if not complied with, may result in loss of nationality.

The article in South African law

All states have the right to determine who their nationals are and how the right to nationality may be lost. This right is, however, not a matter which is solely the decision of a state. Under certain circumstances (for example when there is a conflict between the nationality laws of two states) the right of each state to prescribe rules of nationality may be limited by the application of rules of international law. State rules must conform to international law standards contained in several international laws or conventions such as the Convention on the Reduction of Statelessness, the Convention on the Nationality of Married Women, and the International Convention on the Elimination of all Forms of Racial Discrimination

South Africa's acts of denationalization of approximately eight million South Africans by the process of granting 'independence' to certain 'homelands' has been condemned as contrary to the principles of self-determination (the right of the people of a territory to determine their future). This process has also been condemned as being contrary to rules which prohibit denationalization of persons on the basis of race, religion, ethnicity, or other related grounds.

The process of denationalization of the African people in South Africa started with the National States Citizenship Act of 1970 (formerly called the Black States Citizenship Act). This act created homeland citizenship for all African people in South Africa. Homeland citizenship was determined by one of several criteria such as birth or residence within a homeland area, ability to speak the language or dialects of the area, blood relationship, or identification with a member or members of a homeland area. This idea of a citizenship of regions is unacceptable in constitutional law because citizenship is a product of a sovereign state. Most of the homelands in South Africa (such as KwaZulu, Qwa-Qwa, and Lebowa) are still part of South Africa.

The position of the 'independent' states (such as Transkei) is somewhat different. In terms of South African statutes called the Status Acts, and the corresponding Constitution Acts of each of the 'independent homelands', each of these 'countries' became constitutionally independent. One of the consequences was that citizens of these 'independent' states are considered to be aliens (foreigners) within South Africa. They can therefore be denied property rights, residential rights, and the right to work or seek employment in South Africa. This also means that, in terms of the

Aliens Act, citizens of these countries can be prohibited from entering or remaining in the Republic for the purpose of permanent or temporary residence, unless they possess a valid residence permit. The requirements for visas and residence permits have, in the majority cases, been waived in respect of 'homeland' citizens. The government can, however, withdraw these visa and permit exemptions at any time despite the fact that a section in each of the Status Acts seems to protect certain rights and privileges of 'homeland' citizens who were resident in South Africa at the time of 'independence'.

In one case the Supreme Court confirmed the view that a person who had been denationalized by the Status of Bophuthatswana Act, and who had been resident in South Africa when Bophuthatswana became 'independent', had retained the right of permanent residence in South Africa. In a later case the Appellate Division seems to have given a different decision. The Tshwete case (in 1989) concerned the right of a denationalized person, who was born in South Africa, to live and work in a country of his birth. Tshwete was permanently resident in South Africa at the time of the 'independence' of Ciskei but was declared a Ciskeian national in terms of the Status Act. He continued to live and work in South Africa after the 'independence' of the Ciskei. Nearly three years after Ciskei's independence, he was informed by the Director-General for Home Affairs of the Republic of South Africa that his visa exemption had been withdrawn, meaning that he would, as from that moment, need a visa and a temporary residence permit to re-enter South Africa.

This meant that the rights, privileges, and benefits which were supposed to have been protected by the Status of Ciskei Act (the right of permanent residence in South Africa in this case) were withdrawn by an administrative act of a government official. The court gave approval of this action when it ruled that the Director-General was allowed to issue the notice withdrawing the applicant's visa exemption, thereby terminating the rights, privileges, and benefits that he enjoyed under the Status Act. The practical consequences of this decision for Tshwete were that he could not live in his country of birth without a permit and his continued employment was dependent on having a valid visa and employment permit issued by the South African government.

The above decision may be contrasted with the cases of Tsotsobe (1983) and Gaba (1985) where the Appellate Division confirmed the conviction and death sentences of people who, in terms of statutes, were Transkeian citizens. In Tsotsobe's case the court paid little attention to the accused's defence that he did not owe allegiance to South Africa since he was a citizen of Transkei and therefore could not be convicted of high treason. Instead, the court said that the accused was ordinarily resident in South Africa. In the court's view, the fact that the accused had regarded South Africa as his 'home' meant that he owed allegiance to the South African state. The logic of the court's reasoning in this decision and that of Tshwete is plain: the fact that Africans are granted citizenship rights of an inferior status does not mean that their obligations towards the state are also reduced.

The government has evidently abandoned the grand scheme of separate development and the idea of creating 'independent homelands'. In line with this change of plan the government has made it possible for Africans, who had been denationalized, to resume their South African citizenship under certain conditions. The Restoration of Citizenship Act of 1986 provides that persons who were regarded as citizens of 'independent homelands' can regain South African citizenship on application. There are various grounds on which South African citizenship can be reclaimed. According to the Minister of Home Affairs, over one million people qualify for restoration of South African citizenship under this act.

The position of Indians and 'coloureds' with regard to citizenship rights has also been unsatisfactory. In an attempt to co-opt members of Indian and 'coloured' communities into the government structures, the government created the tricameral parliamentary system in the 1983 Constitution. The participation of these two groups in parliament is mainly limited to 'own affairs' and they have no real say in the central and most important political processes of government. The constitutional basis of the tricameral parliamentary structure is such that Indian and 'coloured' members can never win a vote on any issue of national importance since the white House of Assembly has a built-in majority.

The discriminatory nature of South African citizenship and nationality laws is also evident in the way citizenship is sometimes ascribed to whites. Apart from the ordinary ways of acquiring citizenship such as birth, descent, and naturalization, section 11A of the South African Citizenship Act of 1949 forces citizenship on any white foreigner who has been permanently resident in the Republic for a period of two years. In the case where the foreigner makes a declaration that he or she does not want to acquire South African citizenship, he or she is then regarded as having lost permanent residence in the Republic and is disqualified from ever acquiring South African citizenship in any manner. This is an unusual way of ascribing and denying nationality which can only be explained by the policy of the government to encourage as many white people as possible to become South African citizens so that they can be drafted into the South African army.

The provision is also out of step with current trends in the modern world regarding acquisition and loss of citizenship where the emphasis is on giving the individual the right to choose his or her nationality.

The law of the future

The South African law of nationality falls far below the standards which are contained in a number of international laws or conventions which seek to promote human rights in the world. The International Convention on the Elimination of Racial Discrimination, for instance, requires that all states which undertake to observe the rules contained in the convention should guarantee rights, including the right to nationality, to everyone without discrimination on the basis of race.

The denial of the right to nationality and full citizenship is also a denial of the fundamental right of self-determination. Without full participation in government and decision-making, those who are excluded from these processes cannot determine their future and that of their country.

South Africa's nationality laws and policies of racial discrimination are the causes of the conflict that prevails in the country. There can be no doubt that only laws that respect basic human rights will improve the conditions for peace and prosperity for South Africans. Addressing a meeting that observed the International Day for the Elimination of Racial Discrimination in March 1979, the Secretary-General of the United Nations said:

> More than ever today we understand that the international struggle against racial prejudice, inequality and injustice is very much related to the creation of conditions of stability and well-being which are necessary for peaceful and friendly relations among nations. In essence, these conditions must be based upon respect for the concept of equal rights and self-determination. In South Africa the policies of apartheid are diametrically opposed to this concept. There can be no peace

while the overwhelming majority of its people are deliberately deprived of their human rights and excluded from the mainstream of their country's political, economic and social life.

17
The rights to marriage and a family

Article 16 (1) Men and women of full age, without any limitation due to race, nationality or religion, have the right to marry and to found a family. They are entitled to equal rights as to marriage, during marriage and at its dissolution.

(2) Marriage shall be entered into only with the free and full consent of the intending spouses.

(3) The family is the natural and fundamental group unit of society and is entitled to protection by society and the state.

What this article means

One of the more important aims of this article is to prohibit states from enacting laws which prevent interracial marriages. Article 16 also prevents states from defending discriminatory social practices with regard to marriage and family relationships.

Another requirement of the article is that the partners to a marriage must be treated as equals before the law on entering marriage, while it persists, and when it ends. A goal of the article is to influence states to change their marriage laws so that women are not discriminated against in relation to marriage. Marriage laws have at times tended to be paternalistic towards women, who have often been regarded as possessions of their parents before marriage, and of their husbands after marriage.

Article 16 also proclaims and reinforces the idea that the children of a marriage are members of the society of the future and, as such, need the protection of both laws and society.

The article in South African law

1. 'Men and women of full age'

A person of 'full age' in South Africa is a 'major'. (This is someone who is at least 21 years old.) For these persons to marry, the consent of the parents or guardian is generally not required because the law regards them as having mature judgment.

An exception to this general rule is the case of African customary marriages in Natal and the Transvaal. The Black Administration Act of 1927 provides that a marriage of an African female of 'full age' may not take place unless her father or legal guardian has given his written consent. If the consent is unreasonably withheld, or if she is unable to obtain the consent, the Minister of Development Aid or a judge of the Supreme Court may grant the necessary consent.

The need for consent clearly presents a hardship for some African women, and is a violation of Article 16.

2. 'limitation due to race, nationality or religion'

Before 19 June 1985 a marriage between a white South African and a person of any other race group was invalid. While the removal of this notorious law was welcomed, many of the social results of mixed marriages have not yet been completely addressed. (This will be discussed further below under 'protection of the family unit'.)

A marriage entered into outside South Africa will normally be regarded as valid in South Africa. An exception is that of a polygamous marriage. This is a marriage which allows one partner to have more than one wife or husband, as the case may be. A foreign marriage which, according to South African law, is 'potentially polygamous' will not be recognized even if it is in fact not polygamous.

Marriages by Islamic and Hindu rites are regarded as potentially polygamous and are not recognized under South African law. To make such a 'marriage' legal, the couple must also enter into a legal (civil) marriage. Generally speaking, African customary marriages are in the same legal position as those contracted under Islamic and Hindu rites.

3. 'equal rights as to marriage, during marriage ...'

Since 1 November 1984 the Matrimonial Property Act has brought about major changes with regard to each partner's property and the role of each partner in the marriage. The act acknowledges that both are equal partners in the marriage. Legal domination by the husband has also been lessened.

Since 2 December 1988 all South Africans, irrespective of race, have had the same choices of marriage systems. This means that unless the parties choose to enter into an antenuptial contract, or unless blacks choose a customary marriage, all people marry according to the same marriage law. Furthermore, in the absence of such choices, the legal consequences of marriages for people of all races are the same.

Where the parties choose a customary marriage the legal position of the wife is, however, different. She is still legally regarded as a minor (a person under 21), irrespective of her age, and must be assisted by her husband in any legal action. She does not share in the ownership of her house.

It is possible for a husband and wife in an African customary marriage to change to a civil marriage provided the wife is the husband's only wife. When this happens, the legal consequences of a civil marriage apply.

While the Matrimonial Property Act of 1984 and its amendments have gone a long way to create equality between marriage partners in South Africa, it has still retained the husband's power as the head of the family. This means that the husband has the decisive say in all matters concerning the common life of the partners to the marriage. However, this 'decisive say' must be exercised reasonably.

The husband, as the natural guardian of the children born during the marriage, can deal with the children's legal affairs. He has the final say on questions concerning the children's upbringing. The husband also has the right to decide the place of residence of the family. He may determine the lifestyle of the family, based on the outdated notion that the husband in the 'normal' household is the main breadwinner. With more wives working these days (and, in some cases, bringing home the larger monthly pay cheque) this power is one which threatens the stability of a marriage.

The wife's domicile (the place considered by law to be her permanent home) during the marriage is the domicile of her husband. Once the marriage ends, either by death or by divorce, the wife retains the domicile of her husband until she chooses a new domicile. While it is common practice for the wife to adopt the family name or surname of her husband, in law she is not compelled to use her husband's surname. She may use either her maiden name or any other name she had before the marriage. The children, however, will take the surname of the father.

4. 'equal rights ... at its dissolution'

Whether the partners have equal rights at the end of a marriage (which ends through death of one partner or by divorce) depends upon how they were married. There are variations according to whether the partners were married in community of property or in terms of an antenuptial contract. Whether or not the partner to an African customary marriage has equal rights at the end of a marriage depends upon the circumstances of each case.

5. 'free and full consent of the intending spouses'

The voluntary consent of both the bride and bridegroom is necessary for all marriages in South Africa. The law presumes that there is free and full consent where there is evidence of a ceremony of marriage which is followed by a period of living together. The difficult question is whether free and full consent is present in arranged marriages, or in alliances of families through marriage for financial, social, or any other advantage

The instances of such marriages in South Africa are probably fewer these days than in the past because of the influence of Western ideas of marriage. African customary marriages are also on the decline. It is to be hoped that gradually an increasing proportion of South African marriages will fall in line with the requirement of consent in Article 16.

6. Protection of the family unit

The changes in the laws dealing with interracial marriages have raised new problems concerning the protection of the family unit.

In order to deal with the problem of where a 'mixed' couple is to live, the Group Areas Act has come up with some very unsatisfactory solutions. Where a white man marries a woman of a different racial classification, he receives her racial classification for the purposes of the Group Areas Act. Therefore he is entitled to live in the area classified for her race group. But if a woman marries a man who is not white, she usually takes on the race classification of her husband. They would, therefore, only be entitled to live in the area classified for his race group. Recent indications are that some white people are reluctant to allow persons of other race groups to live in their areas. The application of the law in this regard is extremely unpredictable. The government has attempted to solve this problem in a piecemeal way by declaring certain areas free settlement areas or 'grey' areas.

The Population Registration Act requires all South Africans to be classified in one of the race groups. It is possible for a white male to marry an African female and for their child to be classified 'coloured'. While the father will be permitted to live in an African area, the child should be living in a 'coloured' area. This absurdity is worsened when the child has to go to school, because education is racially segregated. The child would have to apply for a permit to attend a white public school, or may have to travel a great distance to a 'coloured' school, or may be permitted to attend an African school.

While the family is regarded in Article 16 as the 'fundamental group unit of society' and 'is entitled to protection by society and the state', it would be incorrect to say that, in the South African context, this has applied to all family units. The white family has been regarded as a more important unit than those of other race groups when one considers the state expenditure on segregated education, training, and health care.

The law of the future

Recent legal changes have done much to promote equality between marriage partners, both during and at the end of the marriage relationship. In this way the marriage laws meet the objectives of Article 16, namely to do away with unfair treatment of women in marriage. The choice of different types of marriage contracts caters for the needs of different women. But, because of the generally inferior status of the wife in African customary marriages, the phasing-out of these marriages is recommended.

With regard to free and full consent, the law-makers and courts should examine the instances where the practice of arranged marriages may still be present. To the extent that these are still practised, they are a violation of Article 16.

Since many of the laws in South Africa are race-based, the removal of the bar against whites marrying persons from other race groups does not go far enough in promoting the family as the natural and fundamental group unit. Greater protection is required from the state than is the case at present. The call for the total removal of apartheid laws made in other chapters of this book is an urgent one. Only when all these laws are something of the past, and the wider society begins to move away from racial and other forms of prejudice, can the full potential of the principles of Article 16 begin to be realized.

18
The right to own property

Article 17 (1) Everyone has the right to own property alone as well as in association with others.

(2) No one shall be arbitrarily deprived of his property.

What this article means

Although it does not have the force of law, the Universal Declaration is an important statement of international human rights standards. There are other documents which make up the code of international human rights law. In a discussion about the right to property it should be noted that, unlike the Declaration, some of the other documents make no mention of such a right. This is significant, particularly because the two international Covenants of the United Nations — on Civil and Political Rights, and on Economic, Social, and Cultural Rights — are amongst the documents which are completely silent on the right to property.

Why is this so? The most probable explanation is that the whole question of private property, and especially productive property like land, is fraught with controversy. In capitalist, liberal ideology, private property is seen as central to the development of a decent society in which the full worth of the individual is properly recognized. The philosopher John Locke, for example, thought that property, life, and liberty, were the most sacred of all the rights of human beings. By contrast, left-wing ideologies reject the notion of private property, together with the capitalist economic system. In this view all productive property should be vested in the state and used for the benefit of society in general as opposed to the benefit of a few. It is therefore not surprising that Covenants of the United Nations, an organization which represents the community of world states, should fail to agree to recognize the right to property.

Regional human rights documents, however, do tend to recognize the property right. The American Declaration of the Rights and Duties of Man of 1948 proclaims that 'Every person has a right to own such private property as meets the essential needs of decent living and helps to maintain the dignity of the individual and his home'. The American Convention on Human Rights of 1969 says that 'Everyone has the right to the use and enjoyment of his property'. Similarly, the European Convention for the Protection of Human Rights and Fundamental Freedoms states that 'Every natural or legal person is entitled to the peaceful enjoyment of his possessions'. Another important property clause emerges in the African Charter on Human and Peoples' Rights, adopted in 1981. It states that 'The right to property shall be guaranteed'.

Another notable feature of the Declaration is the use of the word 'own' in the phrase 'rights to own property'. Few other documents mention it, choosing instead such words as 'use' and 'enjoyment'. It follows that ownership rights to property, as opposed to other rights which may still be protected under law, are also controversial. Where ownership rights are more strongly protected than rights of use and enjoyment, it might be felt that such protection is not in the best interests of the wider community. For example, there is, universally, a growing awareness of the crucial importance of protecting the environment both for present and future generations. There is a very strong argument that it is quite unacceptable that owners should be allowed to abuse their property in a way which could cause serious environmental degradation.

In some ways the second part of Article 17 of the Declaration, dealing with the *deprivation* of property, has given rise to the most debate. As one writer puts it, 'many speeches have been made and much ink spilt, over questions of compensation for property which is seized by the state'.

There are two closely related issues to consider. The first is under what circumstances, if at all, a government should, under international law, be permitted to expropriate immovable property (such as land). Article 17 states merely that people should not be *arbitrarily* deprived of their property. This, unfortunately, is not particularly helpful because it does not describe the circumstances under which property can be taken in a non-arbitrary way. Certainly, this part of the article *does* mean that expropriation should only be carried out under the machinery of law; for example, in terms of legislation which strictly regulates all aspects of the expropriation process. This itself is an important principle because human rights standards are generally opposed to governments acting in a way which elevates them above the legal system.

Under what circumstances is it legitimate that land be taken away from persons who hold some form of legal title? Other international instruments provide an answer to this, although perhaps not as comprehensively as one might wish. The European Convention for the Protection of Human Rights and Fundamental Freedoms, for example, declares that 'No one shall be deprived of his possessions except in the public interest and subject to the conditions provided for by law and by the general principles of international law'. The African Charter, after declaring that the right to property shall be guaranteed, says that property 'may only be encroached upon in the interest of public need or in the general interest of the community and in accordance with the provisions of appropriate laws'.

The key phrase in these documents is 'public interest'. It is easy enough to see that this includes the right of the state to build dams, roads, and other forms of development which benefit society generally. In these cases the right of the individual must yield to the greater needs of society. But does it mean that a government can expropriate land in order to redistribute the resources of a country among all its people? The answer, it seems, is that under international law there is nothing to prevent a government from expropriating property for this reason.

This is an important issue for the future South Africa. Through apartheid the great majority of the population has been confined to a small proportion of the land.

The second vital issue is the one about compensation. Should people whose land is expropriated in the public interest be paid out the value of the property? Again, Article 17 is not helpful. The American Convention on Human Rights, on the other hand, states quite explicitly that 'just compensation' must be paid when persons are deprived of their property. This issue could be hotly contested in the future South Africa. Under international law the matter is by no means settled. Under the European Convention, for example, the accepted view is that where a state deprives its citizens of their property in the public interest, and in accordance with the appropriate laws, it does not have to pay compensation. The position may be different where foreign property owners are concerned.

The article in South African law

One of the most notorious features of apartheid has been the division of the people of South Africa into racial and ethnic categories. This has largely been achieved through the process of race classification. Alongside this has been an attempt to define the areas in which the various groups may or may not live. This has been the main element of the policy of physical segregation. Now, South Africa consists of a vast patchwork of racial zones, the greatest area of which is reserved for members of the white group.

This aspect of apartheid is a gross violation of Article 17. No persons, not even whites, have the right to own or occupy property where they please. That the Declaration requires this freedom of choice is clear from Article 7, which prohibits discrimination and unequal treatment of any kind. Group areas, black townships, black reserves, and Bantustans all add up to the most blatant form of discrimination.

Exactly how long ago this all started is difficult to say. Some historians claim that the Dutch settlers practised racial segregation from the earliest times of colonization. These practices became more determined, and more evident, in the Boer Republics of the Transvaal and Orange Free State before the turn of the century. Others claim that the government of Natal laid the foundations for modern apartheid when people like Theophilus Shepstone devised a grand scheme to place the Africans of Natal and Zululand into separate reserves in the nineteenth century. Still others argue that the policy of segregation — and with it economic exploitation — was formulated by men such as Cecil Rhodes whose Glen Grey Act of 1894 in the Cape served as a model for future South African governments.

Whatever the origins, there was already by the 1940s an elaborate legal structure which in theory, if not in practice, sought to confine the majority of the African population to rural reserves amounting to no more than 13 per cent of the land. There were exceptions such as 'black spots', a term used to describe sometimes large communities of African people who resided on or owned land outside the areas allocated to them. Also, white-owned farms, mines, and industry needed labour; for these people, rudimentary accommodation was provided where they were needed.

It remained for the National Party to perfect the system after it came to power in 1948. This it tried to do over a period of nearly 40 years, passing numerous property-related laws. Perhaps among the most infamous were the Group Areas Acts (culminating in the 1966 version) and the Prevention of Illegal Squatting Act of 1951. There were many others, some of which were refinements of earlier laws like the Black Land Act of 1913 and the Development Trust and Land Act of 1936. The intention behind these and other laws was essentially two-fold: to provide adequate legal machinery to move people out of the areas where they were said not to belong; and to make racial land segregation into a long-term solution. There were other aspects to the scheme, not least of which was the constitutional one: all 'black' areas were destined, at some stage, to become 'independent states'.

There have been other violations of Article 17. One of these is that the system of land *ownership* has consistently been denied to African people, while it has been freely available to whites, 'coloureds', and Indians. Even in the areas which were allocated for African occupation, full ownership rights were not permitted. In the few instances where there were African owners it was through land purchase around the beginning of the century. Only recently have urban township regulations been relaxed sufficiently to allow residents to gain stronger rights to their property and houses, including those of ownership.

A more significant violation of Article 17 is the highly arbitrary way in which people have been removed, sometimes forcibly, from one race zone into another. Research has shown that well in excess of three million people have been moved in the last few decades. This was always carried out in the interests of putting people into their 'own' areas and included the expropriation of 'black spot' communities without any or adequate compensation. Not only were these procedures carried out under laws which very often could not be challenged (and therefore were not really laws at all), but it was nearly always black people who were the victims of the system.

Recent government statements have indicated that, in 1990, all these racist property laws will be repealed. Were this to happen, it would undoubtedly bring South African law closer to the Declaration, at least as far as Article 17 is concerned. The difficult question, however, is what will happen next?

The law of the future

The most extreme view on the whole land question, often linked to the Pan Africanist Congress, is that all white title is illegitimate and that all land should be restored to its 'rightful owners'. While this view may be rejected by many South Africans (especially whites), there is nevertheless no point in denying the extent of black land demand. This realization has led, in some instances, to far-reaching proposals, including the complete nationalization of all land, so that all persons would be regarded as tenants of the state.

The latter 'solution' has most often been put forward in the context of forging a socialist economy, including state farms and other forms of collective enterprise. Other people in the debate, however, see state ownership of all land as a necessary prerequisite for fair land redistribution to individuals or family groups. Both these approaches stand in stark contrast to the government's own recently-stated position, which is to remove all racial impediments to permit the normalization process to take place under conditions of a free-market economy. There are other positions in the range of options. The African National Congress (ANC), for example, appears to favour an unspecified mix of private property and state intervention in agricultural land.

Debates about what is best for South Africa's rural land economy necessarily elicit differences of opinion on issues such as appropriate levels of food production, the efficiency or inefficiency of white capitalist agriculture, the viability of black peasant agricultural production, and the success or failure of state farms and collectives in other parts of the world.

It is too soon to tell what the future holds. Much depends upon factors such as whether or not the process of change is achieved peaceably, whether influence is exerted from political groups to the left of the ANC, and the impact of the white right wing.

It is realistic to expect that there will, ultimately, be some degree of land redistribution. However, it is perplexing that some of the more radical perspectives on land reform fail to attach any importance to the role of law in the process. For example, advocates of outright nationalization apparently see no need to have the claims and interests of present land-holders evaluated before an independent tribunal, nor is any importance attached to the notion that citizens of the new South Africa should enjoy defensible rights to property. There is a naïve belief that the new democratic order will somehow be able to dispense with the need for fundamental protections. This, of course, would be a grave mistake.

Decades of forced removals and confining people to racial, geographical compartments have demonstrated that there is something fundamentally wrong when organs of government, largely unchecked by the courts, are permitted in this way to determine the fate of individuals and communities. It is therefore not difficult to understand why there is disdain for legal rights and legal process in some quarters. In the wake of an era characterized by what has been dubbed 'lawless law' it will be extremely difficult to convince ordinary people that law is not necessarily a repressive mechanism; that protective law is an essential component of modern society. No society of the future can afford to ignore the lessons of the past.

In recent months a growing interest in court-protected human rights has begun to emerge, especially amongst the white community. There is some irony in this. Through years of apartheid there have been relatively few calls by whites for an entrenched Bill of Rights. Now, with extensive political changes a likely prospect, the notion of a court-protected measure has become singularly attractive.

While a growing rights consciousness is to be welcomed and encouraged, there is danger in bringing present land distribution patterns within the protection of a land clause in a Bill of Rights. The reason for this is obvious: any attempt to give unqualified endorsement to apartheid land patterns in the new order is unlikely to succeed. Furthermore, this could also run the risk of weakening the Bill of Rights itself.

To state the position bluntly, there cannot be unqualified constitutional protection of land which has been made available on a selective racial basis. What is needed, rather, is a property clause which allows the state to expropriate land in the interests of ameliorating the harshness of the old order.

Perhaps the most difficult challenge of all is to create a mechanism by which the difficult decisions can be made about what land should be expropriated, how much compensation should be paid, and who should be placed in possession. The process would also need to take full account of much-neglected environmental issues. One possibility is a special land commission or court, staffed by independent judges together with specialists in agriculture, land use planning, and the environment. Representatives of major political parties would also be needed. The task of the commission would be to make recommendations about the expropriation and re-division of land in the light of principles enacted by parliament.

Whatever procedure is thought to be most appropriate, it is essential that these sensitive, if not potentially volatile issues, are engaged in a way which upholds the best elements of proper legal process. This must necessarily involve the enactment of a law which incorporates some, if not all, of the components of Article 17.

19
Freedom of thought, conscience, and religion

Article 18 *Everyone has the right to freedom of thought, conscience and religion; this right includes freedom to change his religion or belief, and freedom, either alone or in community with others and in public or private, to manifest his religion or belief in teaching, practice, worship and observance.*

What this article means

Article 18 lists three freedoms: freedom of thought, conscience, and religion. While the first part of the article declares the existence of these freedoms, the second sets out some of the implications of one of these freedoms — freedom of religion. This second part indicates clearly that the right to religious freedom is not simply a private or individual matter, but that people should be free both in private and in community to show their religious beliefs in four different ways: by teaching, practice, worship, and observance.

'Teaching' includes the right to give religious instruction, especially to the young, and the right to run educational institutions including schools, colleges, and even universities. 'Practice' includes the freedom to carry out the beliefs and instructions of a particular religion. 'Worship' includes the right to gather and pray and to hold religious services in public and in private. 'Observance' includes the right to carry out requirements of one's religion about special days or seasons on which certain religious duties are to be performed.

Attention should be drawn to the clause about 'freedom to change' a 'religion or belief' because this gave rise to much discussion and controversy when the Declaration was being drawn up. Some delegates even abstained from voting because they were so opposed to this clause. It was, however, included because the right to change one's religion was thought to be an essential aspect of freedom of religion.

The right to religious freedom, freedom of conscience, and

freedom of thought are commonly regarded as the most sacred of all freedoms. The movement to achieve these freedoms preceded every other. It goes back to at least the sixteenth century, if not to the Roman Empire. The right to these freedoms was also one of the first human rights to achieve international recognition and yet it remains one of the weakest from the point of view of general recognition and enforcement. Human beings continue to persecute each other for opinions or beliefs which are regarded as different. Most major world religions have either suffered persecution at some stage or have themselves persecuted others. History shows that we are not satisfied with trying to persuade others to our point of view by reason, preaching, dialogue, exhortation, or example; but frequently make use of force, and sometimes even torture, murder, or massacre in an attempt to achieve this purpose.

Pope John Paul II sees religious freedom as occupying a 'key position' or 'central' place amongst human rights because it directly concerns what is essential in the human person, what 'most fully manifests the person as human, namely the search for the Absolute.' Religious freedom is 'the basic condition and foundation for all other human rights' and the 'fundamental test for the authentic progress' of any society. Respect for religious freedom implies acknowledgment that human beings are more than individuals in a market, cogs in a social wheel, or products of various social forces. Their dignity commands respect because it comes from a deeper than human source.

The definition of religious freedom has become a subject of considerable debate over the last few decades. In some countries, including South Africa, where basic human rights are grossly violated, churches and religious communities have become actively involved in the struggle for justice and human rights on the basis of a sincere understanding of their religious beliefs. If such churches are persecuted for actions undertaken on behalf of security detainees, for example, is this to be regarded as a breach of religious freedom or simply of human rights in general? The authorities in such oppressive countries, who are often sensitive to the charge of denying religious freedom, are understandably extremely reluctant to accept such a broad definition of religious freedom. For example, while many tyrannical regimes would claim that they guarantee absolute freedom of religion in terms of worship, there is generally little freedom in such societies to express the political or social consequences of religion, let alone to take action to put those consequences into practice. Such regimes prefer to regard religion as a private matter relating only to personal morality. They therefore try to limit religious freedom to the narrowest possible definition.

But it has to be admitted that this is a difficult area. If religious freedom is defined too broadly it could open the way to all sorts of unacceptable activities carried out in the name of religion, for example enforced polygamy (having more than one spouse), devil worship, ritual murders, and the ruthless provisions of Shari'at law.

What makes the relationship between religious and political freedom particularly awkward is that both religion and politics embrace in differing ways the whole of human life. Both religious movements and political movements/governments have their own view of what human beings, individually and collectively, should be. While religions stem from and work in areas of inspiration and conviction, political movements are concerned with maintaining the social and legal framework for the human community.

Religion both limits and recognizes political control. Likewise, governments overstep themselves if they try to limit religion by taking on a religious character themselves. While it is not possible to embody such an understanding of the relationship between religion and politics in a legal document such as the Declaration or a constitution, it is essential that those who are concerned about human rights grasp the special nature of religious freedom, which is not simply one other item alongside the right to work, to freedom of association, freedom of movement, etc., but in a sense embraces all rights.

The article in South African law

Visitors to South Africa who regularly watch South African TV or listen to its radio programmes might conclude that religious freedom is alive and well in this country, at least for Christians. In terms of the number of religious broadcasts, they might see no reason to complain about the lack of religious freedom. The numerous religious buildings and institutions of all faiths which appear to function freely, even in the townships, would seem to indicate that this is also the case for people of other faiths.

The 1983 Constitution begins with this grand assertion: 'In humble submission to Almighty God, Who controls the destinies of nations and the history of people; Who gathered our forebears together from many lands and gave them this as their own; Who has guided them from generation to generation.' Section 2 of the constitution stipulates that 'the people of the republic of South

Africa acknowledge the sovereignty and guidance of Almighty God'.

However, it should be noted that the 'humble submission to Almighty God' referred to could only be meaningful if there were some way of testing particular laws and their application against the will of God. It is therefore potentially misleading to begin a constitution with such an assertion because it is impossible to live up to. Since no human institution can claim to represent God fully and entirely, there must be safeguards against infringing fundamental freedoms (such as a Bill of Rights) and there must be a process for changing the law.

It has been claimed that South African law is not intolerant of other religions. For example, the Marriage Act of 1961 allows marriages to be conducted according to Christian, Jewish, and Islamic rites and the rites of any Indian religion. Courts allow people to take the oath in a form which most clearly conveys to them the meaning of the oath, or to make an affirmation instead. The Defence Act of 1957 allows certain people who object on religious grounds to participating in war to be allotted 'as far as is practicable' service in a non-combatant capacity.

However, the preference for Christianity in South African law is clear. For example, the Publications Act of 1974 lays down that the criteria for working out basic standards for the censoring of publications, films, and public entertainment must be determined with due regard to the so-called 'constant endeavour of the population of the Republic of South Africa to uphold a Christian view of life'. This section seems hardly to recognize even the existence of other faiths in South Africa. Similarly, the first 'national goal' listed in the preamble to the 1983 Constitution is that the Republic of South Africa intends 'to uphold Christian values and civilized norms, with recognition and protection of freedom of faith and worship.'

Although the South African government proclaims itself to be Christian, there are many ways in which it has interfered with the work of Christian churches. The government has, for example, made it extremely difficult for missionaries from other countries to enter and work in South Africa. A number of those who have been allowed in have been deported or their work permits not renewed if they have publicly criticized apartheid. The government has also made it difficult for outspoken South African religious leaders to travel overseas by refusing them travel documents.

More blatant interference in the churches' work has been seen during the time of the four states of emergency starting in 1985.

Worshippers have been tear-gassed, services have been banned, and whole congregations were arrested when they gathered to pray on the tenth anniversary of the Soweto uprising. National church leaders were doused by water cannon and a number of them arrested when they attempted to march the short distance from St. George's Anglican Cathedral in Cape Town to Parliament in March 1988. During the 1989 Defiance Campaign a Lutheran religious procession, which was part of an outdoor religious service approved of by a magistrate, was broken up by riot police at the Jabulani Stadium in Soweto. The entrance to the Buitenkant Methodist Church in Cape Town was on one occasion blocked by a Casspir. Police entered St. George's Anglican Cathedral carrying guns and quirts and refused the Dean of that Cathedral access to his own church. St. Alban's Anglican Cathedral in Pretoria was surrounded by barbed wire to prevent people assembling there for a service which was to be followed by a women's march to the Union Buildings. All of this was done in terms of the sweeping powers given to the police by the Emergency Regulations.

Every major world religion sees the treatment of fellow human beings as a central concern of its religious beliefs. Inevitably this has social and political consequences, and the churches in South Africa have been spelling out those consequences with increasing clarity, as well as acting on them and encouraging others to do so. This has inevitably put the churches in direct conflict with the state, which strongly promotes a narrow view of the churches' role.

In March 1988 the activities of major political organizations working for change by peaceful means were restricted. A special meeting of church leaders declared that the restrictions were 'a blow against the heart of the churches' mission'. In this way they stressed that a denial of basic human rights was not only an attack on South African society but on the churches themselves and on religious freedom. The church leaders noted that many of the activities of the restricted organizations, for example assistance to the families of political prisoners, were also duties of the church and they undertook to ensure that such activities would continue in defiance of government-imposed restrictions.

This was the most significant and powerful protest against the restriction of religious freedom since the days of the famous 'Church Clause' of 1958 in terms of which the state had tried to prevent people of different races from worshipping together. The churches' outspoken protest against that clause had prevented it from becoming law. The issue which drew similar outrage from the churches 30 years later was not an attack on the internal life of the church, but on its *social* role and mission — a clear indication of how much more broadly religious freedom is interpreted today by church leaders and theologians.

One of the most glaring examples of the conflict between apartheid and religious freedom is the legislation which has prevented migrant workers from bringing their wives or husbands and families to live with them in urban areas. All churches regard marriage as sacred and some of them view it as 'a sacrament'. The continuation of the migrant labour system over so many years is clear evidence that the South African government has been willing to put short-term political and economic advantage before religious principle.

The very notion that people should be classified by race, and that this should determine where they can live, go to school, be employed, what sort of job they may hold, and how much they may be paid for that work, and whether or not they shall have any say in decision-making — all of which are dictated by law in South Africa — is in fact a fundamental attack on religious freedom.

If one examines these legislative aspects of the South African system from a Christian perspective one quickly discovers how fundamental is the conflict between apartheid and religious freedom. The essence of the Christian religion is that Jesus' death and resurrection and the gift of the Holy Spirit has broken down all dividing walls between people, and that God is calling together into visible community a new people irrespective of race, class, gender, and any form of social distinction. Christians therefore see legislation which prevents the creation of such a community as not only in conflict with human rights in general but as a direct assault on religious freedom. Thus while the repeal of legislation preventing 'mixed marriages' is regarded as a welcome step towards enhancing religious freedom, all apartheid legislation will have to be revoked before the pre-conditions for such freedom may be said to exist in South Africa.

The law of the future

Freedom of religion should be specifically recognized in the new constitution and legislation governing the South Africa of the future. There should be no effort to secure rights or freedoms for Christians which would not be available to all persons, no matter what faith they profess or even if they profess no faith. In the new South Africa, there will be a need for a much greater religious pluralism. This is not just a matter of new legislation but will require a process of education. Once apartheid goes there could be a great danger of religious conflicts breaking out, unless such a process of education is undertaken.

What concrete pointers are there to the future of religious freedom in post-apartheid South Africa? It is not easy to give a definite answer to this question, but some indications can be obtained from a study of South African documents dealing with human rights.

The draft Bill of Rights drawn up by the South African Law Commission in 1989 lays down in Article 2 that 'there shall be no discrimination on the grounds of religion'.

This Bill of Rights also provides (in Article 17) for the right of persons or groups to disassociate from other persons or groups, provided that if this constitutes discrimination on the ground of race, colour, religion, language, or culture no state money shall be provided 'to promote the interests of the person or group which so discriminates.'

Article 21 lays down the right of every person, individually or together with others, freely to practise their culture and religion and to use their language. Article 22 declares the right of every person to be safeguarded from discrimination against their culture, religion, or language and to be safeguarded from preferential treatment of the culture, religion, or language of others. This clause has a proviso that if in court proceedings it is alleged that legislation or an executive or administrative act infringes the cultural, religious, or linguistic values of any individual or group, the court will have to take into account the interests of other individuals or groups.

The Freedom Charter, adopted in 1955, refers to religious freedom in two clauses. The first is that 'All laws which discriminate on the grounds of race, colour or *belief* shall be repealed' (emphasis added). The second is that 'The Law shall guarantee to all their right to speak, to organise, to meet together, to publish, to *preach*, to *worship* and to educate their children' (emphasis added).

There are also two references in the Constitutional Guidelines of the African National Congress (ANC) of 1988. Firstly, 'The Constitution shall include a Bill of Rights based on the Freedom Charter. Such a Bill of Rights shall guarantee the fundamental human rights of all citizens, irrespective of race, colour, sex or *creed* and shall provide appropriate mechanisms for their protection and enforcement' (emphasis added).

Secondly, subject to clauses which outlaw racial discrimination, fascism, Nazism, or the incitement of ethnic or regional exclusiveness, 'the democratic state shall guarantee the basic rights and freedoms, such as freedom of association, *thought*, *worship* and the press' (emphasis added).

The ANC has therefore indicated that it will allow freedom of all religions that do not promote racism, Nazism, fascism, etc. While the idea behind this proviso is positive, it would be best not to put up tests for religions as such. Rather, if any religious organization pursued these objectives — or any similar injustices — then it should be penalized on that basis, and not because it is an unacceptable sort of religion.

It is not clear whether the references to religious freedom in the Freedom Charter and Constitutional Guidelines are in keeping with the modern understanding of religious freedom. In other words, does it encompass not only the freedom to worship and conduct the normal activities of religious faiths, but also to engage in independent comment and action on social and political issues? Such an understanding would help to avoid the difficult situations which have arisen, for example, in post-independence Zimbabwe where the Mugabe government has indignantly responded to criticisms from the Roman Catholic Justice and Peace Commission, though they were very happy when this Commission consistently criticized Ian Smith's regime.

20
Freedom of opinion and expression

Article 19 Everyone has the right to freedom of opinion and expression; this right includes freedom to hold opinions without interference and to seek, receive and impart information and ideas through any media and regardless of frontiers.

What this article means

The rights contained in this article are broadly stated. They include the right to convey opinions and information through speech, theatre, cinema, song, procession, even on a T-shirt. But the main significance of the article lies in its recognition of freedom of the media (the press, radio, and television).

1. Why is freedom of the media so important?

First, because it is in many ways a foundation for all other freedoms. Without freedom of expression, it would be difficult, if not impossible, to protect and ensure compliance with other rights. If the public did not know of violations, no pressure could be brought to bear to bring them to an end.

In a modern democracy, rule by the people and for the people can only be maintained if the people are informed. In the complexity of the modern world, only the media have the resources to gather and disseminate the needed information.

The media can act as watchdog over society. They can expose abuse of power, corruption, fraud. Examples of this role are well known to everyone: Watergate, Irangate, Muldergate.

In education and development the media can also play an important role. This is especially important in a society with Third World elements, where the formal education system is inadequate, literacy is low, and development is urgently needed.

An important role is also played by the media in a deeply divided society. They can publicize the plight of disadvantaged people and emphasize the common humanity which lies below ethnic and cultural differences.

The media can also provide protection for consumers. They can draw public attention to poor products and poor service. They can expose and warn against dangerous drugs, such as Thalidomide, and help to bring their manufacturers to court.

The media can publicize disasters, such as droughts and floods, and highlight the plight of the victims; in this way the media can assist in arranging aid for the needy.

In a society undergoing political transition, the media can encourage public debate. They can analyse ideologies, offer new visions, and expose shortcomings and inconsistencies in the policies of government and opposition. Through this process, they can help the individual members of society to realize their potential as independent, responsible people. The media can help them to think through important issues, and to come to informed and intelligent decisions.

This means that the media are vital to society's well-being. The important tasks of the media cannot, however, be performed if the media are restricted and controlled. Freedom of the media is therefore of critical importance.

2. What is meant by freedom of the media?

Definitions of freedom of the media vary. In essence, however, it means freedom from legal control, especially by the state. It means the liberty to publish without licence or constraint.

The right to freedom of the media may be made absolute, as in the United States Constitution, which provides that 'Congress shall make no law abridging ... freedom of speech, or of the press'. This has been interpreted by some judges as meaning literally 'no law'. However, most interpretations of this provision place some limits on media freedom to enable protection of other rights (such as the right to reputation, to good order, and morality). Most documents which guarantee media freedom recognize these limits.

Article 19, like most international guarantees, is subject to derogation in certain circumstances. (The meaning of derogation is explained at the end of Chapter 32.)

The article in South African law

In South Africa media freedom is not guaranteed. In fact, the media are subject to many restrictions. Some are contained in the common law (for example, the rules against contempt of court). But by far the most significant restrictions are to be found in the many statutes (well over a 100) imposed by the state to prop up its legitimacy and to restrict the flow of information.

The restrictions imposed by the state are wide-ranging. This chapter will briefly examine the provisions of the Internal Security Act and some other important restrictions. In the recent past severe controls on the media were imposed under the state of emergency. Most of these have been lifted.

Restrictions under the Internal Security Act of 1982

This act consolidates and replaces most earlier security legislation, including the Suppression of Communism Act of 1950, the Riotous Assemblies Act of 1956, and the Terrorism Act of 1967. Its restriction of press freedom is extensive and can be analysed under five categories.

1. *Communism and unlawful organizations:* In terms of the act it is an offence (punishable by up to 10 years' imprisonment) to encourage the achievement of any of the objects of communism or to do anything likely to have this effect. The definition of communism provided by the act is extremely broad.

   Similar provisions apply to encouraging the achievement of any of the objects of an unlawful organization. Until 1990 the South African Communist Party, the African National Congress, and the Pan African Congress were among the 20 or so organizations which were declared unlawful under the act.

   Extreme caution must therefore be exercised by the media in publishing any material regarding such organizations, for fear that they may be seen as promoting their objectives. The difficulty experienced by newspapers has been expressed in this way by Richard Steyn, a newspaper editor:

   > The problem with much of this legislation ... is that editors often have to weigh up, not what a court might interpret the law to be, but what some police officer might understand it to be. Does a statement about the African National Congress advance its aims or not? Is reporting the fact of an impending strike inciting people to support it? Does a report about the End Conscription Campaign imply support for the undermining of military service? More and more newspapers are having to adopt the easy way out: when in doubt, leave out.

2. *Publishing the words of 'prohibited' persons:* The act makes it an offence to publish, without prior permission from the Minister of Law and Order, the words of a prohibited person. Prohibited persons fall within three categories. First, there are those who, according to the Minister, have engaged in activities likely to threaten state security or law and order, or to promote 'communism'. Such persons are banned in terms of the act. Secondly, there are those who, on the same grounds, have been restricted by the Minister from attending any gathering. Thirdly, there are those whose names appear on the 'consolidated list'. These are people who are seen to be active supporters of unlawful organizations, or who have been detained under the act. A World Report in 1988, compiled by the Article 19 Organization in London stated:

> Bannings and listings have silenced many hundreds with the effect that an entire spectrum of political opinion has been eliminated from public debate. It has been calculated that approximately 1,500 people have been affected by these orders since the 1950s.

3. *Terrorism and subversion:* The offences of terrorism and subversion are very broadly defined under the act. What is significant, from the viewpoint of the press, is that any person who, for example, incites or encourages this kind of offence is also guilty under the act and subject to the same penalties. (These penalties are severe: the death penalty for terrorism and up to 25 years' imprisonment for subversion.) This means that letters to the editor, advertisements, interviews, or political columns may be seen to be inciting or encouraging terrorism or subversion.

4. *Other offences under the act:* It is also an offence to incite, aid, or encourage any offence by protesting against any law. The provision is very broad so that, again, the media must be careful not to commit the offence unwittingly. A sympathetic comment on a fiery speech against a law (such as the Group Areas Act, which has caused untold hardship) may amount to an offence.

It is also an offence to utter words with intent to cause or encourage feelings of hostility between different population groups. Again, this provision can cause difficulties for the media. Given the differences in wealth, power, and privilege between black and white, any article describing or commenting on these could be seen as encouraging feelings of hostility between the two groups.

5. *Closure of a newspaper under the act:* The Minister of Law and Order has wide powers to investigate and subsequently ban a newspaper for a specified period or altogether. To do so, he must simply be satisfied that the newspaper falls within certain very broad provisions laid down in the act. For example, it is enough if he is satisfied that it 'endangers the security of the state', or 'promotes the spread of communism' or 'expresses views ... calculated to ... encourage feelings of hostility between different population groups'.

Other restrictions

1. *Initial registration:* Registration of a newspaper under the terms of the Newspaper and Imprint Registration Act of 1971 is relatively simple and straightforward. However, registration is not possible unless the newspaper has first paid a deposit, which may be as high as R40 000. Such a deposit is required whenever the Minister of Home Affairs 'is not satisfied' that the newspaper will never be closed (as described above). Should the paper in fact be banned, the entire amount of the deposit, with interest, is generally forfeited to the state.

2. *Regulation through the South African Media Council:* The South African Media Council imposes a form of 'self-control' on registered newspapers. Newspapers which belong to the Newspaper Press Union are exempt from the restrictions of the Publications Act of 1974, but are instead subject to the controls exercised by the Council. The Council has developed a Code of Conduct which its members are expected to obey. The Council operates under frequent threat from the government to tighten its controls.

3. *The Publications Act of 1974:* The Publications Act applies to all unregistered newspapers, as well as to those which have been registered for less than three months. Under the act, complex machinery has been established to prohibit and restrict 'undesirable' publications. What is undesirable is broadly defined and includes matter which is prejudicial to the safety of the state, 'the general welfare', or peace and good order.

4. *Defence, prisons, police, and official secrets:* There are many statutory laws which prevent the public from knowing much about the operations of the Defence Force, the Prisons Service, and the Police Force. Other laws safeguard not only 'official secrets' (as

broadly defined) but also information deemed relevant to state security. As Richard Steyn explains:

> ... Nuclear Energy, Oil, Key Points and Trade are all subjects on which press coverage is strictly controlled. Even the publication of reports about corruption in the Civil Service is now subject to statutory control ... As a [leading South African] editor has dryly remarked: In the old days it used to be publishing untruths which landed one in trouble. Nowadays it is illegal to publish the truth.

5. *Detention and restriction of journalists:* A number of journalists (exact figures are hard to get) have been detained for varying periods. Many have also been subjected to restrictions which make it impossible for them to practise their profession.

The law of the future

If the principles of Article 19 were to be incorporated into South African law, the benefits for individuals and wider society would be profound.

❐ The flow of information would be freed.

❐ Society would hear the words of those who have been silenced. It could better understand and evaluate organizations which in the past have been banned. There could be meaningful debate about ideologies and policies, about the vision of a new South Africa and the best means to attain it.

❐ It would release the information presently withheld, such as that regarding energy, corruption, prisons, and police. It would enable informed assessment of what serves society's best interests.

❐ It would enable the media to uphold free speech and therefore help to counter the disturbing trend to deny the right to expression to those regarded as being 'on the other side'.

The proper role of the media in a democratic society could be demonstrated in a concrete way. This would provide a valuable lesson for both transition and the post-apartheid era. It could help prevent a transfer from one system of coercion to another.

These benefits are vital to South Africa and all its citizens. However, if they are to be attained, the media must be freed. They must be freed not only from restrictive law but also from state ownership. Media such as television and radio — particularly significant in a society largely illiterate — must be made accountable to the community at large, and not used to the benefit of the people in power. Existing state ownership of the media must be ended, and further nationalization should be avoided.

Only when genuine freedom has been given to the media will they be able to fulfil their proper function as the watchdog on the government.

21
The rights to assembly and association

Article 20 *(1) Everyone has to the right to freedom of peaceful assembly and association.*

(2) No one may be compelled to belong to an association.

What this article means

Article 20 consists of the following basic human rights:

❏ Everyone has the right to meet together peacefully without interference from others.

❏ Everyone is entitled to belong to an association of his or her choice.

❏ No one should be forced to belong to an organization.

In general terms these rights are commonly known as the right to free association. Implied in the notion of free association is the principle that the purpose of the association must be legitimate or lawful. The law will not normally protect the right of criminals to associate for the purpose of planning illegal actions. If the right to free association is recognized, the law will intervene to protect the right from outside interference, particularly from state interference.

The right to free association has a positive and a negative interpretation. The positive right is understood to mean the right to have others, with whom you have a common interest, associate with you to achieve a legitimate goal. This right is sometimes not recognized in law because it may conflict with the right of dissociation of those who do not wish to be part of the association. The negative aspect of the right is to ensure the non-interference of others in the lawful activities of your association.

The right to free association, as defined in Article 20, expressly includes the right to dissociate. There are positive and negative aspects to this right. The negative aspect is the right to resist belonging to an association. For example, you may refuse to join a political party and cannot be forced to be a member. The positive right to dissociate is that you may exclude others from your association. The members of an association may decide who may join their association and who may not. This is the positive right of dissociation.

The article in South African law

1. The right to free assembly

Freedom to assemble without the need to get approval from some state authority is a fundamental human and trade union right.

In South Africa there is no requirement to obtain permission for an indoor social gathering, but at present the law requires that all outdoor gatherings be approved by the authorities. Hence all picketing and gatherings of strikers outside their places of work without permission from the authorities constitute unlawful gatherings. The state is empowered to limit or ban political gatherings under various laws.

Trade unions in the mining industry, particularly the National Union of Mineworkers, have in certain instances been effectively prevented from gaining access to members who live in mining compounds on mine property. This is because the only passage to such mines is along private roads which belong to the mine. In such instances the right of mine workers to peaceful assembly is restricted. The presence of the union officials on mine premises, without permission of the mine owner, would be trespassing.

2. Freedom to join associations

1. *Political freedom:* Following the announcements of the South African State President, F. W. de Klerk, on 2 February 1990, various political organizations which were banned in terms of the Internal Security Act of 1951 were declared to be lawful. Since then all political organizations have been allowed to exist and South Africans are free to join any political organization of their choosing.

   Trade unions in South Africa may engage in political activity, and they may administer and utilize their funds as they choose, save that they may not grant financial assistance nor affiliate to a political party or movement.

In terms of the Affected Organizations Act of 1974 the Minister of Justice may declare any organization ineligible to acquire funding, and in terms of the Fund Raising Act of 1978 any person or organization may similarly be declared to be deprived of the right to receive grants of funds.

2. *Trade union freedom:* Workers are entitled to form trade unions of their choosing, and to prepare and adopt their own constitutions. Workers have both the freedom and the right to form their own associations. Unions may be registered in terms of the Labour Relations Act of 1956, or they may choose to remain unregistered. The obligations upon unions which register are no different from those of unregistered unions.

Trade union members are entitled to elect their own representatives. Victimization of employees for trade union membership or activity is forbidden. However, employees who are excluded from the provisions of the Labour Relations Act — public sector employees, farm labourers, and domestic servants in private households — do not have this protection. For employees covered by the act the direct or indirect interference with their right to associate or not associate constitutes an unfair labour practice. This means that an employer may not discourage its employees from belonging to a trade union, and derogatory and misleading tactics by an employer to persuade employees not to associate with a trade union constitutes an unfair labour practice.

There is no law which protects employees from anti-union discrimination in the selection of employees for employment. All the rights and protections provided to workers and trade unions apply once workers have been employed, and not before.

There are no laws regulating the method to be followed by a worker who wishes to resign his or her membership of a trade union. It is not difficult for a worker to cease to be a trade union member, unless there is a statutory closed shop in force in the industry or undertaking concerned.

Trade union practices which infringe freedom of association are outlawed by the Labour Relations Act. The act requires that trade union constitutions provide for the following matters: the circumstances and the manner in which the membership of a worker may be terminated, an appeal procedure against termination, the calling and conduct of meetings and the keeping of minutes, the election of office-bearers, ballot (voting) procedures, the procedures for the removal of officials and office-bearers from office, and the powers and duties of office-bearers and officials.

There is no requirement that officials of trade unions must belong to the occupation in which the trade union functions, nor that they must have been members of the trade union. Trade unions are entitled to elect and re-elect their officials and office-bearers in full freedom. The government's former practice of preventing trade unionists from continuing their work within a trade union by 'banning' them has largely ceased.

Other than as stated above, trade unions are entitled to organize their administration and activities without interference by the public authorities. Trade unions are entitled to make use of experts, and to engage legal counsel, without state interference. Trade unions may join trade union federations, which have the right to be registered, or to remain unregistered. Trade unions may affiliate to international organizations, as may trade union federations.

Trade unionists may leave South Africa to attend international trade union meetings, or to meet with other trade unionists for conferring or for training.

The Industrial Registrar is entitled to cancel the registration of a trade union only if he/she has reason to believe that it is no longer functioning or it has been wound up. This is done by notice in the *Government Gazette*.

3. *Collective bargaining rights:* According to the Freedom of Association Committee of the International Labour Organization:

> The right to bargain freely with employers with respect to conditions of work constitutes an essential element in freedom of association, and trade unions should have the right, through collective bargaining or other lawful means, to seek to improve the living and working conditions of those whom the trade unions represent.

In South Africa the Industrial Court has held that the refusal to recognize a representative trade union and to negotiate with it constitutes an unfair labour practice.

Although the Labour Relations Act does not expressly permit trade union representatives and shop stewards to attend trade union training courses during their employer's time, the practice has become normal in most establishments where trade unions are recognized as the collective bargaining representatives of the employees. Most agreements provide that the shop stewards are permitted to take a certain agreed number of days per year, without loss of pay, to attend union-arranged education courses.

Where disputes have arisen as to which union should represent the employees within a given bargaining unit the Industrial Court has ordered that a secret ballot take place, under the supervision of a neutral person, to determine the most representative trade union.

Although registered trade unions may apply to the Minister of Manpower for an order that an employer remits unions dues to the union through a check-off facility, this legal provision is little used. It has become industrial practice in South Africa for employers to grant this facility to trade unions, as a basic right of recognition. Unregistered unions require the permission of the Minister of Manpower to enjoy the facility.

Registered trade unions in South Africa are entitled to engage in lawful strike activity which is functional to collective bargaining, except in the public sector, in local authorities, and in other essential services. Trade unions are entitled to bargain collectively except on behalf of the public sector, where collective bargaining has not yet been given legal recognition. The right to strike may occur in respect of any matter which has been submitted to a process of statutory conciliation and which concerns a demand regarding terms or conditions of employment which the employer may agree upon or comply with. Hence, strikes over economic and social matters, which are not within the employer's control, are not properly the subjects of a strike, and these strikes are unlawful.

3. The freedom to dissociate

There is no legislation which compels a worker to join a trade union. A statutory closed shop, requiring a worker to belong to a trade union, is permissible only under limited circumstances. Discrimination between employees who belong and those who do not belong to a trade union is forbidden.

The right to exclude others from an association is recognized in law, save that if the association is one with a constitution and members have a legitimate interest in being members (for example, workers may need to be union members in order to retain their jobs) the law will require that the procedures for the expulsion of members are fair.

The law of the future

Article 20 of the Declaration has to a large extent been incorporated within South African law. However, the drastic security legislation which limits the rights of citizens to gather peacefully is an important restriction upon the full application of this article, and clearly only once this drastic legislation is removed will the right to free assembly be properly recognized.

The right to free association is substantially recognized in South African law, both in its negative and positive senses. People may join an association and they may expect to be able to meet without outside interference. They may be able, within certain defined limits, to require those with a common interest to be part of their association.

The negative right to dissociate clearly conflicts with the positive right to associate. In other words, a person's right not to belong to an association such as a trade union may conflict with the right of others to have that person as a member of their association. They may want that person as a member because his or her support is needed to achieve their legitimate object. The law needs to regulate precisely the circumstances in which the positive right to associate should prevail over the negative right to dissociate. To give full effect to the article, the right to dissociate should in general be stronger than the positive right to associate, and the exceptions should be clearly delimited.

A further problem which requires careful regulation now and in the future is the limit upon the positive right of dissociation. The positive right means the right to keep others out of your association. This right can be used to pursue racial or cultural discrimination. For example, a club for white men can exclude all women and blacks under the positive application of the right to dissociate. Should the article be interpreted to include a right to such discrimination, or should the positive right of dissociation be limited to prohibit discrimination on grounds of race, colour, and religion? This is the kind of question which a democratic state will need to address when considering the application of Article 20.

22
The right to democracy in political life

Article 21 (1) Everyone has the right to take part in the government of his country, directly or through freely chosen representatives.

(2) Everyone has the right of equal access to public service in his country.

(3) The will of the people shall be the basis of the authority of government; this will shall be expressed in periodic and genuine elections which shall be by universal and equal suffrage and shall be held by secret vote or by equivalent free voting procedures.

What this article means

The political and civil rights contained in Article 2 are basic first generation rights. This article tries to give practical expression to the saying, attributed to Abraham Lincoln, of government for the people, by the people, and acting in the interests of the people. The article is divided into three sub-clauses which protect different aspects of political and civil rights.

A fundamental feature of any democratic state is that the government governs with the consent of the people. This consent gives the government legitimacy and the power to carry out the functions and duties of state. If a government lacks the support of the majority, as is the position in South Africa, a constitutional crisis of legitimacy is inevitable. A crisis of this kind can potentially result in a strong negative reaction by the majority who may resort to violent means of finding solutions to political grievances as they have no real alternative channels. Under these circumstances, the state often reacts in a repressive manner, with the end result being economic disorder and a state of lawlessness.

Article 21(3) stipulates the basic conditions which have to be met in order to establish the genuine will of the people. Regular elections mean that the government's actions are regularly tested. In this way a government is held to be accountable.

Parliament in South Africa, as in Britain, has a life of five years. The American president has four years in office, and the French equivalent seven years. Effective government would be seriously inhibited if the periods between elections were unduly short; government policies may, in the short term, prove unpopular but in the longer term may be in the best interests of the nation. A period of about five or seven years between elections ensures regular accountability and sufficient periods in office to establish effective government.

The 'secret vote' or 'equivalent free voting procedures' requirements seek to prevent votes being obtained through fear of prejudice or hope of advantage.

The requirement of 'universal and equal suffrage' is the most demanding. It requires that all citizens be regarded as competent to vote unless legitimately and deliberately excluded. Disqualification on irrelevant considerations such as race, gender, lineage, property, and educational qualification are not legitimate. Relevant requirements include the attainment of majority status (turning 18 or 21 years old), citizenship, or the absence of any convictions for electoral offences. Also prohibited are other subtle, but underhand, devices to remove the vote from certain people.

In the early 1960s some southern states of the United States of America, in an attempt to weaken black votes, invented extra requirements before one was entitled to vote. One was that a citizen was entitled to vote only if his or her grandfather was entitled to vote. As the grandfathers of most blacks were slaves or liberated slaves they did not possess the right to vote. Accordingly, without referring to race, this requirement effectively disenfranchised many blacks. Another device was the literacy clause which provided that a person had to read and interpret a section of the constitution to the satisfaction of the electoral officer. Most of these devices were made illegal by the courts of the United States because they were unconstitutional.

The equal suffrage clause is intended to ensure equality in respect of the worth of votes. This does not necessarily mean that each vote must carry exactly the same weight. In a constituency system it is not unusual for one constituency to have, say, 40 000 voters, and another 20 000 voters. And yet if each constituency produces only one elected representative, the value of a vote in the constituency having 40 000 votes is significantly less than the value of a vote in the constituency having 20 000 votes. The equal suffrage condition does not demand strict mathematical equality in the arrangement of constituencies. Substantive equality is sufficient. The goal is to avoid a *substantial* imbalance in the value of votes.

The electoral system used may significantly affect the composition of the government and diminish the value of certain votes. The system used for parliamentary elections in both the United Kingdom and in South Africa is referred to as the 'first past the post system'. In essence this simple system means that the person who gets the most vote wins, even if he or she does not have the support of the majority of people in the constituency. For example, in the United Kingdom general election of 1983, the Social Democratic-Liberal alliance obtained 25,5 per cent of the national vote but obtained only 1 per cent of the seats in parliament. Labour, on the other hand, obtained 27,5 per cent of the popular vote but received 32 per cent of the seats. The more complicated proportional representation system, used in many European countries, ensures that the number of parliamentary seats obtained is directly related to the number of votes cast.

Article 21(1) guarantees the rights both to elect a government and to be part of the government. It insists upon effective representation, and not simply the right to vote. There is a cynical argument that everyone in South Africa has the vote; Africans are able to vote for the legislative assemblies of the self-governing or 'independent' territories, and 'coloureds' and Indians for their separate houses of parliament. In the present system, however, only the white voters enjoy effective representation, as the seat of power is firmly entrenched in the House of Assembly and the State President.

Should the word 'government' in Article 21(1) be widely interpreted to include the right to participate in the *administration* of the country? Many administrative boards make decisions and rules that have serious and far-reaching consequences for ordinary people. Ever-expanding administration is a feature of all developed countries.

The United States of America has tried to accommodate some public participation in its administrative process with the 'notice and comment procedure'. Before the administration adopts any statement of general or particular applicability which is designed to implement or interpret law or policy, it must comply with this procedure. The administrative agency, after explaining the proposed rule, must invite comments from members of the public. When the rule is finally brought into effect, it must be accompanied by a statement indicating the basis and purpose of the rule. It is arguable that Article 21 itself requires some participation by the electorate not only in the legislature and executive but also in the administration.

Article 21(2) requires that the public service be open to all members of the community and not be exclusively staffed by a segment or segments of the society.

The article in South African law

When the Union of South Africa was formed in 1910, an unusual compromise on the voting system was reached. With the exception of the Cape of Good Hope, which retained its qualified multiracial franchise, the rest of the Union adopted an exclusively white franchise. In 1936 the Hertzog-Smuts coalition government removed the African voters from the common voters' roll and placed them on a separate voters' roll. These voters were allowed to vote for three white members of parliament. In 1956 the Nationalist government, after a long struggle with the courts, managed to remove the 'coloured' voters from the common voters' roll and placed them on a separate list. They were allowed to vote for four white representatives.

From this time on government constitutional policy was characterized by commitment to the principle of representation in separate institutions based on race. Alongside this was a firm belief in white domination. Government planners also relied heavily on the colonial strategy of divide and rule. The most important attempts, said to be aimed at satisfying the political aspirations of the African people, were the 'homeland' policies and the tricameral parliament. The rationale behind the 'homeland' policy was to create reservoirs of cheap labour, and to create separate, fragmented entities where Africans would be allowed to exercise their citizenship rights.

Government policy reflected the view that the African population did not constitute a single group, but was an 'unnatural amalgamation of separate groupings' that had to be divided on the basis of language and culture in order to ensure 'peaceful co-existence'. The African population was divided into eight ethnic or tribal units. All existing forms of indirect representation for Africans in the white parliament were removed.

Initially these 'homelands' possessed limited powers and were really only advisory organs to the Minister of Bantu Affairs. Gradually their powers increased as they travelled along the road to 'self-governing' status. At this point legislative assemblies with significantly increased powers were established together with executive councils. The white parliament, however, retained a degree of control. This was 'Grand Apartheid' in the making: because African political rights were accommodated in the homelands there was justification for the total exclusion of Africans from the South African central legislature.

The final stage in the process of African denationalization was the attainment of 'independence' by the 'homelands'. The white statute granting independence to the specific homeland expressly stripped all Africans, who were ethnically linked to that homeland, of their South African citizenship and imposed upon them the citizenship of the 'independent' state. Recent legislation has restored South African citizenship to a limited number of 'homeland' Africans who are resident in South Africa.

The 'homeland policy' has failed for a number of reasons. 'Homelands' suffer from the stigma of being the illegitimate product of apartheid. The success of the policy depended largely on international recognition of the new 'states'. Unanimously, the international community, with the exception of South Africa, has withheld recognition. Further, there has been a widespread rejection of the 'homeland' system by the people upon whom independence has been forced.

After a number of failed attempts to accommodate 'coloureds' and Indians constitutionally, the Nationalist government introduced the ambitious tricameral parliamentary system. This was another refinement of the principle of representation in separate institutions, coupled with white domination. Participation in the parliament is divided on racial lines into three houses and is limited to whites, 'coloureds', and Indians. Built into the constitution are mechanisms designed to ensure the dominance of the white house. The majority of members of the electoral college, which elects the all-powerful State President, come from the white House of Assembly. In order to prevent the 'coloureds' and Indians from having a veto on proposed legislation, the constitution provides that if there is a disagreement between the houses, the President's Council will be a dispute-resolving mechanism. The composition of the President's Council is structured in such a manner that control is retained by the majority party in the white House of Assembly. Therefore the 'coloured' and

Indian vote is of less value and of limited effect compared with the white vote.

The law of the future

Article 21 stipulates the basic or minimum political rights that have to be protected in any democratic order. It does not prescribe a constitutional structure or political system. For this reason compliance with the article is not particularly difficult: most constitutional systems meet these standards.

Recent government pronouncements indicate a policy shift away from white domination to a policy of non-domination and a constitutional order which protects minority rights and interests against majority domination. Fundamental to the Constitutional Guidelines of the African National Congress is the idea of one person one vote in a unitary state. These Guidelines also advocate a multi-party democracy with an entrenched Bill of Rights. In general, the Guidelines envisage a political order that would substantially comply with the requirements of Article 21.

A necessary consequence of the adoption in South Africa of a constitutional system that satisfies the requirements of Article 21 would be black majority rule. Article 21 is unambiguous in its demand that legitimate government is based upon the will of the people. The requirement of universal and equal suffrage will ensure that government would be based upon the will of the majority. It follows that the present political and constitutional order would be fundamentally changed.

23
The right to social security, assistance, and welfare

Article 22 Everyone, as a member of society, has the right to social security and is entitled to realization, through national effort and international co-operation and in accordance with the organization and resources of each State, of the economic, social and cultural rights indispensable for his dignity and the free development of his personality.

What this article means

This article can be read as a preamble to Articles 23 to 27, in which the economic, cultural, and social rights envisioned to enhance the individual's social security are spelt out in more detail.

The Universal Declaration is primarily concerned with first generation rights but this article, together with Articles 23(1), 25, and 26(1) in particular, gives attention to some second generation rights — rights which put a duty on the state to deliver social security in specific spheres.

1. The relationship of Article 22 with other parts of the Declaration

Article 22 claims that every individual has the right to social security and the realization of the economic, cultural, and social rights indispensable for his or her dignity and development. The particular content given to these rights is spelt out in the subsequent articles; hence these also need to be considered briefly.

Social rights can be given a restricted content, and be taken to entail only the support that needs to be provided to an individual in the event of unemployment, sickness, disability, widowhood, old age, 'or other lack of livelihood in circumstances beyond his control' (Article 25(1)). However, by also proclaiming that everyone has the right to a standard of living adequate for health and well-being, including food, clothing, housing, and medical care and the necessary social services, Article 25 gives the concept cf social rights a much broader content.

The economic right to work, so essential to social security, could also be given a more radical content if it is read to imply that there is a duty on the state to provide employment to all. However, in the context of Article 23, where the right to work is proclaimed in the same paragraph as the right to protection against unemployment, it would seem that a more restricted right to unemployment compensation is established. Other economic rights include the right to equal pay for equal work and the right to join or form a trade union.

Free elementary education is proclaimed as a basic socio-economic right, and higher education must be available on the basis of merit. Parents are given a prior right to choose the kind of education their children receive (Article 26).

Cultural rights (Article 27) include not only the right to participate freely in the cultural life of the community, but also the right to protection of the 'moral and material interests' of the author of any scientific, literary, or artistic production.

The right to private property, of which no one may be arbitrarily deprived (Article 17), is clearly also an economic right, but this right, in contrast to the social, economic, and cultural rights contained in Articles 22 to 27, seems to be absolute and not dependent on the resources and organization of the state. The concept of economic rights in Article 22 thus seems to have to do with those rights which enhance social security such as the rights of employment, an adequate standard of living, etc., which are relative to the resources and dependent on the organization of the state, rather than to absolute rights such as that to private property.

2. Is Article 22 'neutral' as regards socio-economic systems?

A number of articles in the Declaration can not in any way be reconciled with a state that exercises central control over the economy. What is interesting, particularly with regard to those second generation economic and social rights contained in Articles 22 to 25, is that these are not all acknowledged in liberal democratic states. Indeed, given the content of Article 22 read with subsequent articles, it could be argued that one-party, centrally-planned socialist states have a better record in recognizing the right to social security than liberal democratic capitalist states. However, this argument seems somewhat unconvincing in the light of the evidence now emerging from Eastern Europe. What is clear is that certain mixed economies, for example the Scandinavian social democracies and the German social market economy, have the best record in realizing these rights.

In theory, centrally-planned economies give the highest priority to the right to social security and economic rights. The right to employment is considered an absolute right, and the prime duty of the state is seen as ensuring that everyone has an adequate standard of living. Although the stipulation that cultural and intellectual production belong to the individual producers, and that parents have the right to choose the type of education their children are to receive, conflicts with the social and economic philosophy of Marxist states, these states do accept 'a standard of living adequate for the health and well-being' of its citizens to be a basic right. In practice the rights to 'free choice of employment' and to form and join trade unions have often been denied, but in theory these states do accept that the right to social security is to be broadly interpreted.

Liberal democratic capitalist states, on the other hand, place the prime responsibility for providing social security on the individual. These states are inclined to allow only a residual role for the state, such as special care for motherhood and childhood, as proclaimed in Article 25. However, the first part of Article 25 does seem to indicate far more substantial rights (including the right to housing), than those acknowledged in liberal democratic societies. Although many of the specific formulations — like the stipulations concerning the freedom to form trade unions and the choice of parents regarding the education of children — seem to be of a liberal democratic nature, social and economic rights in the Declaration are given a content that is broader than that which is accepted in liberal democratic countries. The United States of America, for example, does not provide housing and medical care to all in need, even though it has the resources to do so.

Capitalist countries that are not liberal democracies have often been notoriously bad in denying many of the social, economic, and political rights to which their citizens are entitled according to Article 22. Apartheid South Africa, for one, has denied its citizens not classified as white virtually every one of the rights proclaimed in Articles 22 to 27.

Social democracies have an outstanding record regarding the realization of the right to social security. In Sweden, for example, the state actively intervenes to assure employment and housing for all. For political reasons, however, social democracies have refused to comply with some of the specific articles; for example, the prior right of parents to choose the kind of education given to children is at times questioned. Social market systems, like that of Germany, provide social security which is virtually on a par with that of the Scandinavian countries, and have in practice conformed with the stipulations that are of a liberal democratic nature. Rights like the right to private schools are respected.

The social security rights contained in Articles 22 to 27 are clearly not neutral as regards economic systems. This is not surprising given the different values and practices in societies with different economic systems. It would have been difficult if not impossible to draw up social security rights in the economic, social, and cultural spheres which were simultaneously realizable in different societies.

3. Implementation of rights to social security

In fulfilling second generation rights, there have to be certain trade-offs, not only between one right and another, but also between one generation of citizens and another. A state which attempts to provide everyone with housing may find that it has no resources available to provide even elementary education and medical care. Choosing to provide certain rights at the expense of others may, however, have long-term advantages. For example, more resources for elementary and technical education today may well mean higher rates of economic growth and hence more resources for meeting social security rights in future. The fact remains, though, that trade-offs between different types of social investment are often necessary. Destitute children suffering from malnutrition will have a stronger claim to food than a healthy single adult to a house. Similarly, basic investments in elementary education ought to be given priority over massive expenditure to put a person on the moon.

A court which wishes to enforce a right for basic food will thus have to consider the extent to which such a right may be permitted to override other presently-existing rights or the rights of future generations. This will be a complicated issue, for the court will have to deal with questions on which economists often strongly disagree.

The basic obstacle in the implementation of Article 22 is that the rights on social security can only be exercised in accordance with the organization of the state — a stipulation which, it would seem, leaves the realization of these rights open to the discretion of the particular state.

4. Social security and international co-operation

A number of international organizations promote the realization of the social, economic, and cultural rights. Some of these are attached to the United Nations: UNESCO is concerned with the promotion of the cultural and educational rights of Third World communities; UNICEF is involved with improving the conditions of children; the International Labour Organization is concerned with the position of workers; and various economic commissions, such as the Economic Commission for Africa, try to encourage economic policies and the development of economic institutions which will enhance the economic and social rights of the poor.

The International Bank for Reconstruction and Development, better known as the World Bank, is concerned with similar issues, but is not under the control of the United Nations. It is under the control of a governing body dominated by the richer nations. This has at times led to the question whether the priorities the World Bank has set for the restructuring of Third World economies are in the interests of the social, economic, and cultural rights of the poor in these countries. In terms of actual resources put at the disposal of Third World countries, the World Bank is by far the most significant of all these international organizations.

Article 22 is silent on the nature of international co-operation required to realize the social security goals. It does not seem to impose any specific duties on the richer countries, nor does it declare any specific rights for Third World countries.

The article in South African law

From the 1920s onwards social security rights were increasingly being met in the case of white South Africans. The right to free elementary and secondary education was established. White children from poor families were accommodated in school hostels and provided with a decent education. The rights of white, Indian, and 'coloured' workers to form trade unions and to strike were recognized in law. Subsidized housing was made available to poor whites, and a social welfare system for whites was developed. A provincial hospital system brought medical care to the poorest whites.

By the mid 1940s most of the social, economic, and cultural rights required by Article 22 were, as far as white South Africans were concerned, enshrined in the laws. At the very least, they were recognized in practice. In effect, a 'whites only' social democracy was being established. 'Coloureds' and Indians shared in some of these rights, but Africans were generally excluded.

The Fagan Report of 1946 recommended that many of the social and economic rights be extended to include Africans. The victory of the National Party in the 1948 election prevented the implementation of these recommendations and a new period commenced in which Africans in particular were excluded from existing rights to social security. For example, job reservation laws prohibited Africans from being employed in all but the most menial of occupations.

From the late 1970s onwards, the process of exclusion was reversed. Job reservation was scrapped, and the rights of African workers to strike and organize in trade unions was recognized. Africans now have the right to migrate to urban areas and settle in site and service areas. The permanence of the African population in urban areas has been accepted and there has been a consequent modification in housing policy. In the field of welfare services such as pensions and education the trend in government expenditure has been towards greater equality between the race groups.

However, many discriminatory laws still exist in certain areas. (Some of these are described in the following chapters.) There are, however, clear indications that legalized discrimination in social security will soon be scrapped. Remaining discriminatory government expenditure is likely to be phased out completely.

Because of the implementation of apartheid legislation, South Africa has been expelled from the United Nations organizations concerned with international co-operation in respect of the social, economic, and cultural rights referred to in Article 22. If an internationally-acceptable negotiated settlement in South Africa is concluded, South Africa will be re-admitted to these organizations.

Although South Africa is today still a member of the World Bank, its right to borrow money from the bank has effectively been suspended. The World Bank is presently investigating the possibility of providing loans to finance housing, infrastructure, primary health care, and other services in the black community in the event of a negotiated settlement. This would have positive implications for people's economic, social, and cultural rights.

The law of the future

What is at issue today is the extent to which economic, social, and cultural rights will be enshrined in the new South African constitution. Given the aspirations expressed in the Freedom Charter, it is to be expected that at least one of the major parties negotiating a new constitution will, at the very least, insist on the inclusion of clauses similar to Article 22 and the other articles dealing with social rights.

24
The right to work

Article 23 (1) Everyone has the right to work, free choice of employment, just and favourable conditions of work and protection against unemployment.

What this article means

In summary, this article means that:

❐ When a contract of employment exists between an employer and an employee, not only does the employer have the right to receive services of the employee, but the employee has the right to be allowed to perform his or her employment duties (also called contractual duties).

❐ No person shall be prevented from choosing a career, or from trying to qualify for a job of his or her choice, or from entering a profession of his or her choice.

❐ In a working environment employees are entitled to work under just and favourable conditions. This means that there is a corresponding obligation on the employer to ensure that the conditions of the working environment are just and favourable.

❐ Workers are entitled to security of employment. This means that they must be protected against unfair or unlawful dismissal, retrenchment, or redundancy.

A clearer picture of the requirements of this article emerges from a discussion of the South African context.

The article in South African law

1. The right to work

Unemployment is a massive problem, particularly in developing countries. According to a study by the International Labour

Organization in 1976, there were approximately 300 million unemployed, or underemployed, persons in the Third World. In these countries the right to work protection appears to have little meaning. However, it is almost certainly not correct to interpret this part of the Declaration as an obligation on the state to provide every person with a job. As much as this is desirable, it would seem to be an impossible goal.

Other human rights documents also contain clauses dealing with the right to employment. For example, Article 6 of the International Covenant on Economic Social and Cultural Rights recognizes the right of everyone to have the *opportunity* to gain his or her living by working. The American Declaration of the Rights and Duties of Man speaks of each person having the right to work 'insofar as existing conditions of employment permit'. The European Social Charter, in recognizing that everyone shall have the opportunity to earn a living in an occupation of their choice, requires that states 'accept as one of their primary aims and responsibilities the achievement and maintenance of as high and stable a level of employment as possible, with a view to the attainment of full employment'. The Freedom Charter recognizes the rights and duties of all to work, and also the right to unemployment benefits. The reference to unemployment benefits indicates that the framers of the Charter were not demanding that every person should necessarily be provided with a job.

In South African law a right to work exists once an employee has entered into a contract of employment with the employer. The employer then has the right to receive the services of the employee, who is obliged to render services to the employer in terms of the contract.

The most common examples of employees enforcing their rights to work are in situations where they have been dismissed or retrenched. Dismissals and retrenchments are frequently contested in the courts. Another form of the denial of the right to work is where the employee is suspended from his or her duties. Suspensions are less frequently challenged in the courts because workers are normally paid their wages while under suspension.

2. The right to free choice of employment

All persons should be free to take up the employment of their choice. This means that people are free to choose a job for which they are qualified. Qualification for employment should have absolutely nothing to do with race, ethnicity, gender, or creed. The criteria for the selection of the right person for a particular job should be on merit only.

The right to free choice of employment would be frustrated if the training necessary for that particular kind of work was only available to certain groups of people. This would be the position if the selection criteria took account of race, gender, etc. In other words, all educational institutions must also be opened to all people, so that everyone is free to choose the jobs or careers they wish to pursue.

In South Africa, however, schools and other educational institutions are generally run on racial lines. White schools and technikons, for example, are well equipped, compared with similar institutions for black pupils and students. It follows that whites are in a much stronger position to receive the vocational training of their choice. Black educational and training institutions are characterized by inadequate classes, inadequate subjects (especially those for technical skills), too few qualified teachers, and an unacceptably high student to teacher ratio.

The quality of education, as far as Africans are concerned (see Chapter 29), is so poor that very few African students can truly be said to have had the right to choose proper training for various careers. There are, consequently, too few African accountants, doctors, lawyers, and engineers. There are no African judges. All this is a direct result of the apartheid system. Indeed, the damage caused by 'Bantu Education' has had such a profound effect on South Africa's oppressed people, that the damage will take many years to undo.

Despite these obstacles some African people have managed to rise to high positions in the professions and other fields of work.

3. The right to just and favourable conditions of work

In the early 1980s the law governing the operation of trade unions was changed to make it possible for African workers to use the dispute-settling mechanisms provided in the Labour Relations Act of 1956. Following this, thousands of African workers joined trade unions throughout the country. Almost immediately there was a large increase in trade union activity, including campaigns aimed at improving conditions of work. At about the same time the Industrial Court was established. Its function was to resolve disputes between employers and workers, including those represented by trade unions.

These developments marked a turning point in the life of

millions of African workers. Workers now became aware of their rights to just and favourable conditions of work. Consequently, unions have on the whole successfully negotiated the signing of recognition agreements which contain various worker rights. These agreements include proper disciplinary procedures, retrenchment agreements, and even parental rights, to name but a few. Above all, there have been agreements with employers to the effect that there will be negotiations on a regular basis aimed at improving the conditions of employment of workers, including wage increases. These negotiations are held annually in most cases. As a result, it is now an established practice in most industries throughout the country that employers negotiate their workers' conditions of employment with unions, rather than effect wage increases etc. as they see fit.

Where disputes have arisen on these issues and the parties have been unable to settle their differences through negotiations, these disputes have often been referred to the Industrial Court for a ruling. The Industrial Court has handed down various judgments which have the effect not only of protecting but also promoting the right to just and favourable conditions of work. Some of these judgments are the following:

❐ Where an employer has undertaken to negotiate with a union on wages, it is an unfair labour practice if the employer unilaterally implements wage adjustments without first negotiating with the union.

❐ Where employees strive for just and favourable conditions of work, a strike is a legitimate weapon in the collective bargaining process.

❐ Where an employer fails or refuses to pay wages which are due, employees are entitled to refuse to work, and this refusal does not amount to a strike.

❐ An employer is obliged to consult with employees before closing down its business because such a decision affects the workers' jobs.

❐ The fact that a union is unregistered does not entitle an employer to refuse to negotiate with the union in circumstances where the employer would otherwise be obliged to negotiate.

❐ The fact that a union has not achieved a majority membership of employees in a given bargaining unit does not entitle the employer to refuse to negotiate with the union if the union at least enjoys substantial membership.

The Supreme Court has also made a contribution to the promotion of the right to just and favourable conditions of work. For example, the Supreme Court has said that the working of overtime by employees remains voluntary, unless an agreement to the contrary has been entered into between an employer and employees.

Nobody quarrels with the view that there must be a fair wage and good working conditions. However, controversy arises as to what amounts to a fair wage in any particular case, and what criteria should be used to determine whether a wage is fair. There are various factors which have to be taken into account in determining a fair wage including socio-economic ones. Some of these are:

❏ the needs of workers and their families;

❏ the levels of wages in the industry;

❏ the cost of living;

❏ social security benefits;

❏ levels of productivity; and

❏ the desirability of attaining and maintaining a high level of employment.

Apart from the contributions made by trade unions and the courts to the promotion of the right to just and favourable conditions of work, parliament has also passed the Basic Conditions of Employment Act of 1983 (see also Chapter 25) which sets out the minimum conditions of employment that every employer governed by the act is bound to observe. These include hours of work; minimum periods of annual leave; sick leave; overtime and overtime pay; working on Saturdays, Sundays and public holidays; and minimum notice on termination of employment.

4. The right to protection against unemployment

It is possible to interpret this right in various ways. A common interpretation is that everyone is entitled to receive material (in this case financial) support in the event of being unemployed. In other words there is an obligation on the state to provide some form of unemployment security for people who have either been unable to find employment, or have lost employment. In South Africa there is limited unemployment insurance protection for certain persons who become unemployed. However, there is no general right to state financial support to all people who are unemployed.

The right to protection against unemployment can also be interpreted to mean that all employees have a right not to lose their jobs unfairly. In South Africa the establishment of the Industrial Court has resulted in major advances being made in this respect. The court has frequently come to the assistance of employees who have lost their jobs as a result of employers acting improperly.

The ordinary, or non-statute law (also known as the common law) has shown itself to be inadequate in giving protection to employees who are dismissed without justification. For example, according to the common law, an employer can dismiss an employee without complying with the rules of natural justice. This means that an employee could be dismissed without being given the opportunity to present his or her side of the dispute. According to the common law all that an employer needs to do in order to effect a lawful dismissal is to give the employee proper notice of termination (for example, a month or a week, depending on the contract) or pay wages instead of the notice period. Furthermore, according to the common law, an employer does not have to give reasons for the decision to terminate the employment.

The Industrial Court, acting under powers granted to it in legislation, has developed extensive guidelines on the law of unfair dismissals and retrenchments. The judgments of the court indicate that a dismissal will be regarded as unfair, and re-instatement may be ordered when, for example:

❏ The employer has done no more than comply with the common law requirements of lawful dismissal.

❏ The employer has only complied with the contractual provisions in regard to the termination of a contract of employment.

❏ An employee has been dismissed without being afforded an opportunity to state his or her case.

❏ The employer has failed to be objective and unbiased in applying its mind to the dispute, before deciding on dismissal of the employee.

❏ An employer has dismissed an employee for lawful union activities outside working time.

❏ No right has been given to an employee to appeal against a decision to dismiss him or her, even where it is practicable to give the employee such a right.

☐ There is insufficient evidence to support a finding of guilt, or to warrant dismissal.

☐ Although an employee is guilty of misconduct, dismissal is not the appropriate action.

In the case of retrenchments, the Industrial Court has developed other guidelines. Some of these are that:

☐ The employer must consult with the trade union or an employees' representative body on the question of retrenchment.

☐ The employer must consult with the employees who are affected by the proposed retrenchment.

☐ The criteria adopted in order to select employees to be retrenched must be fair, and one which can be objectively checked.

☐ An employer must take all reasonable steps to try to avoid retrenchment.

☐ The employer must make attempts to assist the retrenched workers to find alternative employment.

Another principle which could soon develop, and which has not yet been decided by the Industrial Court, is that an employer should be obliged to offer employment to retrenched employees before offering positions to other persons.

The right to protection against unemployment, although not fully recognized in South Africa, is being taken far more seriously at the present time.

The law of the future

South African labour law generally requires further development before it can be said that the rights contained in Article 23(1) of the Declaration are fully recognized in South Africa. However, these rights will never be attained as long as the apartheid order, itself a fundamental violation of the Declaration, remains in existence.

25
The right to equal pay for equal work

Article 23 (2) Everyone, without any discrimination, has the right to equal pay for equal work.

What this article means

The purpose of Article 23(2) is to prevent wage discrimination by employers. Employees who do similar work are entitled to equal pay.

This right is a practical example of the effect of Article 1, which declares that 'All human beings are born free and equal in dignity and rights.' Hence, there is a moral foundation to the article, which regards race and gender discrimination to be wrong. Yet attitudes often reflect an indifference to gender discrimination. Karl Marx, for example, suggested that a reason for the discriminatory treatment of women workers was the 'natural' differences of skill and strength. However, feminists argue that the real reason lies in the sexual division of labour in the home — this is reproduced in the workplace and is accepted as quite 'natural.'

It should be emphasized that the right to equal pay is enforceable only if the value or worth of the jobs themselves is regarded as equal. For this reason the 'equal work' aspect of the article requires close examination.

'Equal work' implies that the value of jobs can be measured and, therefore, compared. The value of work is measured through job evaluation systems or job grading. The advantage of job evaluation to the employee is that it prevents arbitrary or purely subjective decisions by an employer about the wage for particular work. It follows that job grading is one way of enforcing the article.

This advantage is, however, overshadowed by two disadvantages. The first problem is the unreliability of job grading. The evaluation runs the risk of being influenced by subjective factors such as the reliability of the job description, decisions about the score to be allocated to a job, decisions about the range of points to be allocated to the different grades, and decisions about the wage payable for each grade. Therefore, precautions are required to ensure the reliability of job evaluation as an objective measure of the value of a job.

The second disadvantage is that job evaluation produces a hierarchy of jobs. This ranking is weighted in favour of factors like decision-making, skill-level, education level, etc., whereas physical effort, repetitive work, or danger are factors which — if considered at all — are not rated highly. The effect of the ranking is permanently to place the disadvantaged at the bottom of the hierarchy, with no hope of breaking out. Where the degree of disadvantage coincides with the division of workers along lines of race or gender, then job grading enforces discrimination.

Therefore, while job grading appears to make it possible to observe the letter of the article, much more is required to conform with its spirit.

The article in South African law

Job reservation, racially discriminatory rates of pay, and the denial of collective bargaining rights to black workers have all been features of apartheid. However, since the Wiehahn Commission Report in 1979 steps have been taken to remove racially-discriminatory laws which apply to labour. But the mere removal of these laws does not guarantee protection from wage discrimination on the basis of race. For example, as recently as 1988 the Industrial Court made a finding of wage discrimination on the basis of race, in the case of *SACWU v Sentrachem* (discussed below).

Regulations made in terms of the Basic Conditions of Employment Act and Machinery and Occupational Safety Act may not differentiate on the basis of race or gender. These regulations deal with conditions of employment. The most general right against discrimination in the employment arena was introduced into the Labour Relations Act during 1988. It is now an unfair labour practice to unfairly discriminate solely on the basis of race, gender, or creed. This means that discrimination on any one of these grounds can be remedied in the Industrial Court.

How effective is the unfair labour practice remedy? The *Sentrachem* decision, referred to above, illustrates one difficulty — the *proof* of wage discrimination. When the case went on review to the Supreme Court it was held that the admission in the evidence of a senior manager that there was wage discrimination did not justify a finding of wage discrimination.

Another problem is that large groups of employees who may suffer from wage discrimination are not covered by the Labour Relations Act. This is the position with domestic workers, farmworkers, and public servants. These workers cannot challenge wage discrimination in the Industrial Court.

Other wage discrimination practices may also exist. For example, although the Labour Relations Act prohibits race or gender discrimination in industrial agreements, it is possible to get around the law in certain circumstances. Such is the case when an Industrial Council agreement is entered into with a racially-exclusive white union. Although the agreement does not refer to race, it can have the effect of wage discrimination if the (white) members of that union receive better wages than black workers who are not part of the union. There is therefore need for a clearer and more universal right to protection against wage discrimination in South Africa.

It is appropriate, in the context of Article 23(2), to consider the distribution of income by race in South Africa. The following statistics for 1988 show the average wages for whites and Africans in various industries:

Sector	Monthly earnings (R)	
	White	*African*
Mining	3 000	500
Manufacturing	2 742	786
Energy, water	2 958	1 120
Construction	2 660	546
Trade	1 813	481
Transport	2 080	708
Finance	2 464	1 155
Services	2 001	748
Public	2 282	760

The mean average African income is in the region of R500 per month, while for whites it is closer to R2 500 per month.

The gap in wages between whites and Africans is huge. However, this is not necessarily evidence that Article 23(2) is being violated. Another explanation for these figures is that the distribution of jobs has a racial character: whites have the most highly-paid jobs. This is confirmed by figures which reveal occupation by race. Of labourers, 88,9 per cent are black and 0,7 per cent white. Of the 66,2 per cent of production workers who are black, most of them are semi-skilled or unskilled, while the 13,9 per cent white production workers are skilled. Only 2,3 per cent of executives and managers are black, while 92,4 per cent are white. Amongst professionals, too, whites are disproportionately in the majority, comprising 70 per cent while blacks make up only 19,2 per cent. (Most of the latter group are teachers.) Hence, there is a link between the wage gap and the distribution of jobs.

Much of the racial imbalance in the distribution of jobs has its origins in job reservation. One of the last remaining laws on job reservation remained in force until as recently as 1988. Until then, black miners could not become blasters. Because job reservation has been used to deny access to jobs on a racial basis, attention must be paid to the right to equal access to employment.

The right to equal pay for equal work will not in itself correct the imbalance in the distribution of jobs. In fact the reverse is true: Article 23(2) in an unqualified form, together with the legacy of Bantu education, may well compound the problem. The reason for this is that job evaluation forms the basis of applying the article. As a result, as explained earlier, the jobs occupied by most blacks are ranked at the lower end of the job scale. The unqualified application of Article 23(2), although providing equal pay for equal work, will maintain the racially-imbalanced distribution of jobs. Consequently, the big wage gap between blacks and whites will remain.

Although the Industrial Court has held that gender discrimination is not permissible, the distribution of women in employment also reveals stereotyped roles. Of the 25,8 per cent women production workers, the majority are employed in the leather and garment industries. While 39,2 per cent of transport and communication workers are women, they are mainly employed as receptionists and telephonists. The main occupations of the 43,7 per cent women sales workers are as counter hands and till operators. Of all clerical employees, 62 per cent are women. Only 12,8 per cent of managers and executives are women. Although 45 per cent of professionals are women, they are largely made up of teachers, nurses, and social workers. These figures also illustrate that equal access opportunities to jobs is a key issue for women.

The law of the future

Equal opportunity rights are needed to prevent the continued imbalance in the distribution of jobs. However, much more is required to change the status quo which job grading maintains. A reassessment of job grading is required, as well as vocational training, affirmative action, and promotions.

In the short term, equal opportunity is meaningless until a uniform education system benefits all. Until then, in order to provide equal opportunity, preferential assistance is required. To this extent then there is no contradiction in implementing equality of opportunity and affirmative action simultaneously.

The problems relating to the objectivity of job grading can be addressed by re-defining job evaluation systems. Such a process can best be achieved by collective bargaining and indeed this process has already begun. The current focus of bargaining includes matters such as the criteria for assessing jobs and union involvement in job descriptions.

The imbalance in the distribution of jobs will have to be dealt with through vocational training schemes. These would be the quickest route to enable all to benefit from equal opportunity until the effects of a uniform education system filters through. Further relief can be achieved through reassessment of promotion criteria. Again this should be negotiable. Areas of possible negotiation would be factors such as seniority and affirmative action.

Certain minimum rights need to be addressed either through a Bill of Rights or legislation. These are equal pay for equal work, equal opportunity, vocational training, and promotion. Against such minimum standards, collective bargaining can shape the exact content of these rights. This is appropriate since the problems being addressed here are really issues which relate to the distribution of wealth — and this is a function of collective bargaining.

26
Social rights

Article 23 (3) Everyone who works has the right to just and favourable remuneration ensuring for himself and his family an existence worthy of human dignity, and supplemented, if necessary, by other means of social protection.

Article 25 (1) Everyone has the right to a standard of living adequate for the health and well-being of himself and of his family, including food, clothing, housing and medical care and necessary social services, and the right to security in the event of unemployment, sickness, disability, widowhood, old age or other lack of livelihood in circumstances beyond his control.

(2) Motherhood and childhood are entitled to special care and assistance. All children, whether born in or out of wedlock, shall enjoy the same social protection.

What these articles mean

What good is it to have freedoms such as speech, movement, and religion if you are hungry and living in poverty? Some say that civil and political rights are almost meaningless to a starving squatter. Therefore social rights come *before* other rights. They say that the poor, wisely or not, would choose a full belly before the right to vote.

It is also said that a person who cannot get basic social goods (food, clothing, housing, and medicine) becomes trapped in a cycle of poverty from which it is almost impossible to escape. A person without money cannot get adequate food. This affects the nutrition of children, which affects their performance in school (which is likely to be sub-standard because of the area in which they are living). Poor education affects the sort of job, if any, that can be obtained on leaving school, which affects the sort of wages that can be earned, which affects not only the quality and location of housing (which affects the family's health and cost of transport) but also the nutrition of the family. Article 25 asserts that human dignity is dependent on a minimum of social goods such as food, clothing, and shelter.

Only the most heartless deny that all people should have basic social goods. Some go further and say that if the government has the resources it has a *duty* to provide these goods. A contentious issue is whether the term *right* should be used to describe a claim to these goods. A right is usually understood as something you can enforce, but a claim to food is conditional on the government having resources. How do you enforce a right to food when none might be available, or the government department's budget does not allow for any more food parcels? This difficulty has led people to say that Article 25 is better described as a 'manifesto' right, a statement of desirable state action, but incapable of being enforced by the court.

Traditionally, the criterion of cost has been used to draw a distinction between (a) civil and political rights (thought to be relatively cheap to enforce) and (b) socio-economic rights (thought to involve enormous government expenditure). This distinction is mistaken because citizens' civil and political rights can also be costly to maintain. For example, expensive state-paid legal representation is essential if poor people are to have a right to a fair trial.

Article 25 amplifies the right to an adequate standard of living by isolating certain factors which together contribute to a decent human existence: health care; food; clothing; housing; social services; provision in the event of unemployment, sickness, disability, or widowhood; old age pensions; and special care for mothers and children. An allied provision is found in Article 23(3) which gives the worker:

> the right to just and favourable remuneration ensuring for himself and his family an existence worthy of human dignity, and supplemented, if necessary, by other means of social protection.

The articles in South African law

1. Health care

There is no national health service in South Africa (as is found, for example, in the United Kingdom), but the Health Act of 1977 places a duty on provincial administrations and local authorities to provide a range of health services and facilities. However, there is no right given to residents to claim these services. So, for example, although provincial ordinances make provision for a superintendent of a hospital to assess the financial circumstances of a patient and to provide free medical treatment to indigent (poor) persons, no one has the right to insist on being admitted to a hospital.

The state of a nation's health services is traditionally measured by factors like the infant mortality rate, the number of hospital beds, and so on. On every index for measuring health services, South Africa remains two different worlds, with distinct standards and consequences. For example, the infant mortality rate (IMR) for whites dropped in 1985 to, for the first time, below 10 in 1 000 while the IMR for Africans in 1985 was 124 in 1 000. There are similar discrepancies in the number of hospital beds and the number of doctors per 1 000 black persons and per 1 000 white persons.

Since the late 1970s there has been a trend towards greater privatization, accelerated by the state's financial crisis and escalating health care costs. This trend directly threatens future standards of medical care for the poor. Another threat lies in the fragmentation of health services (from one Minister of Health in 1973, there are now 14), resulting in a lack of co-ordination and inefficiency. For those on medical aid schemes it is perhaps difficult to appreciate the urgency of demands such as those made in the 1955 Freedom Charter for a preventative health scheme, and free medical care and hospitalization. In the light of current trends, renewed calls have been made for a national health service.

2. Food and clothing

There is no right to food and clothing established under South African law. There does exist provision in terms of the National Welfare Act of 1978 for the temporary giving of 'social relief' to those who find themselves in such material need that they are unable to provide for the primary needs of themselves or their families. Apart from this very limited provision, the problems of hunger and clothing are tackled mainly by charitable organizations. This is an indictment: as the historian Braudel put it, 'Today's society, unlike yesterday's, is capable of feeding its poor. To do otherwise is an error of government.'

3. Housing

Since the 1920s state policy has been to make available some public funds to promote house construction and ownership. This is the closest one comes to any hint of state responsibility for housing.

There is currently a nation-wide shortage of housing, estimated at 1,8 million units. The Urban Foundation estimates that 400 000 units a year will have to be built until the year 2000 for the housing shortage to be eliminated. But housing is still not perceived as a right, and the shortage of housing has become a central and ongoing crisis.

Housing in the 1980s has become privatized and politicized. Rent boycotts, ejectments, massive housing shortages, defiance of the Group Areas Act, continued removals, the selling off of houses owned by the National Housing Commission, and a state policy away from the provision of housing to the provision of land with site and service projects are all dimensions of the issue of housing. The Abolition of Influx Control Act gave, in theory, 10 million Africans the freedom to live and work where they chose, but this measure has not halted the programme of removals. The politics of shelter will remain high on the agenda, especially if the rate of African urbanization rises from the present 35 per cent to a future 75 per cent, as predicted.

4. Social services

The 1985 Report on Welfare Policy declared a commitment to state withdrawal as far as possible from present and future welfare responsibilities. The document categorically rejected the notion of a welfare state or primary state responsibility for welfare. The policy document has two main themes: differentiation and privatization. The first is the 1980s version of apartheid in welfare services; the second is the state's attempt to divest itself of primary responsibility for certain functions.

The 1985 policy document drew strong criticism and was replaced by a cabinet-approved document released in 1988. The new document expresses a commitment to retaining social welfare as an 'own affair' as well as to investigation of possible areas for privatization. But it should also be noted that there is a difference between policy and reality. There are limits to privatization while the unemployment crisis, instead of allowing state withdrawal, requires increasing state intervention in the form of job programmes and poor relief.

5. Provision in the event of unemployment, sickness, disability, or widowhood

In some countries, such as the United Kingdom, any person whose income falls below a certain figure is entitled to receive what has become known as the dole. The idea is to provide a 'safety net' income so that no one starves. There is no such right in South Africa. The closest provision is in the Unemployment Insurance Act of 1966 which sets up a state fund to pay benefits for a period of 26 weeks to people who are unemployed, sick, or to women who have just had a baby. But only those who have been employed and were contributors to the fund for a period of 13 weeks are eligible to receive benefits. This means that if you have never had a job, you can never qualify for benefits.

For a worker who is injured or killed while on duty, the Workmen's Compensation Act of 1941 provides for benefits to be paid to the worker or his or her dependants, if the worker was covered by the scheme. In terms of the Social Pensions Act of 1973, disabled or blind persons are eligible to receive a small but regular pension.

6. Old age pensions

One of the few social rights recognized in South African law is the right to an old age pension. In terms of the Social Pensions Act of 1973 men over the age of 65 and women over the age of 60 are entitled to receive a pension if their income falls below a certain figure (which is adjusted from time to time). However, although there is discrimination between the amount paid to black pensioners and the amount paid to white pensioners, the social significance of these pensions cannot be underestimated. Apart from wages sent by migrant workers, pensions are the only reliable form of income in the 'homelands', and entire families are dependent on them for survival. After defence and education, social pensions is allocated the largest portion of the national budget.

7. Special care for mothers and children

The stark facts in South Africa today are that during the period 1975–88 between 15 000 and 27 000 children under the age of five died from malnutrition. It is estimated that one third of all black children under 14 are underweight and stunted. The infant mortality rate between 1981 and 1985 was 12 in 1 000 for whites, 18 in 1 000 for Indians, 52 in 1 000 for 'coloureds', and 92 to 124 in 1 000 for Africans. Given these facts, it must be asked whether anyone is legally responsible for granting special care to mothers and children.

In terms of the Health Act of 1977, provincial administrations are obliged to provide maternity homes and services; local authorities are obliged to take 'all lawful, necessary and reasonably practical measures' to promote the health of the residents. The free infant and child immunization programme offered by local authorities is the clearest example of the fulfilment of this obligation. No comprehensive service has been offered to address the problem of malnutrition because of the difficulty of providing adequate food within a discriminatory system.

8. Just and favourable remuneration

The government's 1985 policy document on welfare policy specifically rejected the right to a sufficient income, or state responsibility to set minimum wages and ensure a humanly decent standard of living. This statement accords with current government policy of not directly intervening in wage setting or in providing supplementary income. There are many economists who would argue that it is unsound for a government to tamper with minimum wages because this can create unemployment. The argument is that it is far better for someone to be employed at a low wage than be unemployed because the employer cannot afford the stipulated minimum wage. Furthermore, because employers constantly assess whether new technology should replace workers, state intervention in wages tends to push employers towards mechanization.

In spite of this, Industrial Council agreements for specific industries lay down minimum wages for the different groups of employees in that industry. The system covers 97 industries and one million workers. Setting minimum wages does not, of course, ensure that those wages are either just or favourable. In many cases these wages fall below the Household Subsistence Level and even the Poverty Datum Line and this has fuelled calls by trade union federations for a 'living wage'.

The law of the future

Assuming a future government's desire to grant social rights, it will nevertheless be constrained by the enormous cost involved. Someone has called social rights the 'hand-grenade' of our time, having the potential to destroy a government which holds on for too long. Accepting that available finances will be decisive in the *quality* of social rights granted, the problem of enforcing social rights can only be addressed by legislation setting up the machinery for the provision of these rights. Requesting a court to decide if you have been treated fairly in terms of a specific law is in many ways easier than asking it to order the government to give you something which you decide you deserve.

What sort of legislation could be passed to make meaningful provision for social rights? As regards *food*, legislation could be passed setting up food banks for emergency relief and to marshal surpluses and distribute essential foodstuffs. A means-tested approach would be necessary to prevent abuse. State partnership with private enterprise could be an appropriate course of action. As regards *housing*, there must be official recognition that even the cheapest new housing provided by government is not affordable by low-income households. A different approach involving legal recognition, security of land rights, public services, and technical assistance for squatters is essential.

As regards *medical care*, the trend towards the privatization of medical services has to be reversed, and more attention has to be paid to rural areas. Needed also is acknowledgment that the poor will never be able to afford medical treatment and health care. As regards *social pensions*, the present state policy towards equality of pensions must be pursued. As regards *special care for mothers and children*, a full programme of preventative health care, backed by a programme of school feeding, is essential. As regards a *just and favourable wage*, legislation providing for supplementary income to those whose income falls below a prescribed means test could be introduced.

27
The right to form and to join trade unions

Article 23 (4) Everyone has the right to form and to join trade unions for the protection of his interests.

What this article means

The most fundamental of all labour freedoms is freedom of association. In every industrializing society there is an imbalance between the power of owners and managers and the power of isolated workers. The only effective way in which workers can combat oppressive working conditions and promote their interests is by combining their individual efforts through organization. In many countries this type of combination was simply outlawed in the past and heavy penalties, even death sentences, were imposed on those who 'conspired together' to win higher wages and improved conditions. The struggle for freedom of association — the right to form and join trade unions — was very often a bitter one.

Article 23(4) has been expanded upon by Article 22 of the International Covenant on Economic, Social, and Cultural Rights, which provides that no restriction may be placed on labour's rights to freedom of association except by law and when this is necessary 'in a democratic society in the interests of national security or public safety, public order, protection of health or morals or the protection of the rights and freedoms of others'. Article 22 in turn also refers to one of the two most important legal instruments of the world community promoting freedom of association in the context of labour: Convention 87 of the International Labour Organization (ILO). The ILO is a specialized agency of the United Nations and has as one of its general objectives the promotion of the Universal Declaration of Human Rights.

No discussion of freedom of association in general, or of Article 23(4) in particular, can be complete without reference both to Convention 87 (Freedom of Association and Protection of the Rights to Organize Convention, 1948) or Convention 98 (Convention Concerning the Application of the Principles of the Right to Organize and to Bargain Collectively, 1949) of the ILO.

The key provision of Convention 87, Article 2, establishes the fundamental right of workers (and employers) to establish organizations by stating: 'Workers and employers, without distinction whatsoever, shall have the right to establish, and, subject only to the rules of the organization concerned, to join organizations of their own choosing without previous authorization'.

The principal purpose of the article is to promote union autonomy from the state, something emphasized by the phrase 'without previous authorization'. If workers' interests are to be protected, then the independence of those organizations from state control must be guaranteed. It should be noted that a simple set of registration formalities for trade unions is not regarded as an infringement of Convention 87.

The rights enshrined in Convention 87 must apply to all workers ('without distinction whatsoever'). In other words, it would not be permissible for national legislation to deny the right to organize to groups identified on the basis of occupation, gender, colour, race, creed, nationality, or political opinion. The right to organize should also be enjoyed by workers in the agricultural and public sectors, among others. Any legislation which imposes a system of racial discrimination with regard to the right of workers to establish and join trade unions would be in violation of the Convention, as would any legislative limitation arising from a worker's political opinion.

Freedom of choice among trade unions is also implicit in Article 2 of Convention 87. It includes the right to decide on the structure and composition of a trade union; to establish more than one union in any industry or undertaking; and to establish federations according to choice. Although trade union diversity is not an obligation under the Convention, it is a requirement that diversity should remain a possibility. The ILO itself has interpreted the Convention to mean that, while representative trade unions may be given preference for the purposes of collective bargaining, minority organizations must at least have the right to make representations on the behalf of their members and to represent members in cases of individual grievances.

Under Article 3 of Convention 87, workers' organizations have the right 'to organize their administration and activities and formulate their programmes', and 'the public authorities shall refrain from any interference which would restrict this right or impede the lawful exercise thereof'. Under this heading, the ILO has stated that the right to strike is one of the essential means available to workers and their organizations for the promotion and protection of their economic and social interests. In particular, it has found that 'the use of extremely serious measures, such as the dismissal of workers for having participated in a strike and refusal to re-employ them, implies a serious risk of abuse and constitutes a violation of freedom of association'.

Convention 98 on the right to organize and collective bargaining is the second pillar protecting freedom of association. The key article here is Article 1, which provides:

1. A worker shall enjoy adequate protection against acts of anti-union discrimination in respect of their employment.

2. Such protection shall apply more particularly in acts calculated to —
   (a) make the employment of a worker subject to the condition that he shall not join a union or shall relinquish trade union membership;
   (b) cause the dismissal of or otherwise prejudice a worker by reason of union membership because of participation in union activities outside of working hours or, with the consent of the employer, within working hours.

In essence, the article is designed to protect workers in general, and union office-bearers in particular, against acts of victimization by employers and state authorities. Full protection against all forms of prejudicial action, including dismissal, is a vital element of freedom of association.

The article in South Africa law

South Africa has adopted neither the Universal Declaration nor the International Covenant. Although South Africa did ratify certain ILO Conventions before its membership of the ILO was terminated in 1966, it never committed itself to the all-important Conventions 87 and 98.

Although trade unions for African workers were allowed to exist before the labour reforms of 1979, these unions were denied access to the statutory institutions of collective bargaining and their members had very little effective protection against acts of victimization. The same is largely true today of unions organizing farmworkers, domestic servants, and certain state employees.

Most workers in South Africa are covered by the Labour Relations Act of 1956. The statute has three central provisions which promote and protect the freedom of association. Firstly, section 78 prohibits employers from preventing workers from joining trade unions. Secondly, section 66 makes it a criminal offence for an employer to dismiss workers or to prejudice them in any way whatsoever because of their membership of a trade union or because they have taken part in the formation or lawful activities of a union. Thirdly, the unfair labour practice definition, supervised by the Industrial Court, outlaws any action which, amongst other things, 'in an unfair manner infringes or impairs labour relations ', creates labour unrest, unfairly prejudices workers, or interferes with 'the right of employees to associate or not to associate'. The Industrial Court has been very assertive in advancing freedom of association under its unfair labour practice jurisdiction and has been quick to confirm that victimization is not only a crime but an unfair act to boot.

Although domestic labour law is now broadly consistent with Article 23(4) and Conventions 87 and 98, the Labour Relations Act still caters for the racial registration of trade unions and permits unions to exclude workers as members on the basis of race.

It is South Africa's security legislation, however, which continues to offend most directly against labour's freedom of association. Under the Internal Security Act, all open-air meetings have been banned (in the absence of magisterial or ministerial permission) since 1976. It is at least difficult and sometimes impossible for workers to associate freely if they are unable to assemble in the open air. Meetings of large groups of union members have been rendered illegal as a result, something which is a particular problem for workers confined to hostels in the mining industry. The ban on open-air gatherings also effectively prohibits the picketing of employer premises during the course of industrial disputes. The ILO regards the right to organize both meetings and processions (for example, May Day marches) as important aspects of freedom of association. These sorts of events have been severely restricted in recent years under both the Internal Security Act and the Emergency Regulations.

Quite clearly the wide-scale detention of trade union leaders without trial, something which South Africa has experienced over a long period now, constitutes a grave inroad into freedom of association.

The law of the future

During September 1990 the Congress of South African Trade Unions, the National Council of Trade Unions, the South African Consultative Committee on Labour Relations, (an employers' federation), and the South African government entered into an agreement which signified the commencement of a new period of labour reform in the country. Included in that agreement was an explicit endorsement of the principle of freedom of association for workers in all sectors of the national economy and the understanding that future labour law will be brought into line with international labour standards.

There is therefore a very real prospect that farmworkers, state workers, and domestic servants will enjoy adequate rights to freedom of association within the next few years. The parties to the agreement have also committed themselves to removing the racialistic remnants still found in the Labour Relations Act.

Freedom of association in the labour context will only be fully safeguarded once a democratic government has eliminated the restrictions on freedom of assembly and the threat of detention without trial found in the security legislation. Confirmation of the new order will hopefully be heralded by the return of a democratic South Africa to the ILO and by the ratification of Conventions 87 and 98.

28
The right to rest and leisure

Article 24 Everyone has the right to rest and leisure, including reasonable limitation of working hours and periodic holidays with pay.

What this article means

Article 24 of the Universal Declaration, in proclaiming the right of people to rest and leisure, identifies limited working hours and paid holidays as elements of that right. Limited working hours and paid holidays are not by themselves sufficient for the attainment of rest and leisure.

Where people's income is prioritized on subsistence, and where the environment in which rest and leisure are to be exercised is marked by squalor, overcrowding, an absence of peace or privacy, and no electricity or running water, the limitation of the working day is no guarantee of rest or leisure. The meaningful exercise of the rights embodied in Article 24 is dependent upon the attainment of satisfactory standards of living and social security required by the Declaration as a whole.

Save for a fortunate few for whom work is both lucrative and fulfilling, work for the majority of people is alienating, repetitive, and demeaning, and despite all that, poorly paid. The fact that people engage in long hours of unrewarding labour is a consequence of having no alternative means of subsistence. Acceptance by people of employment of the most thankless kind can in no manner be regarded as voluntary in the proper sense. Where unemployment and the prospect of starvation are alternatives to employment, the acceptance of terms and conditions dictated by the employer is inevitable. It is this reality which explains the labour relationship, and the levels of exploitation to which people are prepared to subject themselves.

It is normally only where employees have rare skills, or where they are able to engage in meaningful collective bargaining, that satisfactory conditions of employment are obtained independently of state intervention.

As the ordinary law (called the common law in South Africa) merely accommodates and does nothing to temper the exploitative tendencies of the labour relationship, state regulation is necessary. The introduction of labour legislation providing for occupational health and safety, specified hours of work and holidays, and minimum wages is a reflection of the inability of market forces and the common law to provide for socially-responsible employment standards.

The article in South African law

In South Africa the common law does not restrict the length of the working day. Working hours are regulated by statute. The Basic Conditions of Employment act of 1983 is the general statute which provides for various limitations which cannot be contravened, even by agreement between employer and worker. However, excluded from the provisions of the act are state employees, farmworkers, and domestic workers, to name a few. The employment conditions of various state employees are regulated by other legislation, but farm and domestic workers are entirely unprotected.

The act differentiates between ordinary working hours and overtime, as well as between people employed as guards and other employees. The maximum number of ordinary working hours permitted in terms of the act are as follows:

Per week

Security guards		60 hours
Other employees		46 hours

Per day

Security guards	(in a 5 day week)	12 hours
	(in a 6 day week)	10 hours
Other employees	(in a 5 day week)	9,4 hours
	(in a 6 day week)	8 hours

Overtime is permissible, subject to mutual agreement, and the act provides for a daily maximum of 3 hours and a weekly maximum of 10 hours overtime work. The act specifies the basis of calculation of overtime pay which is one and one third of the employee's basic rate of pay.

Employers regularly make overtime a condition of employment, and prospective employees are forced to choose between compulsory extended working hours or continued unemployment. Where employees are requested to work overtime, which is not compulsory, their decision is invariably determined by material realities. Given the miserable wages of most workers in industry, hopelessly inadequate unemployment benefits, and a general dependency on wage earners, an opportunity to increase income is not lightly foregone. For many, overtime work is critical in the pursuit of a living wage.

In these circumstances overtime for a substantial proportion of workers in South Africa is the norm rather than the exception. Therefore, as most workers perform overtime, the notion of a 46-hour week is deceptive. The reality for many is a 56-hour week, of which the last 10 hours are worked for slightly increased wages.

In South Africa, as in other countries, the working day does not begin and end when workers arrive at and subsequently leave their places of work. This is because of the travelling time between home and work. Peculiar to South Africa, however, is apartheid's physical isolation of workers from the urban industrial centres. It is not uncommon for up to three hours to be spent daily in getting to and from work. This places a large burden on rest and leisure time.

Twelve public holidays are provided for by legislation in South Africa. Employees who work in shops and offices are entitled to be paid leave on all of those holidays, but all other employees covered by the Basic Conditions of Employment Act are only entitled to half of them. Employees can agree to work on public holidays and the act effectively provides for remuneration at double the ordinary rate of pay.

The act provides for at least 14 consecutive days' annual leave on full pay; 21 consecutive days' annual leave are stipulated in respect of guards and certain categories of salespeople.

The purpose of the act is to set protective limits which cannot be violated, even by agreement. However, there is nothing to prevent parties from concluding agreements which make provision for terms and conditions which are more favourable to employees.

For the purposes of comparison with the international standards which are referred to below, it is relevant to note that the agreement of the National Industrial Council for the Iron, Steel, Engineering, and Metallurgical Industry provides for a 45-hour week in respect of ordinary working hours — one hour less than the maximum allowed by the act. The agreement entitles workers to all public holidays, and not only to the six to which factory workers are entitled in terms of the act. It also provides for three consecutive weeks' leave, and for work on public holidays to be remunerated at two and one third times the basic rate of pay. In 1990, agreement was reached regarding a 44-hour week in respect of ordinary time, and, if the agreement is ratified by the Minister of Manpower, it will have the force of law across the industry.

An international comparison of the ordinary working hours and holiday entitlement of employees in the engineering industry, recorded in the table below, illustrates that South African workers are worse off than their counterparts elsewhere.

Country	Normal hours per week	Holiday entit- lement	Public holidays	Total holidays	Net annual working hours
Australia	38	20	11	31	1 748
Austria	38,5	25	11	36	1 789
Belgium	37	20	10	30	1 709
Denmark	39	25	10,5	35,5	1 799
France	38,5	25	9	34	1 748
Germany	38,5	30	11,7	41,7	1 689
Italy	40	25	8	33	1 784
Japan	40	20	10	30	1 848
Netherlands	40	22	7	29	1 752
Spain	40	26	14	40	1 820
Sweden	40	25	12	37	1 792
Switzerland	41	20	9	29	1 902
UK	39	25	8	33	1 778
USA	40	10	11	21	1 920
South Africa	45	15	11	26	2 115

The above table records only the ordinary hours worked by employees in the engineering industry in the countries cited. It does not indicate the actual hours which would include overtime. In the South African engineering industry, where overtime work is common, an even less satisfactory comparison can be drawn.

Present legislation in South Africa also compares unfavourably with the standards of the International Labour Organization (ILO). In 1919, Convention 1 of the ILO gave recognition to the principle of an 8-hour day and a 48-hour week. That convention provided for a maximum of 56 working hours per week, inclusive of overtime which involved work of an exceptional nature.

In 1935, Convention 47, known as 'The Forty Hour Week Convention', proclaimed the ideal of the 40-hour week and motivated its adoption on grounds of widespread unemployment and the hardship suffered by people in consequence of circumstances for which they were not responsible. Fifty-five years later, despite an aggravated unemployment crisis and continuing retrenchment, South Africa has yet to adopt the Forty Hour Week Convention and overtime is the norm rather than the exception in a substantial proportion of industry.

In 1970 the ILO adopted Convention 132 concerning annual holidays with pay, which provided that all employed persons were entitled to no less than three working weeks paid leave per year.

The law of the future

For as long as the majority of South Africans are denied political rights, state policy and legislation will reflect the social and economic priorities of a privileged minority. The extension of political rights and the establishment of a democratic political process is fundamental to the legislative recognition of the rights proclaimed in the Universal Declaration.

In seeking to ensure for South Africans time for rest, leisure, and holidays, an immediate and attainable objective of a responsible political order would be to provide statutory protection limiting hours of work and ensuring holidays for all South Africans. If the Basic Conditions of Employment Act is to remain the general statute regulating working hours, its provisions would need to be extended to provide protection for all persons in employment, including farmworkers, domestic workers, and other categories of employees who are at present not covered by the act.

Adoption of the principle of a 40-hour week would accord with what was declared 34 years ago in the Freedom Charter, as well as international practice and the standards recognized by the ILO. If the 40-hour limit is to be properly applied, overtime work must be prohibited save in exceptional circumstances.

Beyond the basic standards which are guaranteed by legislation, South Africans must be able to improve their conditions of employment by agreement between employer and employee. Statutory promotion of collective bargaining, principally through the right to strike, can provide South Africans with the facility to actively participate in the determination of their conditions of employment, thereby regulating the extent of their working week.

As indicated in the introduction to this chapter, limited working hours and paid holidays are no guarantee of rest or leisure. The realities which exist outside the workplace are beyond the scope of protective labour legislation. With the majority of South Africans housed in ghettos and remunerated at rates barely satisfactory for their own subsistence, rest and leisure in the proper sense will remain the preserve of the wealthy. A 'right' to rest and leisure, if it is to be more than a hollow statement, will require a social and economic transformation in South Africa to create the material conditions which are essential to the exercise of that right.

The development of technology provides society with the means to increase its leisure time as machines secure desired levels of production. Technology, however, is not being used to reduce the workday as much as it is being used to reduce the work-force. Machines are being introduced to reduce production costs through the replacement of people and, in the process, society is being burdened with the increasing stresses of unemployment.

Among the central objectives of any progressive society is to provide for full participation by all in its economic life, to attain optimum levels of productivity, and to ensure an equitable distribution of the benefits of that productivity. The creation of employment is a national priority in South Africa. As technological development threatens to marginalize increasing numbers of workers, one of the challenges to a democratic South Africa will be to ensure the social benefits of technology and not the social costs. Leisure is among those benefits.

29
The right to education

Article 26 (1) Everyone has the right to education. Education shall be free, at least in the elementary and fundamental stages. Elementary education shall be compulsory. Technical and professional education shall be made generally available and higher education shall be equally accessible to all on the basis of merit.

(2) Education shall be directed to the full development of the human personality and to the strengthening of respect for human rights and fundamental freedoms. It shall promote understanding, tolerance and friendship among all nations, racial or religious groups, and shall further the activities of the United Nations for the maintenance of peace.

(3) Parents have a prior right to choose the kind of education that shall be given to their children.

What this article means

It is useful to distinguish between a strong interpretation and a weak interpretation of Article 26. The strong interpretation implies maximum state control, while the weak interpretation implies minimum state control. The strong interpretation emphasizes that people should have the same opportunities to receive the same quality of education. This implies strong state control of the provision of education in terms of finances, what is taught, how it is taught, and by whom. Different kinds of education — such as academic, technical, and commercial — can be provided, but the quality must be the same. The choice of which stream is entered will be made by the state on the basis of social need. Social needs are prioritized over personal needs, and education is seen as a public matter, with equality being regarded as more important than freedom.

The weak interpretation stresses the prior rights of parents and of the individual to choose the kind of education they want. While the responsibility for financing education rests largely with the state, parents and communities are expected to make significant contributions. What is taught, how it is taught, and by whom are determined at a local level by parents and communities. Personal needs are prioritized and education is seen as a private matter. Freedom is emphasized over equality.

Article 26 stresses the moral role of education in the development of the personality and of social attributes like tolerance. No mention is made of the economic functions of education and this omission is highlighted by the failure to refer to schooling as the major provider of education in modern societies. In the last 100 years, education has become strongly linked to schooling. This linkage was forged during the process of industrialization which requires a mass schooling system to provide a labour force with appropriate skills and attitudes, and a child-minding service to enable parents to work.

There are two different approaches to the provision of education. These correspond to the strong and weak interpretations of Article 26. The strong interpretation involves centralized provision of education under state control. Change in education will only occur if there is a change in who controls the state. Political change must precede educational change.

The weak interpretation sees the provision of education decentralized. While the state exerts considerable influence through legislation and the allocation of resources, this is balanced by a greater degree of local and community control. Change in decentralized systems of education can occur in a wide variety of ways and in different forms. A particular community or institution can influence what happens in its local schools. For example, a large industrial company may secure its supply of skilled labour by financing appropriate technical courses in the local schools.

Generally, then, a centralized system of education would be controlled and financed by the state (although, of course, the funding comes ultimately from the community in the form of taxes) and would emphasize equality and uniformity. A decentralized system would allow for a greater degree of freedom of choice on the part of the individual and the community, but would expect a greater direct financial contribution towards the costs of education from individuals and communities.

How does one decide whether or not a schooling system is fulfilling the objectives of Article 26? A practical way of looking at this is to evaluate two aspects of a schooling system. Firstly, who has access to schooling? Do children in a rural area have the same access as those in an urban area? Or, is access in any way dependent on one's colour or socio-economic status? The point is that unequal access directly influences educational achievement.

Secondly, does the process of schooling differ from one school to another? If what is taught and how it is taught differs according to whether the school serves pupils from a particular class, race, or religion, then a particular pupil's educational achievement is dependent not on his or her potential but on the kind of school he or she attends. If the provision of schooling is controlled in such a way that different people have different educational opportunities, then pupils will emerge from the schooling system with very different levels and types of educational achievement.

These inequalities will become even more extreme in a society where the choices of parents and their children are restricted not only by economic criteria but also by race or creed. However, even if a schooling system does provide everyone with equal access to schooling of the same quality, this will not remove the economic inequalities within the society. The performance of children at school and the kind of work they do after leaving school is largely determined by the socio-economic status of their parents.

It is unfortunate that Article 26 makes no mention of literacy and numeracy. However, one can assume that the emphasis on free and compulsory education implies that, where the provision of schooling is insufficient, there is a responsibility to provide alternative opportunities for everyone to become literate and numerate.

The extent to which a society tries to provide equal education, and to ensure that all its members are literate and numerate, depends on its commitment to a strong interpretation of Article 26. Those societies committed to a weak interpretation will accept inequalities as a necessary consequence of the prior right of parents to freedom of choice and will consider the provision of literacy to be the responsibility of communities.

The article in South African law

The most obvious characteristic of South African education is inequality based on racial division. This is a fundamental violation of Article 26. It is a peculiar perversion of apartheid that South Africa has a highly centralized education system with strong state control of all aspects of education for the specific purpose of entrenching inequality.

Education has been one of the major instruments of apartheid and this is reflected clearly in the relevant legislation. The most infamous education law was the Bantu Education Act of 1953 which laid the foundations of apartheid education for Africans and whose consequences are still very much with us today. Prior to 1953, education for Africans was under the control of the provinces and most schools were run by the churches. Although there were not nearly enough schools, the education provided was of a fairly high standard.

The Bantu Education Act centralized control of African schooling in the hands of the government and, in the words of Verwoerd (the Minister of Native Affairs at the time), was designed to ensure that:

the Bantu must be guided to serve his own community in all respects. There is no place for him in the European community above the level of certain forms of labour. ... Up till now he has been subjected to a school system which drew him away from his own community and practically misled him by showing him the green pastures of the European but still did not allow him to graze there.

The effect of this act was to bring about the closure of the majority of the church schools, to strictly peg the financing of African schooling to a very low level (less than 10 per cent of the amount spent on a white pupil), and to ensure rigid control of what was taught in the schools. While there was a massive increase in the numbers attending school, particularly primary schools, the lack of adequate financing resulted in poor quality education.

The creation of the 'homelands' saw a decentralization of the responsibility for the administration of schooling for Africans with each homeland having its own education department, while at the same time control remained in the hands of the central government through its control of financing and examinations. The 1979 Education and Training Act, together with its 1988 amendments, has ensured that the basic features of African schooling remain the same: too few classrooms and schools; poor facilities; very high teacher-pupil ratios; unqualified or underqualified teachers; few books, libraries, and laboratories; inappropriate subject choices; and high drop out and repeater rates. This is accompanied by rigid ideological control over what is taught and how it is taught with a strong racist bias that asserts the superiority of European culture and people and the inferiority of African culture and people.

Schooling for whites, 'coloureds', and Indians did not remain unaffected by apartheid. The National Education Policy Act of 1967 ensured that the Nationalist government's policy of Christian National Education determined what was taught and how it was taught. There was an authoritarian approach to teaching with a strong emphasis on rote learning and the importance of examinations. What was taught emphasized European culture and contained a racist bias against Africans.

The tricameral constitution of 1983 further entrenched the racial division of education with its division of 'own' and 'general' affairs. As with the homelands, the administration of schooling is the responsibility of the racially-specified 'own' affairs departments, but the control of financing, and the standardization of syllabi and examinations remain a 'general' affair under the central government.

As a result of these various laws South Africa now has 17 different departments of education. The actual provision of education in terms of the numbers of schools and teachers and the amount of money spent per pupil varies enormously. Thus, in 1987, in Kangwane the amount spent on education per capita was R280; in Transkei R413; in the Department of Education and Training R477; in 'coloured' education R1 021; in Indian education R1 904; and in white education R2 508. On average, the state spends five times more on a white child than it does on an African child. What is taught and how it is taught remains firmly controlled. The existence of so many departments gives the appearance of decentralization and a form of local control based on ethnicity. However, the Nationalist government maintains strict control over the whole system.

The gross inequalities of apartheid education and the appalling conditions in African schools have led to sustained resistance by African pupils, particularly from 1976 onwards. In response to this resistance and to an increasing recognition by the state, commerce, and industry that the economic future of South Africa is directly related to the quality of its education system, there has been a significant attempt to reform African education. Many of the guidelines for this reform process were spelt out by the De Lange Commission in 1983. However, the reform process has so far produced few positive results. Since the mid 1980s there has been little effective schooling taking place with students, and more recently teachers, expressing their dissatisfaction through boycotts and stayaways.

There have been three major impediments/obstacles to the success of the reform process. Firstly, the consequences of the historical legacy of Verwoerd's policies and the demographic realities combine to create problems of overwhelming proportions. In 1987, there were 6,6 million African pupils at school, compared to 874 000 white pupils; there were, approximately, another 3 million African children who should have been at school but who have dropped out or have been excluded, and another 3 million who have had no schooling. The problems are compounded within the schooling system because more than 75 per cent of African pupils are in primary schools. The African schooling system is like an inverted funnel with over 1,5 million pupils in the first grade and a rapidly decreasing number in each subsequent grade. Only one out of every 100 pupils who enters the first grade will achieve a university entrance matriculation.

This increase in quantity has not been matched by an improvement in quality. In 1987, there were 151 000 African candidates for the matriculation examination. Of these, 56 per cent (85 000) passed, but only 16 per cent (25 000) achieved a university entrance pass. In the same year there were 66 000 white candidates, of whom 95 per cent (63 000) passed with 43 per cent (28 000) achieving a university pass. Of even greater concern than the matriculation figures is the fact that more than 60 per cent of pupils will be excluded or drop out from school before they are functionally literate and numerate.

The second major impediment to the reform process has been the use of Emergency Regulations and the 1988 amendments to the Education and Training Act to apply repressive control measures to schooling. These have included the presence of troops in schools, the detention of pupils, the banning of student representative councils, and strict control of who has access to schooling. The problems of repression have been exacerbated by the increase in violence, particularly in Natal/KwaZulu, which often involves the youth and affects the schools.

The third and probably most important impediment has been the total lack of legitimacy of the Nationalist government's attempts at reform. There has been a collective mistrust of the Nationalist government which has not been helped by the attempts to impose reform rather than to negotiate with those who are regarded as legitimate representatives of the community.

Against this background it is possible to evaluate South African education in the light of Article 26.

Primary education is compulsory for white, 'coloured', and Indian children, but apart from a few exceptions is not compulsory for African children. African, Indian, and 'coloured' parents have always had to pay relatively high fees to send their children to school, while until recently, white schools were free of charge. Thus, for the majority of the population, primary schooling has been neither free nor compulsory.

The provision of technical and professional education has always had a very low priority in the formal schooling system, which has a predominantly academic bias. The government has always regarded the provision of technical education as being the responsibility of industry which has meant that it has not been generally available, particularly for Africans who were barred, until recently, from access to skilled and semi-skilled work by apartheid laws.

As to higher (or tertiary) education, the situation is once again racially differentiated. One example will suffice. The average number of university students per thousand of the population, throughout the world, is 9. In South Africa the figure for the white population is 30 per thousand, while for the African population it is less than 1 per thousand.

As regards the second section of Article 26, which deals with the content of education, the position in South Africa is that the majority of the population have had to accept an education which has asserted their inferiority and which has prepared them for the lowest paying jobs in the labour market. This has not encouraged the full development of the human personality; nor has it promoted understanding and tolerance.

Clearly, parents in South Africa do not have a prior right to choose the kind of education that will be given to their children. The racial definition of education departments forces parents to send their children to schools which differ enormously in the quality of education provided (with the exception of those children who attend non-racial private schools). All parents have to accept that they have very little control over what their children are taught, by whom they are taught, and how they are taught.

The situation for those who have not had access to formal schooling, or who have had to drop out before becoming literate or numerate, is abysmal. There is virtually no state provision of literacy classes, and while there are a number of non-governmental literacy organizations, they have insufficient resources and are only able to scratch the surface of the problem.

Overall, the right to education in South Africa, on either a strong or weak interpretation, has been severely abused.

Education has been more of a privilege than a right, a privilege based primarily on race, and to a lesser degree on economic status. Not surprisingly, those who have had the fewest educational opportunities are Africans living in rural areas. Apartheid education has had severe economic and moral consequences. There has been a tremendous loss of potential skilled and semi-skilled workers which has stifled economic growth, and the inequalities and racist ideologies embedded in the system have caused immense damage to the social fabric of the society.

The law of the future

There have been recent indications by the Nationalist government that, as part of its reform process for education, it intends to achieve greater equality of access, to allow more parental and community control, and to make parents and communities pay more for education. These educational reforms are part of the Nationalist government's overall commitment to a reform process in which privatization of functions presently performed by the state is a major characteristic. This can be understood as a move, on the part of the Nationalist government, from a position in which the right to education was completely ignored in the imposition of apartheid through a highly centralized system of education to a commitment to a weak interpretation of Article 26 and a decentralized system of education.

While this will ameliorate some of the worst features of apartheid education, it will not be sufficient. The combined effects of apartheid have created a society which is divided on racial lines into separate communities with gross economic and social inequalities. A weak interpretation of Article 26 and a decentralized education system will result in wealthy, predominantly white communities, being able to maintain high standards of educational provision. Poor, predominantly African communities, will struggle to improve the quantity and quality of provision. Education will become a privilege dependent on one's wealth.

The African National Congress has shown through the Freedom Charter and its Constitutional Guidelines that it is committed to a strong interpretation of Article 26. This commitment has also been reflected in the demands embodied in people's education. This implies that the state should undertake a strong affirmative action policy to redress the historical inequalities and the ideological effects of apartheid education. The basic features of this policy include the provision of free and compulsory primary education; the opportunity for everyone to have access to some form of post primary education; a radical change in what is taught and how it is taught; and a comprehensive literacy campaign. To achieve this South Africa will require a centralized system of education through which redistribution can take place to remove the existing inequalities.

The tensions between a strong and weak interpretation of Article 26 — and between a centralized and decentralized system — will, hopefully, be resolved as part of the negotiations leading towards a future non-racial South Africa. The interpretation of Article 26 that is adopted will be closely related to the interpretation of other human rights, particularly those related to the political and civil rights that will determine the relationship between equality and freedom. The stronger the interpretation and the more centralized the system, the greater will be the degree of state intervention and control and the prioritization of equality.

Some of the key issues that will need to be resolved include the following:

❐ The financing of education, particularly the balance between state provision and direct local provision is a key issue. Given the need to remove historical inequalities, the use of the state to redistribute wealth through an affirmative action policy of allocating revenue from the wealthy to the poor is likely. However, the extent and rate of redistribution is not clear, although it will have to be substantial to overcome the shortage of classrooms, schools, resources, and teachers.

❐ There will be tension between the need to democratize the control of education through, for example, parent-teacher-student associations, and the need for strong centralized state control to pursue an affirmative action policy.

❐ The removal of all racist ideology from the curriculum is another key issue. This will initially require strong centralized state control, particularly in the design of new syllabi, the publication of new textbooks, the standardization of examinations, and the training of teachers. The degree of freedom that will be allowed to parents to choose the kind of education they want for their children is not clear. Obviously, a racial criterion cannot be used, but to what extent will parents be allowed to make choices on the basis of religion, culture, and language? There is a tension between the need to achieve equality, which implies a degree of uniformity, and the need to respect the diversity of religions, languages, and cultures. There will, almost certainly, be only one national department of education; there will probably be a flexible system of subsidization with freedom of choice being linked to higher costs to the parents. All schools will have to follow a core curriculum which will stress the creation of a single overarching national identity and culture. One of the most difficult problems will be the question of which language or languages should be used as the medium of instruction.

❐ There will need to be the creation of a curriculum which reflects the economic and social needs of the society. Apart from the language issue this will not be too difficult at the primary level. It is at the post-primary level where difficult decisions will have to be made. The majority of people perceive an academic curriculum as having the highest status. However, the economic needs of the society require a far greater emphasis on technical and commercial subjects. It will be necessary to achieve a balance between social needs and individual desires which does not create a new form of privileged schooling, with the children of the wealthy doing academic subjects, and those of the less wealthy doing technical and commercial subjects.

❐ There will need to be a comprehensive national literacy programme to eradicate illiteracy.

Given the reality of scarce economic resources there will have to be clear choices as to which programmes are prioritized. It is here that Article 26 can make a contribution. A clear understanding of a specific interpretation of Article 26, appropriate to the South African context, which provides a resolution to the tension between freedom and equality, and which helps to determine the correct balance between centralization and decentralization, will make a significant contribution to a worthwhile and just future.

30
The right to culture

Article 27 (1) Everyone has the right freely to participate in the cultural life of the community, to enjoy the arts and to share in scientific advancement and its benefits.

(2) Everyone has the right to the protection of the moral and material interests resulting from any scientific, literary or artistic production of which he is the author.

What this article means

This chapter looks at the right to culture in Article 27(1) and (2).

Before discussing the meaning of Article 27 it is essential to define culture. This is very difficult. What are the characteristics of a cultured person? A person learned in, and educated to appreciate, the arts, music, humanities, architecture, philosophy, history, and science springs to mind. Such a person enjoys a high degree of intellectual, moral, and artistic development. This may be described as a commonly held view of a cultured individual. But that degree of development is ultimately derived from the culture of a group or the civilization of a people.

Like most countries, South Africa is a multi-cultural society. There is, for instance, the culture of the working class, the culture of management, the culture of the Third World, the culture of the First World, the culture of religion, and the culture of Marxism. All these cultures can be further sub-divided, and many of them overlap to some extent. Some of these cultures may even transcend the political boundaries of South Africa, and all cultures may be liable to change from time to time, and from state to state. What is more, culture may exist not only in the peaks of human achievement such as what are regarded as great works of art, but also in humble customs like what are regarded as polite eating habits. So, in addition to the traditional view of a cultured individual, a cultured person may also be someone who simply shares in the customary norms of a certain group or particular people.

It should also be mentioned that certain cultural practices may be objectionable for various reasons. They may, for instance, be injurious to health or hygiene, or give rise to discrimination or prejudice, or be contrary to the law of the land.

What emerges from this overview is that culture is immensely variable and virtually infinite, but not always valuable. Moreover, all cultures exist in a flux of mutual enrichment or competition. It is essentially the interaction between cultures that Article 27 of the Universal Declaration aims to regulate. But culture is best regulated if the direction of the flow of culture is determined beforehand. If all cultures are to flow ultimately into a common melting pot, then the regulation of cultural rights is somewhat eased. But if the flow is towards greater cultural diversity, less cultural assimilation, and more cultural competition, then the regulation of cultural rights is much more difficult. There is some evidence for both these trends.

In the United States, the Hispanics, Afro-Americans, and Asian groups increasingly reject the old idea of the cultural melting-pot. Different cultures are being asserted, frequently violently, on a world-wide scale. Consider, for example, the Sikhs in India, the Tamils in Sri Lanka, the Catholics in Northern Ireland, the Muslim and Christian communities in Lebanon, the Lithuanians and Estonians in the USSR, and the Hungarians in Romania.

Why should these cultures be asserted so strongly? Most cultural communities have longer histories than the countries in which they are located. Their allegiance may be to their culture, rather than to their country. Moreover, the process of nation-building, of creating a common culture, is slow. This is because the deep-rooted values and emotional loyalties which are derived from the history of a cultural group are not easily forgotten. It is not surprising, therefore, that state intervention aimed at cultural assimilation is often rejected as trespassing, especially where cultural groups may, as discussed above, be in competition with one another.

While there is much movement towards cultural diversity, there is also the global village phenomenon — the notion of a shrinking world in which there is greater interdependence between states and groups. This may result in more common culture. In South Africa, for instance, the economic interdependence of blacks and whites is clear, at least for the foreseeable future. Thus, the culture of management and the culture of the worker may, in a dawning era of greater worker participation in management, be drawn closer together as common values are discovered. A common culture may also be developed because cultures are often mutually enriching. Furthermore, it is a characteristic of some culture that its value and relevance is neither restricted to time, place, or group even though it may be derived from a particular culture.

If it is accepted that the direction of the flow of culture is complex, uncertain, contradictory, and consensual, then it seems that Article 27 should be interpreted to protect cultural diversity while supporting the development of a common culture. If cultural strife in South Africa is to be avoided, provision must be made for a socially cohesive community that is culturally diverse.

Apart from Article 27 of the Declaration, the right to culture is recognized in many different conventions and political manifestos. Some of these should be mentioned to demonstrate the universal recognition of cultural rights. Article 15 of the International Covenant on Economic, Social, and Cultural Rights of 1966 provides that states recognize the right of everyone 'to take part in cultural life'. The International Labour Organization Convention 107 of 1957 makes provision for the protection of the cultural values of indigenous and tribal populations. Article 5 of the International Convention on the Elimination of All Forms of Racial Discrimination of 1965 obliges states which are parties to the Convention to recognize the right of every person without distinction as to race, colour, or national or ethnic origin to equality before the law in respect of cultural rights. Article 27 of the International Covenant on Civil and Political Rights provides that 'persons belonging to ethnic, religious or linguistic minorities shall not be denied the right, in community with other members of their group, to enjoy their own culture'.

Apart from international conventions, specific political policies may provide for cultural rights. In Britain, for instance, where there is no Bill of Rights, it appears that government policy is to recognize cultural diversity by providing equal opportunity and securing mutual tolerance among the various cultures. In the Freedom Charter of the African National Congress it is provided that 'the doors of learning and culture shall be opened'.

It can be contended that the right to culture is a secondary human right because without, for example, the prior enjoyment of the rights to life, liberty, security of person, freedom of thought, conscience, religion, and education, the right to culture is of little import. The right to education illustrates this point. Since education in one's mother tongue is one of the primary means by which culture is acquired, the right to choose the type of education which a person is to receive is important for the exercise of the right to develop freely one's culture.

The primary meaning of Article 27 is that every individual has the right to cultural freedom regardless of race, gender, religion, or any other such distinction. Implicit in this right is the notion that no culture is superior to another, and that the immense diversity of cultures must be respected. This is essential if one culture is not to dominate the others, as the white, Christian, Afrikaner culture has done in South Africa. Any attempt by a state to evaluate any single culture for the purposes of preferring or assimilating any culture would be rejected, perhaps even violently, by the members of the disaffected cultures. The right to culture secures the right to be different. It also is a classical negative right in that it imposes no positive duty on the state other than to ensure that legislation must not infringe the right to culture. But, as discussed below, both the right to be different and the negative character of that right require further qualification.

The right to be culturally different cannot be an absolute right for certain cultural practices may, as mentioned above, be injurious to health or hygiene, or result in discrimination or prejudice, or be objectionable for some other reason. Objectionable cultural practices may even conflict with some other rights. While Article 27 provides for the protection of cultural pluralism, it cannot be interpreted to limit the other human rights which are also enshrined in the Declaration, especially where these are first generation rights (such as life, liberty, and expression). Furthermore, the exercise of objectionable cultural practices may also impair the rights of others to their cultures. Here, again, objectionable cultural practices should be condemned or outlawed. When judging what is objectionable, care should be taken not to be culturally biased. Instead, culture should be judged to be objectionable by notions of universal human rights, especially as set out in international conventions.

Cultural rights are usually said to be group rights. But how is a group to be defined? Many criteria may be used. Language, religion, social custom, beliefs, traditions, and a common history may all, for instance, be employed to determine a cultural group. But to delineate a cultural group based purely on colour, as has been done in South Africa, is arbitrary, irrational, and discriminatory. The right to culture is best regarded as the right of an individual, without discrimination of any type, to freely participate in and develop further his or her culture. Of course, the right to participate freely in culture extends only to activities which are cultural in character. Since, as already pointed out, culture is difficult to define, that definition should be left to the determination of a court of law as and when the need arises. Otherwise, any legislative definition of culture is sure to be incomplete, even misleading.

Because the right to culture in Article 27 is a negative right, the state has only to protect *individual* rights to culture. It is then assumed that one culture is thereby protected against another. But this may not be achieved by such a negative right. To exercise fully the right to develop the various cultures in South Africa will require enormous human and financial resources. Such resources may well be far beyond the means of the individuals and groups concerned. If Article 27 provides only for the non-prohibition or protection of the right to culture, it may well be that the right to culture cannot be fully enjoyed. In other words, mere protection of equal rights to culture at the juridical level may allow the rich to develop their culture, while the poor cannot do the same. But, it seems that no positive action is imposed on the state by Article 27. In the European Court of Human Rights in the *Belgian Linguistics* case of 1968 it was held that Belgium was not obliged under Article 2 of the First Protocol of the European Convention on Human Rights (which provides that no person shall be denied the right to education) to provide education in French where parents did not wish their children to be educated in Flemish. Since Articles 2 and 27 are similarly worded, it may be that Article 27 would also be construed as conferring only a negative right on individuals to participate freely in culture.

But if this view is wrong, and the state is indeed required by Article 27 to support and fund culture actively, problems may arise. It is clear that public funds should not be used to promote a culture which practises discrimination, for this would infringe the other human rights which are enshrined in the Declaration. But for example, should the state, in an attempt to ensure equal opportunities for all cultures, prohibit all private cultural organizations and provide instead free state-run institutions to cater for all cultures? If so, should the state fund the implementation of cultural rights at the expense of first generation rights? Would the state not be tempted to favour the culture of the majority political party in government as the 'official' culture so that the culture of minority political groups would be disadvantaged in practice? Is not the monopoly of culture by a government anti-democratic, even where such a government is democratically elected? Many examples could be cited where a state like South Africa has supported or suppressed culture in accordance with a political ideology. On the other hand, should the state set up schools of cultural programmes in order to strengthen respect for the various cultures? Whatever the meaning of Article 27, state involvement in the development of culture is a reality. It is also a necessity to some extent. But whenever it occurs, an important concern should be to avoid a type of cultural apartheid, of separate and unequal cultures lacking in equal opportunity.

Certain cultures have international dimensions. Where that is so, does the state have a duty to protect the rights of its citizens to participate in a culture to be found in another sovereign state? Where the foreign state is also a party to the Universal Declaration it may respect the right of foreigners to participate in its culture. If so, does the South African state have an obligation to fund and support its citizens in developing a culture which exists in another country as well? Conversely, what respect should be paid to foreign cultures in South Africa? In England judges have emphasized that foreign cultures must be respected, subject to notions of reasonableness and public policy. Thus foreign customs are not recognized or applied in England if they are considered repugnant or otherwise offend the conscience of the court. Why should South African courts not be persuaded to follow this approach?

The law of the future

It is imperative that Article 27 be implemented in South Africa in a Bill of Rights. This would be the most effective means by which the rich diversity of cultural groups in South Africa could be protected. Anything short of such protection would simply be undemocratic. While such a Bill of Rights would also outlaw cultural practices which are universally objectionable, it would also allow a common culture to grow unimpeded.

31
The right to international peace and security

Article 28 *Everyone is entitled to a social and international order in which the rights and freedoms set forth in this Declaration can be fully realized.*

What this article means

The Declaration aims to secure the protection of human rights in the national legal systems of states and in the international legal order.

Article 28 uses the term 'social order' instead of 'national legal order' so as to emphasize that everyone is entitled under domestic law to the social and economic rights set out in the Declaration, as well as to the political and civil rights that it expounds. The purpose of this article, in the first place, is to make each state aware of its moral obligation to create a legal system in which these rights are respected and remedies are provided for their enforcement.

Before 1948 few states contained Bills of Rights in their constitutions. However, since 1948, many states have adopted new constitutions or amended their old constitutions to provide for the legal protection of fundamental rights and freedoms. In 1949 India and West Germany adopted constitutions with Bills of Rights. Later, as decolonization swept Asia and Africa, many new states included Bills of Rights in their constitutions. In 1982 Canada adopted a Charter of Rights and Freedoms. There can be no doubt that the Declaration has inspired many of these constitutions.

The international legal order has also changed radically to take account of this new concern for human rights. Before the Second World War there were a number of international treaties that sought to provide international protection to workers, ethnic minorities, and the people of mandated territories (such as what was then South West Africa); but there were no treaties that imposed legal obligations upon states to recognize the basic rights and freedoms of their own citizens. To make matters worse, international law still recognized the right of each state to exclusive control over its own national domain. This meant that the international community was precluded from intervening in the domestic affairs of a state to protect the citizens of that state against its own government.

The Charter of the United Nations set the scene for a new world order in Articles 55 and 56 which recognize the obligation of states to promote human rights. The Declaration took this commitment a step further by calling upon states to respect and to promote certain specific civil, political, social, and economic rights. Since then a number of regional and universal treaties have been signed which not only recognize the rights contained in the Declaration, but also provide legal machinery for the protection of these rights. In 1950 Western European states signed the European Convention on Human Rights, which creates a Commission and a court to enforce human rights. A similar convention was adopted by the Latin American States in 1969, and in 1981 the African Charter on Human and Peoples' Rights was signed.

Universal treaties, signed by large numbers of states from the different regions of the world, have been adopted to advance civil and political rights (International Covenant on Civil and Political Rights, 1966) and economic and social rights (International Covenant on Economic, Social, and Cultural Rights, 1966); and to outlaw racial discrimination (International Convention on the Elimination of all Forms of Racial Discrimination, 1966) and torture (Convention against Torture, 1984). In 1975, East and West European nations, and North American States, approved the Helsinki Final Act which seeks to establish peace and security in Europe based on respect for human rights. In this historic agreement 35 nations, including the United States and the USSR undertook to 'act in conformity with the purposes and principles of the Charter of the United Nations and with the Universal Declaration of Human Rights'.

These developments, inspired by the Declaration, have changed the nature of international law and relations. No longer can states claim that the manner in which they treat their own nationals is a domestic issue. A wide range of international agreements have 'internationalized' human rights. The methods for enforcing these rights against governments that suppress human rights are still undeveloped; but today no state can claim to be without international obligations in the field of human rights. Moreover, states that consistently violate human rights do so at their peril — as shown by the political and economic isolation of South Africa.

Principal international human rights instruments

The United Nations Charter
❏ Signed on 26 June 1945.

The Universal Declaration of Human Rights
❏ Adopted on 10 December 1948.

The International Covenant on Civil and Political Rights
❏ Completed 1954, adopted 1966, came into force 23 March 1976.

The International Covenant on Economic, Social, and Cultural Rights
❏ Completed 1954, adopted 1966, entered into force on 3 January 1976.

The European Convention on Human Rights and Fundamental Freedoms
❏ Adopted 4 November 1950, entered into force on 3 September 1953.

The European Social Charter
❏ Signed in 1961, entry into force on 26 February 1965.

The American Declaration of the Rights and Duties of Man
❏ Adopted in 1948.

The American Convention on Human Rights
❏ Signed in 1969, entry into force on 18 July 1978.

The African Charter on Human and Peoples' Rights
❏ Adopted on 26 June 1981, entry into force on 21 October 1986.

The United Nations Charter was the first multilateral treaty to deal with the whole range of human rights, and to date has the most signatories. It demonstrates the concerns of the international community to encourage and respect human rights, and begins by reaffirming its faith in fundamental human rights, the dignity and worth of human beings, the equal rights of men and women, and of nations large and small. Article 55 of the Charter states: '... the United nations shall promote ... universal respect for, and observance of, human rights and fundamental freedoms for all without distinction as to race, sex, language, or religion'.

The Universal Declaration of Human Rights, as a basic statement of human rights, continues to be the inspiration of all other human rights instruments.

The article in South African law

South Africa has until recently ignored the developments in the protection of human rights that have dominated international relations in the post-war period. Successive South African constitutions have failed to provide legal protection for human rights; and South Africa is one of the few states in the modern world that has not signed any international human rights treaty. But it has paid heavily for this approach in the form of international isolation and economic sanctions.

The law of the future

Today South African leaders accept that the new South African order must be founded on respect for human rights. Both the 1988 Constitutional Guidelines of the African National Congress and the 1989 South African Law Commission report on human rights recognize this obvious truth. When South Africa creates a legal order premised on respect for human rights and fundamental freedoms and signs the principal international human rights conventions, it will once more be admitted to the community of nations. On the domestic level, millions of South Africans will at last be able to live their lives in a society in which liberty and freedom have replaced discrimination and repression.

32
Restrictions and limitations on human rights

Article 29 (1) Everyone has duties to the community in which alone the free and full development of his personality is possible.

(2) In the exercise of his rights and freedoms, everyone shall be subject only to such limitations as are determined by law solely for the purpose of securing due recognition and respect for the rights and freedoms of others and of meeting the just requirements of morality, public order and the general welfare in a democratic society.

What this article means

Article 29 can only be understood in the context of the rest of the Universal Declaration. Articles 1 and 2, arguably the fundamental articles of the Declaration, emphasize the *individual* as the bearer of rights and freedoms. In doing so, attention is given to the individual's desire for liberty and legal personality. Individuals, however, also live in communities and are capable of both compassion and cruelty. Reconciling the needs of communal life with the liberty of the individual is therefore a fundamental philosophical and political problem which has to be addressed. It is for this reason that the Declaration closes with Articles 29 and 30, which deal with this and related problems.

In Article 1 it is stated that people 'should act towards one another in a spirit of brotherhood.' This ideal is unfortunately seldom realized. Although the world is becoming increasingly unified on a technological level, it is in so many other ways divided. The essence of the approach in Article 29(1) is that whatever people's feelings, they have a *duty* to those around them. This is to be performed in return for the freedoms and rights people exercise as individuals.

What is the nature of this duty to the community? On one level it means a duty to recognize the rights of others, and perhaps also to tolerate the differences which those very rights allow. On another level it means an acceptance that individual rights have to be subject to limitations. It is very interesting to note, however, that nowhere does the Declaration state that performing one's duty is a pre-condition for enjoying one's rights. This is perhaps understandable since, although human rights belong to individuals, protection of these rights is the obligation of the state.

The state as supreme power must enact and enforce laws which will maximize the protection of a person's rights. Obviously this will have to mean placing limits on the power of the state itself, since it is from the supreme power of the state that people need the most effective protection. In Article 29(2) the basis on which limitations should take place are set out. These are 'the just requirements of morality, public order and the general welfare in a democratic society.' It is against this yardstick that the acceptability of any limitation on individual freedom should be measured. In imposing limitations the state should have to show that it actually had good reasons for doing so. It is not enough that people high in government *thought* they had good reasons. This distinction is important because state tyranny has sometimes sought justification on grounds best described as paternalistic. In South Africa this distinction should not be forgotten; for decades people's freedoms were removed supposedly in order to do what was best for them.

Article 29(2) also requires that any limitations must be determined by law. These words are important because they prohibit the use of arbitrary or unproclaimed rules by the government. It also means that the content of the law which imposes limitations should not only be made available to those affected by it, but must be clearly understandable. Furthermore, any limitation imposed upon an individual must be narrowly and strictly interpreted by the courts.

How does one define a concept such as 'morality' in order to give effect to Article 29; and, is it acceptable that a human rights document, which is intended for international application, espouse a particular political philosophy — democracy? In regard to the latter question one can say that democracy is perhaps humankind's best attempt to have both good government and personal liberty. The Declaration promotes pluralism, tolerance, and broadmindedness — the hallmarks of democratic society. While democracy could produce a tyranny by the majority, this would be an abuse of democracy. As Paul Sieghart states:

> Although individual interests must on occasion be
> subordinated to those of a group, democracy does not simply

mean that the views of a majority must always prevail: a balance must be achieved which ensures the fair and proper treatment of minorities and avoids any abuse of a dominant position.

A democratic attitude on the part of the state can perhaps therefore be seen as a pre-condition for the exercise of human rights.

With regard to the first question, the morality of the society as a whole, as well as the morality of an individual or group of individuals, needs to be considered. Here, the role of the courts will be central in interpreting the 'just requirements of morality' at the time.

The article in South African law

The apartheid system has over the years imposed more illegitimate limitations on human rights than could ever be mentioned here. It has also stunted the growth of the idea of all South African people living as one community. This has been done by underlining racial, ethnic, and tribal divisions, and by enforcing geographic isolation and separate facilities such as schools. Little opportunity has existed to build common interests, hopes, ideals, and morals.

South Africans need to search for and identify values they hold in common rather than those which differentiate between different groups of people.

The law of the future

A future South Africa must be free from a system which minimizes self-esteem and opportunity. Only then will people begin to develop a broader sense of community, which will in turn work to the benefit of all. A society which allows and encourages self-fulfilment is a society which will survive because its own citizens will strive to ensure its survival. It is important, however, that human freedoms be protected in a Bill of Rights. This document must include a prohibition against limiting rights further than is absolutely necessary to give 'recognition and respect for the rights and freedoms of others'.

Postscript: derogation

One further matter remains to be discussed. Article 29 deals with limitation of rights but not with what is known as 'derogation of rights'. When a right is limited it means that it is not absolute, that there are in fact limitations which are necessary in a just and democratic society. Derogation describes the practice of restricting rights in situations of public emergency or public need. Some rights can never be subject to derogation: examples include the freedoms from slavery and arbitrary deprivation of life, which can never be 'cancelled', even in time of national emergency.

In other situations derogation can take place without destroying the foundations of the system. Sometimes derogation is for the benefit of society. One example is the expropriation of property to widen a dangerous public road. Another is restricting freedom of movement to prevent the spread of contagious disease. Derogation should only arise in exceptional circumstances, and should be temporary in nature.

Although the Declaration does not deal with this question, many other human rights documents do. These documents are most concerned with derogation in a political context and try to establish the limits within which derogating measures may be permitted. Derogation clauses normally place these limits at actual or imminent public emergency, a threat to the life of the community as a whole, or an exceptional crisis which cannot be dealt with using the ordinary measures available to the state. Derogation should only be used strictly to deal with the emergency itself, and a court must be given wide powers to review the state's actions to prevent abuse.

33
Abuse of human rights

Article 29 (3) These rights and freedoms may in no case be exercised contrary to the purposes and principles of the United Nations.

Article 30 Nothing in this Declaration may be interpreted as implying for any state, group or person any right to engage in any activity or to perform any act aimed at the destruction of any of the rights and freedoms set forth herein.

What these articles mean

Articles 29(3) and 30 are designed to prevent states and individuals from using human rights for an improper purpose. As with other legal rights, human rights must be exercised in good faith: any attempt to exercise them for an improper purpose constitutes an abuse of those rights and is prohibited.

In terms of these articles an improper purpose is present when the right is exercised contrary to the principles of the United Nations; or when it is exercised with the aim of destroying any of the human rights contained in the Universal Declaration. The effect of the articles is to prohibit anyone taking advantage of the rights guaranteed under the Declaration to carry out acts aimed at depriving other people of their rights.

An example of an abuse of human rights is this: a group of individuals form a political party which aims to establish a dictatorship in which citizens are to be deprived of human rights. Although the individuals in this group have the human rights to freedom of thought (Article 18), opinion, expression (Article 19), and association (Article 20(1)), Articles 29(3) and 30 prohibit them from using these rights for an improper purpose. The promotion of a dictatorship offends the purposes and principles of the United Nations — which centres on the promotion of an international society in which all human beings enjoy just treatment — and a dictatorship denies its subjects human rights. Therefore the members of the political party are abusing their human rights by advocating a dictatorship.

If a state were to ban the political party, its members could therefore be prevented from relying on their rights to freedom of expression and association because they had used those rights for an improper purpose. To give members of the political party the protection of Articles 18, 19, and 20 — so that they could encourage a situation in which people were denied human rights — would defeat the whole purpose of the Declaration.

On the basis of an article (like Article 30) in the Council of Europe Convention for the Protection of Human Rights and Fundamental Freedoms, the European Commission of Human Rights (EUCM) upheld a German court's decision to dissolve the German Communist Party. The EUCM did not consider the dissolution of the German Communist Party as contrary to the rights and freedoms guaranteed under the Convention because the aim of the party was the establishment of a dictatorship and, therefore, would mean the suppression of the rights and freedoms of the Convention.

The human rights of freedom of opinion and expression (Article 19) are also abused when a person argues that other people should be denied human rights. Because this is an abuse, it may not be a denial of the right to freedom of speech if such a person is prevented from putting forward these views publicly.

The prohibition on the abuse of human rights is of particular relevance in South Africa. Supporters of racism and apartheid policy constantly abuse their rights to freedom of speech in terms of international law. Statements of support for racism have been held by the International Court of Justice to be contrary to the purposes and principles of the United Nations and amount to a denial of a person's right not to be discriminated against on the basis of race or colour (Articles 2, 7, and 23(2)). For this reason, one may argue that supporters of apartheid are correctly excluded when they are denied the right to address audiences inside South Africa and abroad. This has indeed happened at various universities, especially outside South Africa.

The position in South African law

Given the obvious disregard for human rights in apartheid legislation, it is not surprising that provisions guarding against the abuse of human rights are difficult to find in South African law. Yet

Some major apartheid laws still in force*

Some of these laws are fundamental to the apartheid order, while others contain provisions which allow people to be treated in a racially discriminatory way. All these laws (along with others not listed here) will have to be repealed or amended before apartheid can be said to be completely eradicated. Some of these laws depend for their operation on other racial statutes, while many permit the making of racially discriminatory regulations, which have the same force as ordinary laws.

Black Administration Act 38 of 1927
Black Affairs Act 55 of 1959
Black Authorities Act 68 of 1951
Black Communities Development Act 4 of 1984
Black Land Act 27 of 1913
Black Local Authorities Act 102 of 1982
Coloured Persons Education Act 47 of 1963
Coloured Persons Settlement Act 7 of 1946
Community Development Act 3 of 1966
Development Trust and Land Act 18 of 1936
Education and Training Act 90 of 1979
Electoral Act 45 of 1979
Free Settlement Areas Act 102 of 1988
Group Areas Act 36 of 1966
Identification Act 72 of 1986
Indian Advanced Technical Education Act 12 of 1968
Indian Education Act 61 of 1965
National States Citizenship Act 26 of 1970
Population Registration Act 30 of 1950
Promotion of Development of National States Act 46 of 1968
Provincial Government Act 32 of 1961
Referendums Act 108 of 1983
Republic of South Africa Constitution Act 110 of 1983
Rural Coloured Areas Act 24 of 1963
Self Governing Territories Act 21 of 1971
Status of Bophuthatswana Act 89 of 1977
Status of Ciskei Act 110 of 1981
Status of Transkei Act 100 of 1976
Status of Venda Act 107 of 1979
Technikons (Education and Training) Act 27 of 1981
Transvaal Asiatic Land Tenure Amendment Act 30 of 1963

*Most of these laws have been amended many times, but the amending statutes are not listed here.

it is interesting to note that the Internal Security Act of 1982 (which itself permits the violation of certain fundamental human rights) also contains provisions against the abuse of human rights. Of note is section 5(1)(f) which provides that if the Minister of Law and Order is satisfied that any publication expresses views which are calculated to cause or encourage feelings of hostility between different population groups of the Republic, he may prohibit the book or magazine from being published.

Even though this law seems to prohibit the publication of racially inflammatory speech (and therefore prevents the abuse of the right to freedom of speech) it would be wrong to assume a right to free speech in South Africa (see Chapter 20).

The law of the future

If South Africa is ever to become a society in which human rights are guaranteed, it is important that some provision be made to guard against the abuse of these rights. In the Constitutional Guidelines of the African National Congress (ANC), the organization proposes that the state guarantee, amongst others, the right to free thought and association. However, in order to prevent the abuse of these rights, the ANC expressly provides that advocating or practising racism, fascism, Nazism, or inciting ethnic or regional exclusiveness will be outlawed.

This means that where a party is formed which, for example, argues for racism, it would be prevented from participating in the political system because it would be abusing its right of free thought and association. A policy of racism denies people their fundamental right not to be discriminated against on the grounds of race. To allow a party to advocate racism would defeat the purpose of the state in guaranteeing people the right to be free from racial discrimination.

In the ANC's Guidelines the advocacy or practice of sexism and homophobia are abuses which are not prohibited. Perhaps a general clause similar to that of Articles 29(3) and 30 may therefore be better. This would allow the judiciary, in future years, to decide what other forms of prejudice should be prohibited.

Articles 29(3) and 30 are important provisions because they reinforce the protection of human rights. The aim of human rights is to encourage respect for humanity and, therefore, any attempts to undermine this purpose must be prohibited.

Glossary

African customary marriage: A marriage conducted according to African custom; the marriage differs in many respects from a civil law marriage and is given only limited recognition by the legal system.

alien: A person who is a citizen of a foreign state.

antenuptial contract: A written document, certified in a special way, which specifies aspects of the marital relationship; most commonly it governs matters affecting the ownership and division of property, and **marital power**.

anti-discrimination instruments: Laws which prohibit the practice of discrimination in various forms.

arbitrary arrest and detention: The arrest and detention in prison of a person for insufficient reason or on grounds not permitted by law.

associational rights: Rights of persons to associate freely with other people of their choice.

autonomous institution: An institution independent of, and not accountable to, another institution or person for the work it does; e.g. a court of law in the process of making judgments.

bargain in good faith: To bargain honestly, and with the serious intention of reaching an agreement.

bargaining unit: A group of workers on behalf of whom a union is entitled to conclude an agreement.

Bill of Rights: A legal document, usually, but not necessarily, part of a country's constitution, which stipulates which basic human rights are recognized in the country and therefore should be protected by the courts.

capital offence/crime: An offence/crime, punishment for which carries the death penalty.

collective bargaining: The process of bargaining between management and workers; in this bargaining relationship the union acts as an agent for the group of workers; the process almost always takes place independently of any state interference and can take place around any issues of mutual interest to both employers and workers.

common law: That part of South African law which had its origins in the Roman-Dutch law and, to some extent, English law; it is regarded as unwritten (as opposed to **statute law**) and is different from African customary law, the origins of which pre-dated white colonization.

constituent state: A state which is part of a larger political grouping of states which make up, e.g., a federation such as the USA.

constitutional crisis of legitimacy: A crisis which arises within a state when there is significant opposition to the laws and government, usually because the latter is not regarded as properly representative.

constitutional protection: This is a broad description for any kind of protection contained in a constitution which aims to check the authority of the state in the interests of the individual; one such form of protection could be a **Bill of Rights**.

court-martial conviction: The finding or pronouncement of guilty by a military court.

deportation: Expulsion of a non-citizen from a country.

disenfranchisement: The removal of the right to vote.

due process: Procedures carried out in accordance with established legal rules; the term is similar to **rule of law**.

enact laws: The process of law-making by parliament, followed by promulgation (publication).

equal suffrage: Equality of voting, i.e. a system in which all persons have an equal right to vote; *see also* **universal suffrage**.

expropriation: The compulsory deprivation of a person's right in land and usually, but not necessarily, with compensation.

extradition: The process in terms of which a person is handed over on request by one country to another; to be tried for crimes alleged to have been committed in the requesting country.

first generation rights: Civil and political rights such as the right to life, equal treatment, and freedom of movement, expression, and religion.

group areas: Land and buildings which may be owned or occupied only by persons who are regarded as belonging to a particular race group; in accordance with the Group Areas Act 36 of 1966.

in community of property: *see* **marriage in community of property**.

inalienable rights: Rights which may not be alienated, i.e. taken away or interfered with by any state organ.

independent judiciary: A system of courts and judges (or other judicial officers) which is said to be independent of the government so that its decisions are not influenced by the government or any other persons or institutions.

interdict: An order given by a court, sometimes as a result of an urgent request, which prevents a person from performing an action regarded as potentially harmful to the person making the request.

judicial commission of inquiry: A special inquiry ordered by the government to establish the facts of a controversial event, or to investigate something of importance, and to make recommendations to the government; headed by a judge, who may be assisted by other commissioners and who has powers to order the attendance of witnesses and to secure other kinds of evidence.

judicial execution: The process of killing a person who has been sentenced to death by a judge.

judicial punishment: The punishment, e.g. hanging, imprisonment, fine, ordered by a judge after finding a person guilty of a crime.

judiciary: Collectively, the judges in office.

juridical: Relating to the law or concerning judicial procedures.

jurisdiction: Generally, the power of a court, both with regard to area and type of authority, to hear disputes and to make orders.

jurisprudence: This word has two meanings: (1) the philosophy of law; (2) a body of legal principles used by e.g. the courts; the word is used in the second sense in this book.

justiciable: Subject to the **jurisdiction** of the court, capable of being dealt with and pronounced upon in legal proceedings.

lead evidence: The presentation of evidence before a court, nearly always by the examination (and cross-examination) of witnesses appearing in person.

legal capacity: The ability to act (e.g. sign a contract, make a will, marry, etc.) in a way which will be recognized as valid in terms of the law.

legal personality: The condition of being recognized by the law as being capable of performing legal acts (*see* **legal capacity**).

legislative: Relating to the **legislature**.

legislature: the state body which is responsible for making laws, e.g. parliament.

legitimate: In the context of this book, an institution (e.g. court, parliament, government) which is regarded as authentic, representative, or democratic.

marital power: The rights which a husband possesses to decide on matters concerning the marriage and the family; also, the rights of the husband over the person and property of his wife.

marriage in community of property: A marriage in which the property of the spouses (land, belongings, money) is pooled; when the relationship ends on death or divorce, each partner is entitled to one half share of the joint estate.

means test: An assessment carried out to determine a person's income, assets, and liabilities, for the purpose of deciding whether he or she qualifies for support (legal, financial, etc.).

naturalization: The legal process by which a person, previously an **alien** is granted the nationality of the country concerned.

positive law: The rules of law actually in force, distinguishable from rules of morality or religion.

procedural protections: Legal principles which prescribe that a legal process takes place in a certain way; these protections are usually for the benefit of the individual in that they prevent the abuse of power by public authorities.

pro deo **counsel:** An advocate, paid by the state, to defend a person charged with a crime before the Supreme Court.

proportional representation: An electoral system which can take various forms; typically, the number of seats in parliament obtained by a political party is allocated on the basis of the party's overall support country-wide, e.g. if a party obtains 35 per cent of the popular vote, it will receive 35 per cent of the seats in parliament.

proviso: A clause in a legal document which begins with the words 'provided that —'; similar to a condition.

ratify: Approve a decision or agreement which has previously been made.

recover damages: The process of gaining compensation, as a result of a court order, for a loss or harm that has been suffered.

repeal: The act of abolishing a **statute**.

rights culture: A tradition of respect for the rights of other people; where the **rule of law** is ignored or abused and people fail to assert their rights, this may be evidence of the absence of a rights culture.

rule of law: The notion that individuals and society are best served in a system in which rights are fairly and equally respected by everyone, including officials of the state; the notion that society is best governed under fair and equal laws, rather than at the arbitrary whim of state officials.

second generation rights: Typically, economic and social rights to food, clothing, shelter, and education; also known as socio-economic rights and distinguishable from civil and political rights (**first generation rights**).

sovereign: Supreme, unlimited in power; a sovereign parliament is one which can make any laws it chooses, unrestrained by a **Bill of Rights**; or other **constitutional protections**; a sovereign parliament is restrained only by its own procedures.

statute/statute law: Laws made by the **legislature**.

statutory conciliation: A preliminary step in the statutory procedures provided in the Labour Relations Act of 1956 for the resolution of industrial disputes; the aim of statutory conciliation is to resolve disputes through **collective bargaining** rather than through industrial action or court procedures.

statutory institutions: Boards, committees, organizations, etc. established by **statute**.

treasonable activities: Activities which amount to treason, i.e. activities aimed at overthrowing the state.

unfair labour practice: Any practice in the industrial arena which the Industrial Court decides to be unfair; the Industrial Court exercises its **jurisdiction** in terms of the definition of 'unfair labour practice' in the Labour Relations Act 28 of 1956.

universal suffrage: A system in which each adult person has an equal vote in parliamentary elections; *see also* **equal suffrage**.

veto: The right to reject a statute in the process of being enacted, having the effect of defeating the proposed law.

Selected reading list

Brownlie, I. (ed.) *Basic Documents on Human Rights* (1981) Clarendon Press

Cranston, M. *What are Human Rights?* (1973) Bodley Head

Dugard, J. *Human Rights and the South African Legal Order* (1978) Princeton University Press

Henkin, L. (ed.) *The International Bill of Rights* (1981) Columbia University Press

Henkin, L. *The Rights of Man Today* (1979) Steven & Sons

Mathews, A. S. *Freedom, State Security and the Rule of Law* (1986) Juta

Meron, T. *Human Rights Law-making in the United Nations* (1986) Clarendon Press

Meron, T. (ed.) *Human Rights in International Law* (1985) Oxford University Press

Ramcharan, B. G. (ed.) *Human Rights: Thirty Years After the Universal Declaration* (1979) Martinus Nijhoff

Robertson, M. K. (ed.) *South African Human Rights and Labour Law Yearbook 1990* (1990) Oxford University Press

Rycroft, A. *et al.* (eds.) *Race and the Law in South Africa* (1987) Juta

Sieghart, P. *The International Law of Human Rights* (1983) Oxford University Press

Sieghart, P. *The Lawful Rights of Mankind* (1985) Oxford University Press

South African Institute of Race Relations *Race Relations Survey* (1985), (1986), (1987/8)

South African Law Commission *Working Paper 25 Project 58: Group and Human Rights* (1989)

Appendix 1
The ANC's Freedom Charter

Preamble
We, the people of South Africa, declare for all our country and the world to know:

That South Africa belongs to all who live in it, black and white, and that no government can justly claim authority unless it is based on the will of the people;

That our people have been robbed of their birthright to land, liberty and peace by a form of government founded on injustice and inequality;

That our country will never be prosperous or free until all our people live in brotherhood, enjoying equal rights and opportunities;

That only a democratic state, based on the will of the people, can secure to all their birthright without distinction of colour, race, sex or belief;

And therefore, we, the people of South Africa, black and white, together — equals, countrymen and brothers — adopt this Freedom Charter. And we pledge ourselves to strive together, sparing nothing of our strength and courage, until the democratic changes here set out have been won.

The people shall govern
Every man and woman shall have the right to vote for and stand as a candidate for all bodies which make laws;

All the people shall be entitled to take part in the administration of the country;

The rights of the people shall be the same regardless of race, colour or sex;

All bodies of minority rule, advisory boards, councils and authorities shall be replaced by democratic organs of self-government.

All national groups shall have equal rights
There shall be equal status in the bodies of state, in the courts and in the schools for all national groups and races;

All national groups shall be protected by law against insults to their race and national pride;

All people shall have equal rights to use their own language and to develop their own folk culture and customs;

All apartheid laws and practices shall be put aside.

The people shall share in the country's wealth
The national wealth of our country, the heritage of all South Africans, shall be restored to the people;

The mineral wealth beneath the soil, the banks and monopoly industry shall be transferred to the ownership of the people as a whole;

All other industries and trade shall be controlled to assist the well-being of the people;

All people shall have equal rights to trade where they choose, to manufacture and to enter all trades, crafts and professions.

The land shall be shared amongst those who work it
Restriction of land ownership on a racial basis shall be ended, and all the land redivided amongst those who work it, to banish famine and land hunger;
The state shall help the peasants with implements, seed, tractors and dams to save the soil and assist the tillers;
Freedom of movement shall be guaranteed to all who work on the land;
All shall have the right to occupy land wherever they choose;
People shall not be robbed of their cattle; forced labour and farm prisons shall be abolished.

All people shall be equal before the law
No one shall be imprisoned, deported or restricted without fair trial;
No one shall be condemned by the order of any Government official;
The courts shall be representative of all the people;
Imprisonment shall be only for serious crimes against the people, and shall aim at re-education, not vengeance;
The police force and army shall be open to all on an equal basis and shall be the helpers and protectors of the people;
All laws which discriminate on grounds of race, colour or belief shall be repealed;
The preaching and practice of national, race or colour discrimination and contempt shall be a punishable crime.

All shall enjoy equal human rights
The law shall guarantee to all their right to speak, to organise, to meet together, to publish, to preach, to worship and to educate their children;
The privacy of the house from police raids shall be protected by law;
All shall be free to travel without restriction from countryside to town, from province to province, and from South Africa abroad;
Pass laws, permits and all other laws restricting these freedoms shall be abolished.

There shall be work and security
All who work shall be free to form trade unions, to elect their officers and to make wage agreements with their employers;
The state shall recognise the right and duty of all to work, and to draw full unemployment benefits;
Men and women of all races shall receive equal pay for equal work;
There shall be a forty-hour working week, a national minimum wage, paid annual leave, and sick leave for all workers, and maternity leave on full pay for all working mothers;
Miners, domestic workers, farm workers and civil servants shall have the same rights as all others who work;
Child labour, compound labour, the tot system and contract labour shall be abolished.

The doors of learning and of culture shall be opened

The government shall discover, develop and encourage national talent for the enhancement of our cultural life;

All the cultural treasures of mankind shall be open to all, by free exchange of books, ideas and contacts with other lands;

The aim of education shall be to teach the youth to love their people and their culture, to honour human brotherhood, liberty and peace;

Education shall be free, compulsory, universal and equal for all children;

Higher education and technical training shall be opened to all by means of state allowances and scholarships awarded on the basis of merit;

Adult illiteracy shall be ended by a mass state education plan;

Teachers shall have all the rights of other citizens;

The colour bar in cultural life, in sport and in education shall be abolished.

There shall be houses, security and comfort

All people shall have the right to live where they choose, to be decently housed, and to bring up their families in comfort and security;

Unused housing space shall be made available to the people;

Rent and prices shall be lowered, food plentiful and no one shall go hungry;

A preventative health scheme shall be run by the state;

Free medical care and hospitilisation shall be provided for all, with special care for mothers and young children;

Slums shall be demolished and new suburbs built where all have transport, roads, lighting, playing fields, creches and social centres;

The aged, the orphans, the disabled and the sick shall be cared for by the state;

Rest, leisure and recreation shall be the right of all;

Fenced locations and ghettos shall be abolished, and laws which break up families shall be repealed.

There shall be peace and friendship

South Africa shall be a fully independent state, which respects the rights and sovereignty of all nations;

South Africa shall strive to maintain world peace and the settlement of all international disputes by negotiation — not war;

Peace and friendship amongst all our people shall be secured by upholding the equal rights, opportunities and status of all;

The people of the protectorates — Basutoland, Bechuanaland and Swaziland — shall be free to decide for themselves their own future;

The right of all the peoples of Africa to independence and self-government shall be recognised, and shall be the basis of close co-operation.

Let all who love their people and their country now say, as we say here;

'These freedoms we will fight for, side by side, throughout our lives, until we have won our liberty.'

Appendix 2
The ANC's Constitutional Guidelines for a Democratic South Africa

The Freedom Charter, adopted in 1955 by the Congress of the People at Kliptown near Johannesburg, was the first systematic statement in the history of our country of the political and constitutional vision of a free, democratic and non-racial South Africa.

The Freedom Charter remains today unique as the only South African document of its kind that adheres firmly to democratic principles as accepted throughout the world. Among South Africans it has become by far the most widely accepted programme for a post-apartheid country. The stage is now approaching where the Freedom Charter must be converted from a vision for the future into a constitutional reality.

We in the African National Congress submit to the people of South Africa, and to all those throughout the world who wish to see an end to apartheid, our basic guidelines for the foundations of government in post-apartheid South Africa. Extensive and democratic debate on these guidelines will mobilise the widest sections of the population to achieve agreement on how to put an end to the tyranny and oppression under which our people live, thus enabling them to lead normal and decent lives as free citizens in a free country.

The immediate aim is to create a just and democratic society that will sweep away the centuries-old legacy of colonial conquest and white domination, and abolish all laws imposing racial oppression and discrimination. The removal of discriminatory laws and eradication of all vestiges of the illegitimate regime are, however, not enough; the structures and the institutions of apartheid must be dismantled and be replaced by democratic ones. Steps must be taken to ensure that apartheid ideas and practices are not permitted to appear in old forms or new.

In addition, the effects of centuries of racial domination and inequality must be overcome by constitutional provisions for corrective action which guarantees a rapid and irreversible redistribution of wealth and opening up of facilities to all. The Constitution must also be such as to promote the habits of non-racial and non-sexist thinking, the practice of anti-racist behaviour and the acquisition of genuinely shared patriotic consciousness.

The Constitution must give firm protection to the fundamental human rights of all citizens. There shall be equal rights for all individuals, irrespective of race, colour, sex or creed. In addition, it requires the entrenching of equal cultural, linguistic and religious rights for all.

Under the conditions of contemporary South Africa 87% of land and 95% of the instruments of production of the country are in the hands of the ruling class, which is solely drawn from the white community. It follows, therefore, that constitutional protection for group rights would perpetuate the status quo and would mean that the mass of the people would continue to be constitutionally trapped in poverty and remain as outsiders in the land of their birth.

Finally, success of the Constitution will be, to a large extent, determined by the degree to which it promotes conditions for the active involvement of all sectors of the population at all levels of government and in the economic and cultural life. Bearing these fundamental objectives in mind, we declare that the elimination of apartheid and the creation of a truly just and democratic South Africa requires a Constitution based on the following principles:

The State

a South Africa shall be an independent, unitary, democratic and non-racial state.

b Sovereignty shall belong to the people as a whole and shall be exercised through one central legislature, executive, judiciary and administration. Provision shall be made for the delegation of the powers of the central authority to subordinate administrative units for purposes of more efficient administration and democratic participation.

c The institution of hereditary rulers and chiefs shall be transformed to serve the interests of the people as a whole in conformity with the democratic principles embodied in the constitution.

d All organs of government, including justice, security and armed forces, shall be representative of the people as a whole, democratic in the structure and functioning, and dedicated to defending the principles of the constitution.

Franchise

e In the exercise of their sovereignty, the people shall have the right to vote under a system of universal suffrage based on the principle of one person/one vote.

f Every voter shall have the right to stand for election and be elected to all legislative bodies.

National identity

g It shall be state policy to promote the growth of a single national identity and loyalty binding on all South Africans. At the same time, the state shall recognise the linguistic and cultural diversity of the people and provide facilities for free linguistic and cultural development.

Bill of Rights and affirmative action

h The Constitution shall include a Bill of Rights based on the Freedom Charter. Such a Bill of Rights shall guarantee the fundamental human rights of all citizens, irrespective of race, colour, sex or creed, and shall provide appropriate mechanisms for their protection and enforcement.

i The state and all social institutions shall be under a constitutional duty to eradicate race discrimination in all its forms.

j The state and all social institutions shall be under a constitutional duty to take active steps to eradicate, speedily, the economic and social inequalities produced by racial discrimination.

k The advocacy or practice of racism, fascism, nazism or the incitement of ethnic or regional exclusiveness shall be outlawed.

l Subject to clauses (i) and (k) above, the democratic state shall guarantee the basic rights and freedoms, such as freedom of association, thought, worship and the press. Furthermore, the state shall have the duty to protect the right to work and guarantee the right to education and social security.

m All parties which conform to the provision of (i) to (k) above shall have the legal right to exist and to take part in the political life of the country.

Economy

n The state shall ensure that the entire economy serves the interests and well-being of the entire population.

o The state shall have the right to determine the general context in which economic life takes place and define the limit to the rights and obligations attaching to the ownership and use of productive capacity.

p The private sector of the economy shall be obliged to co-operate with the state in realising the objectives of the Freedom Charter in promoting social well-being.

q The economy shall be a mixed one, with a public sector, a private sector, a co-operative sector and a small-scale family sector.

r Co-operative forms of economic enterprise, village industries and small-scale family activities shall be supported by the state.

s The state shall promote the acquisition of management, technical and scientific skills among all sections of the population, especially the blacks.

t Property for personal use and consumption shall be constitutionally protected.

Land

u The state shall devise and implement a land reform programme that will include and address the following issues: Abolition of all racial restrictions on ownership and use of land; Implementation of land reform in conformity with the principle of affirmative action, taking into account the status of victims of forced removals.

Workers

v A charter protecting workers' trade union rights, especially the right to strike and collective bargaining, shall be incorporated into the Constitution.

Women

w Women shall have equal rights in all spheres of public and private life and the state shall take affirmative action to eliminate inequalities and discrimination between the sexes.

The family

n The family, parenthood and children's rights shall be protected.

International

y South Africa shall be a non-aligned state committed to the principles of the Charter of the OAU and the Charter of the UN and to the achievement of national liberation, liberation, world peace and disarmament.

Appendix 3
The ANC's Bill of Rights for a Democratic South Africa (Working Draft for Consultation)

Article 1. General
1. All South Africans are born free and equal in dignity and rights.
2. No individual or group shall receive privileges or be subjected to discrimination, domination or abuse on the grounds of race, colour, language, gender, creed, political or other opinion, birth or other status.
3. All men and women shall have equal protection under the law.

Article 2. Personal rights

The right to life
1. Every person has the right to life.
2. No-one shall be arbitrarily deprived of his or her life.
3. Capital punishment is abolished and no further executions shall take place.

The right to dignity
4. No-one shall be subjected to slavery, servitude or forced labour, provided that forced labour shall not include work normally required of someone carrying out a sentence of a court, nor military service or national service by a conscientious objector, nor services required in the case of calamity or serious emergency, nor any work which forms part of normal civil obligations.
5. The dignity of all persons shall be respected.
6. No-one shall be subjected to torture or cruel, inhuman or degrading treatment or punishment.
7. Everyone shall have the right to appropriate protection by law against violence, harassment or abuse, or the impairment of his or her dignity.

The right to a fair trial
8. There shall be no detention without trial.
9. No persons shall be arrested or detained for any purpose other than that of bringing them to trial on a criminal charge.
10. Arrest shall take place according to procedures laid down by law, and persons taken into custody shall immediately be informed of the

charges against them, shall have access to a legal representative of their choice, and shall be brought before court within 48 hours or, where that would be a Sunday or a public holiday, on the first working day thereafter.

11. Bail shall be granted to awaiting-trail persons unless a court rules that in the interests of justice they should be kept in custody.
12. No-one shall be deprived of liberty or subjected to other punishment except after a fair trial in public by an independent court.
13. Trials shall take place within a reasonable time.
14. Everyone shall be presumed innocent until proven guilty.
15. No conduct shall be punished if it was not a criminal offence at the time of its occurrence, and no penalty shall be increased retrospectively.
16. No-one shall be punished twice for the same offence.
17. Accused persons shall be informed in writing of the nature of the allegations against them, and shall be given adequate time to prepare and conduct their defence.
18. Everything that is reasonable shall be done to ensure that accused persons understand the nature and the import of the charges against them and of the proceedings, that they are not prejudiced through illiteracy or lack of understanding, and that they receive a fair trial.
19. Accused persons shall have the right to challenge all evidence presented against them, to be defended by a legal practitioner of their choice, and if in custody, to have access to a legal practitioner at all reasonable times.
20. If a person is unable to pay for legal representation, and the interests of justice so require, the State shall provide or pay for a competent defence.
21. No persons shall be required to give evidence against themselves, nor, except in cases of domestic violence or abuse, shall persons be required to give evidence against their spouses, whether married by civil law or custom, their parents or their children.
22. No evidence obtained through torture or cruel, inhuman or degrading treatment shall be admissible in any proceedings.
23. Juveniles shall be separated from adult offenders.

The right to judicial review

24. Any person adversely affected by an administrative or executive act shall have the right to have the matter reviewed by an independent court or tribunal on the grounds of abuse of authority, going beyond the powers granted by law, bad faith, or such gross unreasonableness in relation to the procedure or the decision as to amount to manifest justice.

The right to home life

25. No-one shall be deprived of or removed from his or her home on the

grounds of race, colour, language, gender or creed.

26. The privacy of the home shall be respected, save that reasonable steps shall be permitted to prevent domestic violence or abuse.

27. People shall have the right to establish families, live together with partners of their choice and to marry.

28. Marriage shall be based upon the free consent of the partners, and spouses shall enjoy equal rights at and during the marriage and after its dissolution.

The right to privacy

29. No search or entry shall be permitted except for reasonable cause, as prescribed by law, and as would be acceptable in an open and democratic society.

30. Interference with private communications, spying on persons, and the compilation and keeping of secret files about them without their consent, shall not be permissible save as authorised by law in circumstances that would be acceptable in an open and democratic society.

The right of movement

31. Everyone shall have the right to move freely and reside in any part of the country, to receive a passport, travel abroad and to emigrate or return if he or she wishes.

The right to conscience

32. The right to conscience shall be inviolate, and no-one shall be penalised for his or her beliefs.

Article 3. Political rights

1. South Africa shall be a multi-party democracy in which all men and women shall enjoy basic political rights on an equal basis.

2. Government at all levels shall be subject to the principles of accountability to the electorate.

3. Elections shall be conducted in accordance with an electoral law which shall make no distinction on the grounds of race, colour, language, gender or creed.

4. Elections shall be regular, free and fair and based on universal franchise and a common voters' roll.

5. All men and women entitled to vote shall be entitled to stand for and occupy any position or office in any organ of government or administration.

6. All citizens shall have the right to form and join political parties and to campaign for social, economic and political change, either directly or through freely chosen representatives.

Article 4. Freedom of speech, assembly and information

1. There shall be freedom of thought, speech, expression and opinion,

including a free press which shall respect the right to reply.

2. All men and women shall have the right to assemble peacefully and without arms, and to submit petitions for the redress of grievances and injustices.

3. All men and women shall be entitled to all the information necessary to enable them to make effective use of their rights as citizens or consumers.

Article 5. Rights of association, religion, language and culture

Freedom of association

1. There shall be freedom of association, including the right to form and join trade unions, religious, social and cultural bodies, and to form and participate in non-governmental organisations.

Freedom of religion

2. There shall be freedom of worship and tolerance of all religions, and no State or official religion shall be established.

3. The institutions of religion shall be separate from the State, but nothing in this Constitution shall prevent them from co-operating with the State with a view to furthering the objectives of this Constitution, nor from bearing witness and commenting on the actions of the State.

4. Places associated with religious observance shall be respected, and no-one shall be barred from entering them on grounds of race.

Language rights

5. The languages of South Africa are Sindebele, Sepedi, Sesotho, Siswati, Setswana, Afrikaans, English, Tsonga [Shangaan], Venda, Xhosa, and Zulu.

6. The State shall act positively to further the development of these languages, especially in education, literature and the media, and to prevent the use of any language or languages for the purpose of domination or division.

7. When it is reasonable to do so, one or more of these languages may be designated as the language to be used for defined purposes at the national level or in any region or area where it is widely used.

8. Subject to the availability of public and private resources, and limitations of reasonableness, primary and secondary education should wherever possible be offered in the language or languages of preference of the students or their parents.

9. The State shall promote respect for all the languages spoken in South Africa.

Creative freedom

10. There shall be freedom of artistic activity and scientific enquiry,

without censorship, subject only to such limitations as may be imposed by law in accordance with principles generally accepted in open and democratic societies.

The right to sporting, recreational and cultural activities

11. Sporting, recreational and cultural activities shall be encouraged on a non-racial basis, drawing on the talents and creative capacities of all South Africans, and autonomous organisations may be established to achieve these objectives.

Article 6. Worker's rights

1. Workers shall have the right to form and join trade unions, and to regulate such trade unions without interference from the State.

2. Workers shall be free to join trade unions of their choice, subject only to rules of such unions and to the principles of non-discrimination set out in this Constitution, and no worker shall be victimised on account of membership of a union.

3. The right to organise and to bargain collectively on any social, economic or other matter affecting workers' interests, shall be guaranteed.

4. In the furtherance of these rights, trade unions shall be entitled to reasonable access to the premises of enterprises, to receive such information as may be reasonably necessary, and to deduct union subscriptions where appropriate.

5. No law shall prevent representative trade unions from negotiating collective agreements binding on all workers covered by such agreements.

6. Workers shall have the right to strike under law in pursuance of their social and economic interests subject to reasonable limitations in respect of the interruption of services such as would endanger the life, health or personal safety of the community or any section of the population.

7. Workers shall have the right to peaceful picketing, subject only to such reasonable conditions as would be acceptable in a democratic society.

8. Trade unions shall have the right to participate in lawful political activities.

9. Trade unions shall have the right to form national federations and to affiliate to international federations.

10. Employers shall be under a duty to provide a safe, clean and dignified work environment, and to offer reasonable pay and holidays.

11. There shall be equal pay for equal work and equal access to employment.

12. The State shall make provision by way of legislation for compensation to be paid to workers injured in the course of their

employment and for benefits to be paid to unemployed or retired workers.

Article 7. General rights

1. Men and women shall enjoy equal rights in all areas of public and private life, including employment, education and within the family.
2. Discrimination on the grounds of gender, single parenthood, legitimacy of birth or sexual orientation shall be unlawful.
3. Positive action shall be undertaken to overcome the disabilities and disadvantages suffered on account of past gender discrimination.
4. The law shall provide remedies for sexual harassment, abuse and violence.
5. Educational institutions, the media, advertising and other social institutions shall be under a duty to discourage sexual and other types of stereo-typing.

Article 8. Disabled persons

1. There shall be no discrimination against disabled persons.
2. Legislation shall provide for the progressive opening up of employment opportunities for disabled men and women and for the removal of obstacles to the enjoyment by them of public amenities and for their integration into all areas of life.

Article 9. Children

1. All children have the right to a name, to health, to security, education and equality of treatment.
2. The State shall, to the maximum of its available resources, seek to achieve progressively the full realisation of these rights.
3. No child shall suffer discrimination or enjoy privileges on the grounds of race, colour, gender, language, creed, legitimacy or the status of his or her parents.
4. In all proceedings concerning children, the primary consideration shall be the best interests of the child.
5. Children are entitled to be protected from economic exploitation and shall not be permitted to perform work that is likely to be hazardous or harmful to their education, health or moral well-being.
6. It shall be unlawful to oblige children to work or perform services for the employers of their parents or other family members.

Article 10. Social, educational, economic and welfare rights

General

1. All men and women have the right to enjoy basic social, educational, economic and welfare rights.

2. The State shall, to the maximum of its available resources, undertake appropriate legislative and executive action in order to achieve the progressive realisation of basic social, educational, economic and welfare rights for the whole population.

3. Such State action shall establish standards and procedures whereby all men, women and children are guaranteed by law a progressively expanding floor of enforceable minimum rights, with special attention to nutrition, shelter, health care, education and income.

4. In order to achieve a common floor of rights for the whole country, resources may be diverted from richer to poorer areas, and timetables may be established for the phased extension of legislation and minimum standards from area to area.

5. The State may collaborate with non-governmental organisations and the private sector in achieving these goals, and may impose appropriate responsibilities on all social and economic bodies with a view to their materialisation.

6. In circumstances where persons are unable through lack of means to avail themselves of facilities provided by the State, the State shall, wherever it is reasonable to do so, give appropriate assistance.

Freedom from hunger

7. In order to guarantee the right of freedom from hunger, the State shall ensure the introduction of minimum standards of nutrition throughout the country, with special emphasis on pre-school and school feeding.

The right to shelter

8. In order to guarantee the right to shelter, the State shall, in collaboration with private bodies where appropriate, dismantle compounds, single-sex hostels and other forms of accommodation associated with the migrant labour system, and embark upon and encourage an extensive programme of house-building.

9. The State shall take steps to ensure that energy, access to clean water and appropriate sewage and waste disposal are available to every home.

10. No eviction from homes or from land shall take place without the order of a competent court, which shall have regard to the availability of alternative accommodation.

The right to education

11. In order to guarantee the right to education, the State shall, in collaboration with non-governmental and private educational institutions where appropriate, ensure that:

- there shall be free and compulsory primary education for all, with a school-leaving age of sixteen,
- there shall be progressive expansion of access by all children as a right to secondary education,

- there shall be progressive increase in access to pre-school institutions and institutes of vocational training and of higher learning,
- there shall be increasingly extensive facilities to enable adults to overcome illiteracy and further their education.

11. Education shall be directed towards the full development of the human personality and a sense of personal dignity, and shall aim at strengthening respect for human rights and fundamental freedoms, and promoting understanding, tolerance and friendship among all South Africans and between nations.

The right to health

12. In order to guarantee the right to protection of heath, the State shall establish a comprehensive national heath service linking health workers, community organisations, State institutions, private medical schemes and individual medical practitioners so as to provide hygiene education, preventative medicine and health care delivery to all.

The right to work

13. In order to guarantee increasing enjoyment of the right to work, the State shall, in collaboration where appropriate with private bodies and non-governmental institutions:
- make technical and vocational training available to all,
- remove the barriers which keep large sections of the population out of technical, professional and managerial positions,
- and promote public and other works with a view to reducing unemployment.

The right to a minimum income and welfare rights

14. In order to guarantee the achievement of a minimum income for all, the State shall introduce a scheme of family benefits and old age pensions financed from general revenue.

15. In order to guarantee the enjoyment of basic welfare rights, in particular unemployment benefits, compensation for injury, superannuation or retirement pensions, the State shall, in collaboration where appropriate with private bodies, establish a system of national insurance based upon contributions by employers, employees and other interested persons.

Article 11. The economy, land and property

1. Legislation on economic matters shall be guided by the principle of encouraging collaboration between the State and the private, co-operative and family sectors with a view to reducing inequality, promoting growth and providing goods and services for the whole population.

2. All men and women and lawfully constituted bodies are entitled to the peaceful enjoyment of their possessions, including the right to acquire, own, or dispose of property in any part of the country without distinction based on race, colour, language, gender or creed.

3. All natural resources below and above the surface area of the land, including the air, and all forms of potential energy or minerals in the territorial waters, the continental shelf and the exclusive economic zone of South Africa, which are not owned by any person at the time of coming into force of this Constitution, shall belong to the State.

4. The State shall have the right to regulate the exploitation of natural resources, grant franchises and determine royalties, subject to payment of appropriate compensation in the event of interference with any lawfully vested interest.

5. The State may by legislation take steps to overcome the effects of past statutory discrimination in relation to enjoyment of property rights.

6. There shall be no forced removals of persons or communities from their homes or land on the basis of race, colour, language, gender or creed.

7. No persons or legal entities shall be deprived of their possessions except on grounds of public interest or public utility, including the achievement of the objectives of the Constitution.

8. Any such deprivation may be affected only by or pursuant to a law which shall provide for the nature and the extent of compensation to be paid.

9. Compensation shall be just, taking into account the need to establish an equitable balance between the public interest and the interest of those affected.

10. In the case of a dispute regarding the amount of compensation or its mode of payment, provision shall be made for recourse to a special independent tribunal, with an appeal to the courts.

11. The preceding provisions shall not be interpreted as in any way impeding the right of the State to adopt such measures as might be deemed necessary in any democratic society for the control, use or acquisition of property in accordance with the general interest, or to preserve the environment, or to regulate or curtail monopolies or to secure the payment of taxes or other contributions or penalties.

Article 12. Environmental rights

1. The environment, including the land, the waters and the sky, are the common heritage of the people of South Africa and of all humanity.

2. All men and women shall have the right to a healthy and ecologically balanced environment and the duty to defend it.

3. In order to secure this right, the State, acting through appropriate

agencies and organs shall conserve, protect and improve the environment, and in particular:

i. prevent and control pollution of the air and waters and degradation and erosion of the soil;

ii. have regard in local, regional and national planning to the maintenance or creation of balanced ecological and biological areas and to the prevention or minimising of harmful effects on the environment;

iii. promote the rational use of natural resources, safeguarding their capacity for renewal and ecological stability;

iv. ensure that long-term damage is not done to the environment by industrial or other forms of waste;

v. maintain, create and develop natural reserves, parks and recreational areas and classify and protect other sites and landscapes so as to ensure the preservation and protection of areas of outstanding cultural, historic and natural interest.

4. Legislation shall provide for co-operation between the State, non-governmental organisations, local communities and individuals in seeking to improve the environment and encourage ecologically sensible habits in daily life.

5. The law shall provide for appropriate penalties and reparation in the case of any direct and serious damage caused to the environment, and permit the interdiction by any interested person or by any agency established for the purpose of protecting the environment, of any public or private activity or undertaking which manifestly and unreasonably causes or threatens to cause irreparable damage to the environment.

Article 13. Affirmative action

1. Nothing in the Constitution shall prevent the enactment of legislation, or the adoption by any public or private body of special measures of a positive kind designed to procure the advancement and the opening up of opportunities, including access to education, skills, employment and land, and the general advancement in social, economic and cultural spheres, of men and women who in the past have been disadvantaged by discrimination.

2. No provision of the Bill of Rights shall be construed as derogating from or limiting in any way the general provisions of this Article.

Article 14. Positive action

1. In its activities and functioning, the State shall observe the principles of non-racialism and non-sexism, and encourage the same in all public and private bodies.

2. All benefits conferred and entitlements granted by the State shall be distributed on a non-racist and a non-sexist basis.

3. The State and all public and private bodies shall be under a duty to prevent any form of incitement to racial, religious or linguistic hostility and to dismantle all structures and do away with all practices that compulsorily divide the population on grounds of race, colour, language or creed.

4. With a view to achieving the above, the State may enact legislation to prohibit the circulation or possession of materials which incite racial, ethnic, religious, gender or linguistic hatred, which provoke violence, or which insult, degrade, defame or encourage abuse of any racial, ethnic, religious, gender or linguistic group.

5. All organs of the State at the national, regional and local levels shall pursue policies and programmes aimed at redressing the consequences of past discriminatory laws and practices, and at the creation of a genuine non-racial democracy in South Africa.

6. Such policies shall include the implementation of programmes aimed at achieving speedily the balanced structuring in non-racial form of the public service, defence and police forces and the prison service.

7. Without interfering with its independence, and with a view to ensuring that justice is manifestly seen to be done in a non-racial way and that the wisdom, experience and judicial skills of all South Africans are represented on the bench, the judiciary shall be transformed in such a way as to consist of men and women drawn from all sectors of South African society.

8. In taking steps to correct patterns or practices of discrimination, special attention shall be paid to rectifying the inequalities to which women in South Africa have been subjected, and to ensure their full, equal, effective and dignified participation in the political, social, economic and cultural life of the nation.

9. Legislation may be enacted requiring non-governmental organisations and private bodies to conduct themselves in accordance with the above principles.

Article 15. Limitations

1. Nothing in the Constitution shall be interpreted as implying for any group or person the right to engage in any activity or perform any act aimed at the destruction of any of the rights and freedoms set forth in the Constitution, or at their limitation or suppression to a degree other than is authorised by the Constitution itself.

2. Nothing in this Constitution should be interpreted as impeding the right of the State to enact legislation regulating the manner in which fundamental rights and freedoms shall be exercised, or limiting such rights, provided that such regulation or limitation is such as might be deemed necessary in an open and democratic society.

3. Any restrictions permitted under the Constitution to fundamental

rights and freedoms shall not be applied to or used as a cover for any purpose other than that for which they have been expressly or by necessary implication authorised.

4. Any law providing for any regulation or limitation of any fundamental right or freedom shall:

i. be of general application;

ii. not negate the essential content of the right, but simply qualify the way that right is to be exercised or the circumstances in which derogation from the right is permitted;

iii. as far as practicable, identify the specific clauses of the Constitution relied upon for the limitation of the right and the specific clauses of the Constitution affected by the legislation;

iv. specify as precisely as possible the exact reach of the limitation and the circumstances in which it shall apply.

Article 16. Enforcement

General

1. The fundamental rights and freedoms contained in this Bill of Rights shall be guaranteed by the courts.

2. Provision shall be made for the establishment of a constitutional court.

3. The terms of the Bill of Rights shall be binding upon the State and organs of government at all levels, and where appropriate, on all social institutions and persons.

4. All persons who claim that rights guaranteed them by the Bill of Rights have been infringed or threatened, shall be entitled to apply to a competent court for an order for the declaration or enforcement of their rights, or for the restraining of any act which impedes or threatens such rights.

5. Any law or executive or administrative act which violates the terms of the Bill of Rights shall be invalid to the extent of such violation, save that the Court shall have the discretion in appropriate cases to put the relevant body or official to terms as to how and within what period to remedy the violation.

Human Rights Commission

6. Parliament shall have a special responsibility for ensuring that the basic social, educational, economic and welfare rights set out in this Bill of Rights are respected.

7. Parliament shall establish by legislation a Human Rights Commission to promote observance of the Bill of Rights.

8. Such Commission shall have the right to establish agencies for investigating patterns of violation of any of the terms of the Bill of Rights and for receiving complaints and bringing proceedings in court where appropriate.

9. The Commission shall monitor proposed legislation with a view to reporting to Parliament on its impact on the realisation of the rights set out in the Bill of Rights.

Ombudsman

10. With a view to ensuring that all functions and duties under the Constitution are carried out in a fair way with due respect for the rights and sentiments of those affected, the office of Ombudsman shall be created.
11. The Ombudsman shall be independent in the carrying out of his or her functions and may open offices in different parts of the country.
12. The Ombudsman shall receive and investigate complaints from members of the public concerning abuse of power or unfair, insensitive, capricious, harsh, discourteous or unduly delayed treatment of any person by any official of government at national, regional or local level, or any attempt by such official to extort benefits or corruptly to receive favours.
13. In accordance with his or her findings, the Ombudsman may initiate legal proceedings, refer the matter for prosecution, negotiate a compromise, or make a report to the department or organ concerned containing recommendations with a view to remedying the improper conduct, preventing repetition, and, where appropriate, making amends, including compensation.
14. Recourse to the Human Rights Commission or to the Ombudsman shall not oust the jurisdiction of the courts to hear any matter.

Appendix 4
The South African Law Commission's draft Bill of Rights (Working Paper 25: Group and Human Rights)

Part A: Fundamental rights

The rights set forth in this Part are fundamental rights to which every person in the Republic of South Africa shall be entitled and, save as provided in this Bill, no legislation or executive or administrative act of any nature whatever shall infringe these rights.

Article 1
The right to life: Provided that legislation may provide for the discretionary imposition of the sentence of death in the case of the most serious crimes.

Article 2
The right to human dignity and equality before the law, which means that there shall be no discrimination on the ground of race, colour, language, sex, religion, ethnic origin, social class, birth, political or other views or any disability or other natural characteristic: Provided that such legislation or executive or administrative acts as may reasonably be necessary for the improvement, on a temporary basis, of a position in which, for historical reasons, persons or groups find themselves to be disadvantaged, shall be permissible.

Article 3
The right to a good name and reputation.

Article 4
The right to spiritual and physical integrity.

Article 5
The right to be recognised legally, economically and culturally as having rights and obligations and as having the capacity to participate in legal, commercial and cultural affairs.

Article 6
The right to privacy, which shall also mean that a person's property or place of residence or employment shall not be arbitrarily entered, that he shall not be arbitrarily searched, that his property or possessions shall

not be arbitrarily seized and that there shall be no arbitrary interference with or interception of his correspondence or any other form of communication used by him.

Article 7
The right not to be held in slavery or subjected to forced labour: Provided that legislation may provide for such labour as may be prescribed to be performed during detention resulting from a person's being sentenced to imprisonment by a court of law, or such compulsory military or civil service as may reasonably be acceptable in a democratic state.

Article 8
The right to freedom of speech and to obtain and disseminate information.

Article 9
The right freely to carry out scientific research and to practise art.

Article 10
The right to freedom of choice with regard to education and training.

Article 11
The right to the integrity of the family, freedom of marriage and the upholding of the institution of marriage.

Article 12
The right to move freely within the Republic of South Africa and therein to reside, to work, or to carry on any lawful business, occupation, trade or other activity.

Article 13
The right of every citizen not to be
(a) arbitrarily refused a passport
(b) exiled or expelled from the Republic of South Africa
(c) prevented from emigrating.

Article 14
The right freely and on an equal footing to engage in economic intercourse, which shall include the capacity to establish and maintain commercial undertakings, to procure property and means of production, to offer services against remuneration and to make a profit.

Article 15
The right to private property: Provided that legislation may in the public interest authorise expropriation against payment of reasonable compensation which shall in the event of a dispute be determined by a court of law.

Article 16
The right to associate freely with other groups and individuals.

Article 17
The right of every person or group to disassociate himself or itself from other individuals or groups: Provided that if such disassociation constitutes discrimination on the ground of race, colour, religion, language or culture, no public or state funds shall be granted directly or indirectly to promote the interests of the person who or group which so discriminates.

Article 18
The right of citizens freely to form political parties, to be members of such parties, to practise their political convictions in a peaceful manner and to be nominated and elected to legislative, executive and administrative office, and to form and become members of trade unions: Provided that no person shall be compelled to be a member of a political party or a trade union.

Article 19
The right to assemble peacefully, to hold demonstrations peacefully and to obtain and present petitions.

Article 20
(a) The right of all citizens over the age of eighteen years to exercise the vote on a basis of equality in respect of all legislative institutions at regular and periodical elections and at referendums.
(b) Subject to paragraph (a) hereof, the composition of the legislative institutions of the country shall be determined in the constitution.

Article 21
The right of every person, individually or together with others, freely to practise his culture and religion and use his language.

Article 22
The right of every person to be safeguarded from discrimination against his culture, religion or language and to be safeguarded from preferential treatment of the culture, religion or language of others: Provided that legislation may determine the official languages of a region: Provided further that when in proceedings instituted by an interested person or persons it is alleged that legislation or an executive or administrative act infringes the cultural, religious or linguistic values of any individual or group of individuals, the court shall in adjudicating such allegations have regard to the interests of other individuals or groups of individuals.

Article 23
The right to personal freedom and safety, which shall also mean that no person shall be deprived of his freedom, save in the following cases and in accordance with a generally applicable prescribed procedure whereby his fundamental rights to spiritual and physical integrity are not denied:
(a) Lawful arrest or detention of a person effected in order to cause him

to appear before a court of law on the ground of a reasonable suspicion that he has committed a crime or whenever it may on reasonable grounds be deemed necessary to prevent the commission of a crime.

(b) Lawful detention upon conviction by a court of law or for non-compliance with a lawful order of the court.

(c) Lawful detention of a person in order to prevent the spread of infectious diseases.

(d) Lawful detention of a person whom is mentally ill or one who is addicted to narcotic or addictive substances, with a view to his admission, in accordance with prescribed procedure, to an institution or rehabilitation centre.

(e) Lawful detention of a person in order to prevent his unauthorised entry into or sojourn in the Republic of South Africa or with a view to the extradition or deportation of a person in accordance with prescribed procedure.

Article 24
It shall be the right of every person under arrest —

(a) to be detained and fed under conditions consonant with human dignity:

(b) to be informed as soon as possible, in a language which he understands, of the reason for his detention and of any charge against him;

(c) to be informed as soon as possible that he has the right to remain silent and that he need not make any statement and to be warned of the consequences of making a statement;

(d) within a reasonable period of time, but not less than forty eight hours or the first court day thereafter, to be brought before a court of law and in writing to be charged or in writing to be informed of the reason for his detention, failing which he shall be entitled to be released from detention, unless a court of law, upon good cause shown, orders his further detention;

(e) within a reasonable period after his arrest, to be tried by a court of law and pending such trail to be released, which release may be subject to bail or guarantees to appear at the trial, unless a court of law, upon good cause shown, orders his further detention;

(f) to communicate and to consult with legal representatives of his choice;

(g) to communicate with and to receive, in reasonable measure, visits from his spouse, family, next of kin or friends, unless a court of law otherwise directs;

(h) not to be subjected to torture, assault or cruel or inhuman or degrading treatment.

Article 25
The right of every accused person —

(a) not to be convicted or sentenced unless a fair and public trial before a court of law has taken place in accordance with the generally applicable procedural and evidential rules;

(b) to be treated as innocent until the contrary is proved by the state;

(c) to remain silent and to refuse to testify during the trail;

(d) to be assisted by a legal representative of his choice and, if he cannot afford this, and if the case is a serious one, to be defended by a legal representative remunerated by the state;

(e) not to be sentenced to inhuman or degrading punishment;

(f) not to be convicted of an offence in respect of an act or omission which did not constitute an offence at the moment when it was done and not to receive a penalty heavier than that which was applicable at the time when the offence was committed;

(g) not to be convicted of a crime of which he was previously convicted or acquitted, save in the course of appeal or review proceedings connected with such conviction or acquittal;

(h) to have recourse by appeal or review to a court superior to the court which tried him in the first instance: Provided that if a Division of the Supreme Court of South Africa was the court of first instance it may not be prescribed that leave to appeal shall first be obtained from that court or from the Appellate Division;

(i) to be informed as to the reasons for his conviction and sentence.

Article 26

The right of every person convicted of a crime and serving a term of imprisonment in accordance with a sentence of a court of law —

(a) not to be subjected to torture, assault or cruel or inhuman or degrading treatment;

(b) to be detained and fed under conditions consonant with human dignity;

(c) to be given the opportunity of developing and rehabilitating;

(d) to be released upon expiry of the term of imprisonment imposed by the court of law.

Article 27

The right to cause civil disputes to be settled by a court of law and to appeal to a court of law by way of review against executive and administrative acts and against quasi-judicial decisions.

Article 28

the right to have the rules of natural justice applied in administrative and quasi-judicial proceedings and to have reasons furnished for any prejudicial decision.

Article 29

The right that the South African law, including the South African international private law, shall apply to all legal relations before a court of law; Provided that legislation may provide for the application of the law of indigenous groups or the religious law of religious groups in civil proceedings.

Part B

Article 30
The rights granted in this Bill may by legislation be limited to the extent that is reasonably necessary in the interests of the security of the state, the public order, the public interest, good morals, public health, the administration of justice, the rights of others or for the prevention of disorder and crime, but only in such measure and in such a manner as is acceptable in a democratic state.

Article 31
The Supreme Court of the Republic of South Africa shall have jurisdiction upon application by any interested person acting on his own behalf or on behalf of a group of interested persons to determine whether any legislation or executive or administrative act violates any of the rights herein set forth or exceeds any of the limitations herein permitted and, if so, to the extent that the violation or excess takes place, to declare invalid the legislation in question or to set aside the executive or administrative act in question: Provided that finalised executive and administrative acts by which effect has been given to legislation declared invalid and which are not the subject of the proceedings concerned, shall not automatically become void.

Article 32
The provisions of the Bill shall apply to all existing and future legislation and to all executive and administrative acts done after the date of the introduction of this Bill.

Article 33
The provisions of this Bill, including this article, shall not be amended or suspended save by a three-quarter majority of those members who are entitled to vote in each House of Parliament and who have been directly elected by the electorate: Provided that the addition of further fundamental rights or the extension of existing fundamental rights may be effected by a simple majority.

Index